Retur[n]
Other Side [of]

Further Reflections of
India 44's Peace Corps Volunteers

Volume II

Developed by

Mary Jo Clark
Thomas Corbett
Michael Simonds
Kathy Kelleher Sohn
Haywood Turrentine

A GROUP PROJECT OF INDIA 44 A & B

Strategic Book Publishing and Rights Co.

Strategic Book Publishing and Rights Co.
12620 FM 1960, Suite A4-507
Houston, TX 77065
www.sbpra.com

ISBN: 978-1-62516-059-1

Book Design: Suzanne Kelly

Dedication

We dedicate this volume to the memory of President John F. Kennedy who inspired a generation of young (and not so young) Americans to pursue the concept of service to country and to the ideal of working toward a better world. We also dedicate this book to the memory of Sargent Shriver who through his boundless energy and imagination turned a vague concept into a living program. We want to once again recognize our fellow volunteers who no longer are with us—Gary Gruber and Robert Proffit—they are fondly remembered. We also dedicate this work to past and future volunteers. Their legacy, and ours, is a better understanding between people, even on the small scale we were able to achieve. Each volunteer, in his or her own way, chose to brave worlds they barely understood to make our world a slightly better place for all. Finally, this work is dedicated to our spouses and significant others who graciously endured the reliving of adventures and misadventures acted out over four decades ago. Their patience and forbearance were greatly appreciated.

Acknowledgments

We want to acknowledge all of the dedicated Peace Corps staff who helped to prepare us for the rigors of India. They took a group of unskilled and naïve college students and helped us to confront the challenges of volunteering for two years in a demanding, sometimes uncompromising, culture. In particular, we would like to thank Dennis Conta, our stateside training director, who brought together a superb staff who exposed us to a curriculum that stretched us well beyond our comfort zones. We also wish to express our appreciation to the many Indian officials who extended courtesy and friendship to a bunch of well-intentioned, but not always competent, volunteers who landed in their villages. In addition, we extend thanks to our fellow volunteers who did not directly contribute to this volume but helped make it a reality in so many subtle ways. Many of them verbally shared stories that helped stimulate our own memories, and all of them encouraged us to develop this second volume of recollections. The Institute for Research on Poverty, located at the University of Wisconsin-Madison, in particular, Robin Snell, also provided invaluable assistance in the development of the manuscript. Finally, we wish to thank Elisabeth Garofalo for her excellent editing assistance and Jennifer Seubert for her wonderful work on the cover design.

Table of Contents

Preface

United States Senator Christopher Dodd, who served as a volunteer in the Dominican Republic, wrote about the Peace Corps as follows:

> *Every American of goodwill we send abroad is another chance to make America known to a world that often fears and suspects us. And every American who returns from that service is a gift—a citizen who strengthens us with firsthand knowledge of the world.[i]*

These words are likely to strike a responsive chord with most volunteers, intimating a core truth about the meaning of Peace Corps. Its significance does not lie in large or visible projects with easily measured markers of success. No, the significance of Peace Corps is found elsewhere…in much smaller things like the personal relationships developed with those we met in our host sites and in the bonds forged with fellow volunteers. It is about modest contributions we might have made in villages and city slums largely invisible to the wider world, tiny gifts to others unnoticed at the time. And perhaps most importantly, Peace Corps is about understanding life in some broader sense including how we came to view ourselves and how willingly each of us embraced subtle lessons we then treasured for the remainder of our lives.

In this volume, the Peace Corps volunteers of India 44 continue their personal journey of self-discovery originally initiated with the 2011 publication of *The Other Side of the World: Vision and Reality*. The release of that first volume of reflections on the 50th anniversary of the Peace Corps surprised us in some special ways.

First, we learned so much about one another. Most of us knew our fellow volunteers only tentatively at best, our awareness of each other too frequently encumbered by the uncertainties and defensiveness of youth. Four decades later we could approach one another more honestly and with a maturity flowing from full and successful lives.

Second, the reaction to the first volume deeply pleased us. Those who read it, even if they had no previous connection with the Peace Corps, were virtually universal in their praise. They found the reflections intimate, revealing, informative, occasionally funny, and sometimes quite sad. Many mentioned how much they had learned about us, about Peace Corps, about India, and about that special time so long ago. We clearly had not wasted our time or our energies in putting together that first set of reflections. In fact, the work seemed unfinished in many important ways.

Finally, our reflections permitted us to return to a special moment in our own lives as well as the lives of those born to our generation. Those of us who served in the 44th Peace Corps group to be sent to India arrived back in the United States at the end of the 1960s. We returned during a turbulent time in our country's history. The Vietnam war was raging as was the domestic discontent generated by that war. Minority groups continued their search for a more equitable share of the American dream, their aspirations sometimes spilling over into spasms of rage that left a number of cities scarred by wounds that would last a generation or more. Women also sought a measure of equality and respect long denied their gender, expressing legitimate grievances that left many men confused and frightened. Others—victims because of their sexual orientation or physical and mental limitations—would assert their right to pursue the American dream.

Who of that generation could forget the assassinations that occurred during our tenure abroad? Dr. Martin Luther King and Robert Kennedy, two men who eloquently expressed our hopes for what this country should be and could be, were gunned down in acts of brutal insanity. For those of us observing these events from the 'other side of the world,' it looked as if the country had gone mad and was literally tearing itself apart.

Perhaps not surprisingly, we returned from the most compelling and transformative experiences of our young lives with rather strong feelings of trepidation and anticipation. Many of us were, in fact, quite eager to share with others what we had just experienced as well as how the challenge of India helped us grow. We naïvely thought those back home might be interested in what we had to say.

What we largely encountered, however, was indifference and incomprehension. There were no easy ways to communicate what we had been through and, to be honest, our tribulations and triumphs in a remote land were not terribly compelling to those struggling to make sense of the troubles evident all around them. For the most part, no one really seemed to care.

Besides, most of us harbored a dark secret. We believed that, at the end of the day, we had contributed far too little to India when our intent had been so noble and our ambitions so expansive. Perhaps just a small touch of shame and guilt pushed us to misplace those Peace Corps years in some distant and hidden place.

We quietly went on with our lives while putting India somewhere beyond our consciousness. It was not until May of 2009, some 40 years after returning from two years of service in either Rajasthan or Maharashtra, that many of us saw one another again. That reunion proved for many, if not most of us, to be the first real opportunity to tell our stories. It became a weekend that opened us up to our pasts, permitting memories that had been stuffed inside for over four decades to flow in small measures before merging together as emotional rivers of feeling. That shared need to express ourselves, to make better sense of things that yet gripped us despite the passage of time, culminated in the publication of our first volume of reflections.

While that book was cathartic, redemptive, and even transformative for us, both as individuals and as a group, we sensed that the process of dealing with our Peace Corps lives was somehow incomplete. In September of 2011, on the 50th anniversary

Before Indian Embassy Reception

of the founding of the Peace Corps experiment, we met again as a group...this time in Washington D.C.

The magic of mutual sharing touched us in some compelling way for a second time. Some who had not contributed to the first volume now wanted to express their feelings and thoughts in writing. Others, even those who had contributed to the first volume, wanted to say more or perhaps say it in a different way. Still others recalled new vignettes or feelings that now seemed important to share.

We discovered one additional truth about ourselves after publishing the first volume: some of us found that our original recollections, when tested against recently rediscovered letters and diaries from that period, proved to be not very accurate narratives of our Peace Corps experiences. Apparently, the process of recalling significant events is quite untidy. Steven Johnson, in describing the 'ah ha' moments surrounding scientific breakthroughs, observed that "...people tend to condense the origin stories of their best ideas into tidy narratives, forgetting the messy, convoluted routes to inspiration that they actually followed."[i] Apparently, we did the same with our most compelling memories of India. As a result, some of us wanted a second chance at getting our narratives right.

Still, there was another motivation for putting our recollections and feelings to paper, even when it was neither easy nor necessarily pleasant. If the truth were to be told, we are aging. In the not too distant future, these experiences and memories will be lost to us. Several of us mused on that reality and shared a private hope. These reflections are a legacy of sorts, something we can leave to those who come behind us...our loved ones and our children. When we can no longer share our tribulations and triumphs in person, these reflections will remain to serve as a testimony and a testament to a moment in our lives that remains so special to us all. Perhaps this, above all, is why we have put together these two volumes.

And so, a second volume of reflections took flight. We invite you to join us once again in *Return to the Other Side of the World: Further Reflections of the Peace Corps Volunteers of India 44.*

—The Volunteers of India 44

ORIGINAL MEMBERS OF INDIA 44-A & B

*[Those who flew to India in 1967 whether or not
they were later sworn in as volunteers.]*

John Alexander (B)
David Bauer (B)
Don Carter (B)
Mary Jo (Dummer) Clark (A)
Carolyn (Jones) Cullen (A)
Tom Corbett (B)
Sheryl (Taub) Dale (A)
David Dell (B)
Roger Edwards (B)
Lynne Graham (A)
Michael Goldberg (B)
Gary Gruber (B) (Deceased)
Cheryl Hanks (A)
Diane (Hamilton) Jeffcott (A)
Pat (Gorski) Johnson (A)
Sylvia (Bray) Larque (A)
Diane (Logefiel) Lauro (A)
Mary (Welch) Krackenberger (A)
John Lievore (A)
David Lubbs (B)
Gareth Loy (B)
Tom McDermott (B)
Terry Merriman (A)
William Muhler (B)
Don Nordin (B)
Harry 'Hap' Pedigo (B)
Robert Proffit (B) (Deceased)
Sam Rankin (A)
Robin (Schatzberg) Samsel (A)
Donnie Schatzberg (A)
Michael Simonds (B)
Nancy Simuel (A)
Kathy (Kelleher) Sohn (A)
Susie Spence (A)
Randall Stoklas (B)
Marilyn Topp (A)
Haywood Turrentine (B)
Carolyn T. Watanabe (A)
Jerold (Jerry) Weiss (B)
William (Bill) Whitesell (B)
Gerald (George) Wilson (B)
Susan (Krawiec) Young (A)

CHAPTER 1

Returning to
'The Other Side of the World'
India 44

*The road is strewn with many dangers. First is the
danger of futility; the belief there is nothing one man
or woman can do against the enormous array of the
world's ills. Yet, each time a man stands up for an
ideal, or acts to improve the lot of others, or strikes out
against injustice, he sends forth a tiny ripple of hope,
and crossing each other from a million different centers
of energy and daring, those ripples build a current that
can sweep down the mightiest walls of oppression and
injustice.*

Robert F. Kennedy

*We are people of this generation, bred in at least
modest comfort, housed now in universities, looking
uncomfortably to the world we inherit.*
Port Huron Statement ... 1962

Abraham Lincoln, in his first inaugural address, allegorically spoke of the 'mystic chords of memory.' In his own
eloquent way, he was suggesting to the nation that there is a kind
of collective memory, deeply felt images and feelings along
with shared values, which can bind a community, perhaps even
a nation, together. At the time, he was attempting to remind his

Home Sweet Home in the Desert

countrymen of their own special kinship with one another just as deep cultural and political divides inexorably pushed the nation toward an apocalyptic civil war.

At a more profane level, any group sharing a compelling collective experience can evoke common memories and connections. Those of us who served in India as members of the 44th Peace Corps group sent to that enchanted and demanding land developed such a bond. India proved to be an extraordinarily difficult Peace Corps site. The culture of India was complex and exacting while our mission required technical skills in which we were sadly lacking. Our training, no matter how well done, could not possibly overcome our obvious shortfalls.

In addition, most of us were assigned to remote village sites where we endured extended bouts of intense isolation amidst a relentless heat, breeding a loneliness punctuated only by the occasional bout of dysentery. In many if not all cases, we were deprived of the usual comforts of modern living...running

2

water, flush toilets, electricity, communication with the outside world, a diet that included meat, and (that most coveted article of western decadence) toilet paper.

During a 2009 gathering in the Berkeley, California area, we were reminded once again of those bonds forged by the common challenges encountered more than four decades earlier. As it turned out, that reunion was much more than a venue for renewing old friendships. It became an opportunity to shape and solidify those 'mystic chords of memory' that had fallen into disuse over the intervening decades. At some fundamental level, the gathering became an opportunity to first recall, and then to engage, memories and feelings that had been part of us for so long and yet had been pushed aside by the touches of guilt and regret they inevitably brought with them. That reunion also became a place where long suppressed feelings and fears could be expressed to others who might actually understand and perhaps even empathize.

Slowly, long-held fears and feelings emerged, tentative at first, and then with more confidence. Instead of bewildered or uncomprehending looks, each bit of sharing was acknowledged and accepted with knowing nods and an intimate acceptance. Laughs were shared over common failings and tears over bonds of affection renewed after so many years. We realized that decades meant little when you were with those who had also survived what had to be the most profound experience of our young lives.

We also realized something else, something perhaps a bit disturbing. Most of us brought back from India a deep sense of failure. We thought we failed the program, our mission, our fellow volunteers, the people of India and, most importantly, ourselves. Encumbered by the hubris of the young, it had been virtually impossible to admit and talk about this internalized sense of 'failure' privately borne for so long. Rather, we stuffed these doubts and all the attendant anxieties deep inside and moved on with our lives.

Those of us at the 2009 India 44 reunion quickly appreciated that a minor miracle was taking place. We were, in fact,

India 44 reunion, Oakland, CA, May 2009

experiencing something special where those 'mystic chords of memory' were being stirred and refreshed along with all the related emotions, good and disturbing, that inevitably attach themselves to something so irreplaceable in one's life. And so, at some point during that weekend, the notion of publishing a set of personal reflections was born.

It was never clear at first whether anything would really happen. But slowly, and sometimes painfully, personal expressions were transformed into shared written testimonies. Each reflection served to both illuminate our shared adventures and encourage further exploration of our interior lives. More than anything else the reflections were the start of a healing process that offered a promise of redemption for perceived failures most of us ascribed to personal shortcomings, to the folly of our youthful exuberance.

A little over two years after the 40th reunion of our return to the States, we published *The Other Side of the World: Vision and Reality*, just in time for our second reunion in Washington DC on the 50th anniversary of the founding of the Peace Corps. Not everyone had contributed to the first set of reflections. Some had doubted whether anything would actually materialize in print. Others were still struggling with whether they could express what was inside them. Others of us had not had the benefit of the first reunion or the stirring of those deeper emotions that occurred there.

Eventually, an inescapable conclusion emerged…the members of India 44 would continue this redemptive process by developing a second volume of reflections. Some would take this as a first opportunity to express themselves; others would push their own private envelopes just a bit further or in a different direction altogether.

One thing became clear during the creation of the first volume. The mystic chords of memory are elusive and sometimes illusory. Our memories, it turns out, are quite elastic. We easily impose order on narratives about our pasts where order doesn't exist. At the same time, our marvelous brains are quite fallible, generating questionable interpretations of our pasts that often do not conform to the actual evidence.

Thus, for some of us, volume two (*Return to the Other Side of the World*) is a second chance to get our personal narratives right and more importantly to take from those stories the true substance and significance of our experiences. Consequently, in this volume, some of us rely more heavily on diaries and letters and on memories that have been tested against the recollections of our peers. Moreover, we spend more time in this volume thinking about how our experiences as members of India 44 shaped the trajectories of our future lives.

We start, however, by reviewing the context of our service in the Peace Corps during that turbulent decade of the 1960s. Who were we back then, and what did we face in that fascinating, enigmatic place we know as India? Just what was it that motivated each of us to forego ordinary comforts to search for something that none of us could easily define?

5

A Compelling Concept

Arguably, the embryonic concept of a Peace Corps might be traced back to sentiments reflected in remarks Kennedy made on the Sunday morning news show *Meet the Press* when he began his first run for the U.S. Senate in 1951. During this interview, scheduled shortly after a fact-finding tour of the Far East as a Congressman, he mused that we needed to recruit more well-rounded young Americans to better represent the country abroad. He may well have been referring to careers in the Foreign Service but Chris Mathews, in his recent biography of Kennedy, thought the candidate's remarks reflected the first stirrings of a concept that would later emerge as the Peace Corps:

> *This call to service for young Americans—especially as they might affect the developing world—marked the beginning of an idea that, a decade later, inspired the country. It was one of many emblematic ideas evolving in his mind even now.*[i]

Later in the 1950s, a vague notion of something akin to a Peace Corps was surfaced by others...the redoubtable liberal warrior Hubert H. Humphrey for one and a Wisconsin Congressional representative named Henry Reuss for another. Reuss actually drafted legislation based on that concept but nothing happened. It was an idea whose time had not yet come.

The actual inception of Peace Corps, although seemingly accidental in many respects, reflects and embodies the special times that were the 1960s. In the third Presidential debate between Kennedy and Vice President Nixon, the Republican standard bearer taunted the Democrat by arguing that Presidents from his party had led the country into war three times over the past half-century while challenging Kennedy to name one Republican President to have done the same over that period.

Stung by Nixon's charge, then Senator Kennedy next flew to Ann Arbor, home of the University of Michigan. Although late at night and behind schedule, a boisterous crowd of some 10,000, mostly students, awaited the youthful candidate who paused for several minutes to make some rather impromptu remarks.

Kennedy reached back to that idea first entertained a decade ago…that America's youth might serve the country by going abroad, not in the name of war, but in the name of peace. He then threw out what appeared at the time to be an innocuous challenge:

> *How many of you who are going to be doctors are*
> *willing to spend your days in Ghana? Technicians and*
> *engineers? How many of you are willing to work in the*
> *Foreign Service and spend your lives traveling around*
> *the world? On your willingness to do that—not merely*
> *to serve one year or two in the (military) service—but*
> *on your willingness to contribute part of your life to*
> *this country, I think will depend the answer whether*
> *our society can compete.*[ii]

In effect, would these young students be willing to sacrifice a life of relative ease and privilege to bring their skills, knowledge, and perspectives to developing countries as a way of making the world a safer and more humane place? Would they consider volunteering for something like a Peace Corps although, in fact, he never used those precise words on that fateful evening?

Kennedy's offhand comments were made at the dawn of the 1960s. Something special was in the air, something that would touch off a movement that would not easily die. During a panel discussion at the 50th anniversary of Peace Corps in Washington DC, one of the participating panel members (a student who was there that night so long ago) recalled her thoughts and reactions to Kennedy's words. She was electrified by the candidate's challenge, as were many others in the crowd that raw October night in 1960.

The next day, she posted notices across campus asking, in effect, if other students would be willing to sacrifice their comfort and delay their careers to work toward a better world. Of course, this was the days before Facebook and Twitter and all the other social networks that make communications seamless. She expected a few replies at best so had no reservation about listing her phone number on the notice.

Her phone did not stop ringing. Within days, she was overwhelmed by some 800 'volunteers' for a program that did not even exist. As she mentioned during the panel discussion in which she took part over a half-century later, she had no concept how deeply Kennedy's call for sacrifice would resonate with her fellow students. It took a while but eventually she and others reached the President-elect with feedback about this extraordinary response to his late night throw-away campaign line. Even without prompting, Kennedy continued to warm to the idea. In a major address that November, he focused on two issues: nuclear disarmament and his plans for "...this new corps of Americans working for peace throughout the world."[iii]

This quickly emerging 'movement' was not confined to the Michigan campus. Word spread to campuses across the country and within months some 25,000 inquiries about this new Peace Corps concept were received by the Kennedy administration. A vague notion had morphed into a movement. The moment had come to turn this vague political concept into a living reality. On March 1, 1961, the Peace Corps was established by Executive Order.

A Unique Moment in Time

As we think back on it, the response to Kennedy's invitation to help shape our world was not merely about him, his charm, or his charisma, though such attributes surely were there in abundance. It was also about the times.

The quarter-century or so after the Second World War, from about 1947 through 1973, witnessed a remarkable period in U.S. history. It was an era of decreasing income inequality as well as a period of economic growth that lifted up all segments of American society, rich and poor alike. Real (after adjusting for inflation) median income doubled during this period, and income poverty was falling from peaks that may have exceeded 60% during the depths of the 1930s depression to about 11% in 1973; the lowest rate we would ever see in this country.

At the dawn of the 1960s, we were in the midst of this economic and social transformation. As a consequence, our generation came of age when a growing middle class had an opportunity to put the very real and legitimate economic obsessions of prior generations on the back burner. Although we may not have been fully cognizant of this at the time, we could think about college, the meaning of life, and about seeking ways to make a contribution to society without guilt or embarrassment. Our parents, on the other hand, had to focus on finding jobs and developing some sense of security in a precarious world. Their sacrifices provided possibilities for us that few of them could have entertained.

Not long after Peace Corps came into being, another group of students, many of them also from the University of Michigan, drafted what was called the Port Huron Statement, which became the founding document of the Students for a Democratic Society (SDS). Although the organization would eventually spiral down to a nihilistic self-implosion, the original intent was "… nothing less than the spiritual enrichment of American Society—not through prayers or love-ins, but by diminishing the power of dominant economic institutions and the materialistic obsessions that obstructed individual fulfillment."[iv]

More than anything else, the statement flailed against the apathy that seemed to grip the country in the previous decade. It strove to reengage society through something called a 'participatory democracy,' a concept that would live long after the organization that gave it birth self-destructed. In the end, the drafters of the Port Huron Statement were responding to a growing fear of an apocalyptic nightmare made real, a fear solidified by childhoods partly spent huddling under school desks in a silly attempt to ward off an anticipated nuclear Armageddon. The final line of the statement captures that inchoate sense of doom: "If we appear to seek the unattainable, as it has been said, then let it be known that we do so to avoid the unimaginable."[v]

Both Peace Corps and that fledgling agent of youth-driven societal change within America (SDS in its early manifestation at least) reflected a singular underlying impulse. Both initiatives proposed to transform the world, and both posed a challenge: What can each of us do to remake society and make our world a fairer and more humane place, perhaps even a safer place? Both asked similar questions: What does it mean to be a good citizen and how can each of us contribute to something beyond our own, narrow self-interest?

We simply were fortunate to come of age when more of our generation, perhaps for the first time, could look out over the wider world and envision something better. We could confront the larger purposes of our own lives and even entertain that wild, idealistic notion that each of us, somehow, might participate in building that just society to which we aspired.

Some of us, at least, could consider a world larger than some zero-sum game, larger than some Darwinian struggle for survival where a few would enjoy much at the expense of the many. After all, as we looked around us in the early 1960s, we could see levels of affluence and opportunity not witnessed by those who had come before us. Perhaps, it was simply time to share all this munificence in a more equitable way.

Peace Corps loomed as a natural way to satisfy these restless impulses. The program was being birthed by a group of extraordinary young leaders....Sargent Shriver (President Kennedy's brother-in-law and future VP candidate), Bill Moyers (advisor to Kennedy and Johnson and brilliant author), Richard Goodwin (speech writer to John and Robert Kennedy as well as Johnson), Charles Peters (a respected political insider and editor of the *Washington Monthly*), Warren Wiggens (who articulated a large, ambitious Peace Corps vision), and so many other icons of that age.

Right from the start bitter infighting took place to make this developing initiative independent, aggressive and, most importantly, big. Size, it would appear, would be equated with significance. While Kennedy initially conceived of Peace Corps as an extension of the State Department and U.S. foreign policy,

Shriver and Wiggens fought for a different vision. In their minds, the program must be independent, both institutionally and politically, and should encompass enough volunteers to make a difference in the developing world. Shriver received strong support for an independent Peace Corps from Vice President Lyndon Johnson who blustered that "You put the Peace Corps into the Foreign Service and they'll put striped pants on your people when all you will want them to have is a knapsack and a tool kit and a lot of imagination."[vi]

For almost a decade, this vision of an independent, unconventional, and strong volunteer corps had traction. The Peace Corps, both inside and outside of Washington, was perceived as a powerful and unique institution. It was seen as a counterweight to a hardening cold war and a shift in U.S. policy away from an over-reliance on military force on the international stage. If anything, Peace Corps was the international 'butter' in the ongoing tension of whether guns or butter might be the preferred response to international pressures.

J. Larry Brown, former India volunteer and top Peace Corps official, has noted that the 1960s were the 'wild west' era of the Peace Corps. A vibrant energy and sense of risk-taking coursed through the program. Ideas were tried and discarded. The same hubris that drove college students to think that they might reshape American society prompted early PC volunteers and officials to believe that they might reshape the world through sheer will and audacity. The agency itself was years away from the kind of bureaucratic sclerosis that diminishes organizational responsiveness until it loses sight of what the program is all about.[vii]

But for us, this was the sixties after all…the decade of energy and excess. Everything was possible, and we just might make the impossible happen. In 1963, while speaking to students from around the world, Richard Goodwin defined Peace Corps as befitting the spirit and tone of the times. Peace Corps, he said, illuminates a conviction that:

> …*touches on the profoundest motives of young people throughout the world…tells them…that idealism,*

high aspirations, and ideological convictions are
not inconsistent with the most practical, rigorous,
and efficient of programs—that there is no
basic inconsistency between ideals and realistic
possibilities—no separation between the deepest
desires of heart and mind and the rational application
of human effort to human problems...It will be easy
to follow the familiar paths—to seek the satisfaction
of personal action or financial success...But every
one of you will ultimately be judged—will ultimately
judge himself—on the effort he has contributed to the
building of a new world society, and the extent to which
his ideals have shaped that effort.[viii]

This was the spirit of the sixties and of the Peace Corps vision...at least before war, assassinations, riots, and reality brought us back to earth. As students entering college in 1963, this was our world.

The Hubris of Youth

Most of us, if not all, applied for the Peace Corps in 1965 during our junior year in college. By intent, or by coincidence, each of us was accepted into what was called an Advance Training Program (ATP), which is described more fully in our first volume of reflections titled *The Other Side of the World: Vision and Reality.*[ix]

Designated India 44, we were actually two distinct programs destined for the same country. The 44A program was to do rural public health work in Maharashtra, a province located in western India. The 44B program was initially to be trained as poultry experts (later switched to agricultural development) and destined to serve in Rajasthan, a northwestern province bordering on Pakistan.

Briefly, the ATP concept was a short-lived experiment designed to strengthen the training experience and thereby improve the preparation of prospective volunteers. In theory,

India 44 Advanced Training Program, Milwaukee, 1966

this extra training would enhance their potential contribution to the host country and reduce the dropout rate. Like many Peace Corps ideas, the concept made sense on paper. We would receive our first round of training at the University of Wisconsin-Milwaukee between our junior and senior years of college. Returning to college for our final year, we would, on paper at least, continue our training by taking relevant courses, if available, and continuing to improve our language skills through instructional materials made available to us.

After graduation, we would return for a second summer of preparation in Wisconsin before heading off to India for even more training. At the end of this long and intensive marathon, the survivors would be sworn in as Peace Corps Volunteers in September, 1967 and be sent to their permanent sites.

Whatever the intent, the reality of the ATP experiment was less encouraging. While the program was more costly relative to the normal training regimens, the anticipated beneficial outcomes did not materialize. Whether or not we were better prepared for

13

our PC tenures is unclear. What is certain is that many trainees were lost along the way. A number voluntarily left the program, with quite a few dropping out during their senior year of college as career considerations or the pull of significant others diverted their attentions. Others were deselected (involuntarily terminated) from the program, often for reasons that were totally incomprehensible to those deselected and to most of us who survived. In any case, the ATP experiment soon withered and died.

Nonetheless, the ATP concept did manage to bring a bunch of young, idealistic, and painfully inexperienced college students to the campus of the University of Wisconsin-Milwaukee on June 24th, 1966. The original roster of India 44 contains the pictures and brief biographies of 85 trainees.[x] Recalling who we were then is humorous and even a bit painful. We were so innocent and unpolished and, at the same time, so hopeful and full of audacity.

Looking out from the faded pictures in the 1966 roster are faces of enthusiastic college students caught up by the Kennedy call to "…do what you can for your country." The roster reveals a reasonable representation of what America's youth had to offer at the time. There were more females than might be expected (48) but that is easily explainable by the fact that one of the two programs focused on public health, still largely thought of as women's work in those very early days of the feminist revolution. And there were ten minority trainees, nine African Americans and one Asian female.

A little more than half (44) were designated for the exciting field of poultry development (group 44B), which then contained 11 young women. The remaining trainees (41) would be prepared for work in rural public health (group 44A). Only four males were slotted for this program. Later in the training, it would be determined that India did not need more help in the poultry arena and the 44B group would shift its training focus to agricultural development. At that point, all the females in that program were shifted to the public health group.

These kids came from all over the country, north and south, east and west, city and rural. Glancing through the roster, you find home towns such as Clay Center, Kansas; Pine Bluff, Arkansas; Prairie View, Texas; Kimberly, Idaho; Cheyenne, Wyoming; Okemos, Michigan; Winton, North Carolina; Franklinton, Louisiana; Billings, Montana; and Maplesville, Alabama. Others came from big cities and sophisticated suburbs, such as New York City, Los Angeles, Denver, Oakland and San Francisco and San Jose, Chicago, Seattle, Scottsdale, and Honolulu.

Some were attending the best universities our country offered, such as Yale, Columbia, Northwestern, Smith College, Cornell, the University of Wisconsin-Madison, and the University of California-Berkeley. Others attended smaller or less prestigious schools such as Fort Hayes State College, Johnson C. Smith University, MacMurray College, or the Prairie View Agricultural and Mechanical College.

Some wrote about modest life ambitions such as teaching first grade or kindergarten, becoming a high school coach or a wrestling coach, doing social work, or working in the arts. Others had set their sights on becoming physicians, or becoming academics at the college level, or doing international development work, or becoming corporate executives. Moreover, unlike today, when colleges offer so many opportunities for study abroad, few, if any, had travelled much or seen much of the world beyond our borders.

The bottom line is that the 'kids' who arrived at the University of Wisconsin-Milwaukee in the summer of 1966 were an incredibly diverse lot, though strikingly similar in their lack of experience and sophistication. Schools of higher education can stimulate young adults through new people and ideas, thereby testing their prevailing world views, but there is no guarantee that they will. However, as some contributors to volume one of our reflections have noted, nothing in their experience to date prepared them for what they were about to encounter in that summer of '66. Half-formed kids were to be thrown into a grueling test of their skills and perseverance along with others drawn from radically different backgrounds and cultures. It was like being thrown into a volatile petri-dish and being asked to grow or, frankly, go home.

All of us remember well that summer, and the next, and what was to come when we finally arrived on the sub-continent. From day one, we would be pushed, prodded, and continually reviewed. But the pushing and prodding would not merely come from the designs of Peace Corps. It would also be generated by a wonderfully heterogeneous set of peer trainees, each of whom would bring his or her own values, perspectives, and skills to the mix. The diversity within the group made our training a marvelous learning laboratory and helped the training experience become a transformative moment in our lives.

Some 45 years later, it is quite difficult to look over our young faces and not wonder what brought us to Milwaukee that summer of '66 and what we really were thinking. Now, that era almost seems like some strange, alien world. With your average income of slightly over $7,000, you could get a new house for about $14,000, a new car for $2,700, attend Harvard for less than $1,900 in tuition costs, and fill up your gas tank for less than $5.00.

You probably would marvel at a new consumer convenience called a microwave oven, most likely would approve the fact that an African American finally sat on the Supreme Court (Thurgood Marshall), and perhaps would wile away an evening watching the Dean Martin Show in 'living' color. You were definitely not surfing any web or updating your Facebook status, and you might actually recall the 'party' telephone line that you shared with other households.

You might also be aware of deeper and sometimes more disturbing changes. In Southeast Asia, starting in the spring of 1965, actual combat units were sent to Viet Nam for the first time…an escalation that ultimately would bring terrible devastation to those we proposed to help and would tear apart our own country later in the decade. The Voting Rights Act signed by President Johnson would deal a substantive blow to de facto apartheid in America but, at the same time, accelerate a political realignment in the South that would more accurately reflect the country's deep divides along normative and cultural lines. And horrific acts of violence, the assassinations of Martin Luther

King and Robert Kennedy, eventually would wring the last vestiges of innocence from a decade that started out with such hope.

Each of us, looking out onto a world in mid-decade when the future remained fresh with promise, retained our hubris and our innocence. We sought to make a difference, the kind of difference reflected in Kennedy's iconic call for personal sacrifice over a narrow self-absorption that would dominate some subsequent decades. As Stanley Meisler noted in his excellent history of the Peace Corps:

> *For a young American, joining the Peace Corps would become a way to infuse some meaning into an awful, senseless death. It would be a way of making a sacrifice, of performing a powerful service at the calling of a fallen hero. The 'ask not' mantra would have more meaning and more verve than ever before.*[xi]

Each of us made the decision to apply for the Peace Corps at a moment when the Kennedy call was still fresh and when hope for a better America, embodied in the successes of the Civil Rights Act and the call for a Great Society by President Johnson, rang in our ears. We, however, were not so prescient as to be able to anticipate the demise of that decade's largest hopes or the retrenchment in Peace Corps' grandest dreams. Rather, we prepared for that incredible adventure that was India.

Our Destination

We looked forward to our destination...India, surely a land of enchantment, mystery, and possibility. It was also a destination that evoked uncertainty and anxiety and many unsettling questions.

One lesson we eventually would learn, often with considerable pain, is that it is one thing to read about a country, a culture, and a people, and quite another to really understand those things. The magic and mystery of India would challenge and fascinate us, leaving a residue of ambivalent perceptions and emotions. For us, India would be the classic Russian doll with layers upon layers of complexity to be uncovered before one realized just how much more remained to be revealed. Moreover, fully appreciating India is so very dependent on when you happen to look at her.

Today, the average American typically thinks of India only when calling for computer tech support and someone claiming to be Harold from Wichita starts responding to their concerns in a suspiciously strange-sounding accent. Somewhere in the back of the average American's mind, India is one of those countries on the move, still beset by many problems but also overflowing with enormous potential. It is a member of BRIC (Brazil, Russia, India, and China) where entrepreneurship and promise show signs of breaking free from structural impediments that had constrained growth in the past.

Economic reforms in the early 1990s began to unleash for India a potential long stymied by a surreal mix of "Soviet stupidity, British pedantry," and a home grown version of semi-socialistic sclerosis. Given a continuation of recent economic growth rates, however, India could well become the world's third biggest economy within the next generation.

In 2005, Thomas Friedman characterized the new India as...

A country of buzzing entrepreneurs and start-ups, turbocharged by the internet, outsourcing and global communications—a kind of giant Silicon Valley with worse roads and spicier food. In the years since, perhaps reflecting the woes of the west and the rise of China's state-backed approach, some observers have been less restrained, celebrating a reassuring India of a billion innovators who, through a bottom-up revolution, would propel their country to prosperity.[xii]

But the India that first captured our imagination, and which attracted us as young volunteers, was closer to the inchoate image of a vast subcontinent teeming with too many people (the population eventually passed the one billion mark in 2000), a fantasy land deeply imbued with profound mystical thought and graced with both physical beauty and architectural splendor. It would be a fairy tale place for us that stretched some 1,960 miles from north to south, from the Himalayan mountains and Thar Desert in the north through the vast triangular Deccan plateau built on a granite and basalt foundation to the lush landscape of the tropical south, all framed with 4,700 miles of coastline touching upon the Indian Ocean and the Bengal Sea.

India is also home to a civilization that stretches back to the beginnings of recorded history, witnessing countless invasions that made it a melting pot of people, traditions, cultures, and ideas. Evidence of organized, settled life in the Indus Valley can be traced back to 4,000 years BCE (Before the Common Era). The Aryan tribes pushed south out of central Asia around 1,500 BCE to usher in the subcontinents 'modern' era, to be followed by the Persians in 326 BCE, the Muslim dynasties beginning about 1,000 CE (the Common Era), and the British Raj that lasted from 1757 to 1947.[xiii]

Each major incursion brought new thoughts and ideas which were subsequently absorbed into a rich and chaotic tapestry of existing thought and belief. New understandings wrought by the clash of cultures and ideas were periodically codified into epic literary and philosophical works. As the early Aryan invaders settled into agricultural domesticity, they had more time to solidify centuries of oral speculation into the Vedas around 800 BCE; the Upanishads around 700 BCE, which articulated an impersonal, timeless essence of the universe (Brahman); and the Bhagavad Gita, which emerged as a foundational statement for Hinduism around the 1st century BCE. And who could forget the first manual devoted to the erotic arts, the Kamasutra, which first appeared about 150 CE. The subcontinent also produced epic poetry such as the Mahabharata and Ramayana around 400 (CE) along with the works of Rabindranath Tagore who won the Nobel Prize for Literature in 1913.

The India of our imagination was also a deeply spiritual place, or so we thought at the time. Buddhism, Jainism, and Hinduism were all well-established before the birth of Christ. Islam and Christianity were later imports along with too many offshoots to even mention (e.g., Sufism, Tantrism, Sikhism, etc). As we were preparing to encounter the mystery that was India, numerous so-called gurus had migrated to the west to preach forms of meditation and enlightenment. Even the political movement for self-rule led by Mahatma Gandhi was wrapped around an ascetic message of self-denial, non-violence, and liberation as a spiritual quest.

The India we would confront would be a conundrum, seductive and repulsive at the same time. Along with deeper strains of spirituality and stunning beauty, there would be chaos and unimaginable poverty. Along with profound philosophical traditions, there remained disturbing conventions such as a rigid caste system rationalized by a seemingly indifferent fatalism that argued one's position in this life, no matter how execrable, was simply a reasonable outcome associated with one's behavior in a prior life.

There were abhorrent practices such as mutilating children so that they would look more pitiable as beggars, or the murdering of recent brides who violated the expectations or demands of their new mothers-in-law, or vestiges of the traditional practice of 'suttee' in which widows joined the funeral pyres of their deceased husbands. And there were the small everyday cultural clashes, the same questions asked over and over again, the buses that never arrived despite the promise that it was 'just now coming,' or being cheated one more time by a street vendor.

And yet, so many Indians would accept and befriend us despite our obvious lack of experience and skills, our incomplete language skills, and our sometimes awkward attempts at integrating ourselves into a foreign culture. They opened their hearts, and often their homes, to these clumsy Americans who sometimes behaved with incorrigible stupidity and, on occasion, unfathomable insensitivity.

Nancy Tschetter, whose husband was to become the Peace Corps Director in 2006, recalls their arrival in New Delhi in 1966 as newly minted volunteers.

We flew all night to Delhi, India. I will never forget when we arrived, stepping off the plane: the smoky haze that rose from hundreds of small brown huts; the exotic smell of dinner prepared over wood fires; the pungent tropical air. We were truly on the other side of the world in a culture very different from our own.[xiv]

We also were to descend into the 'other side of the world' one year later to find a place equally profound and profane, seductive and sordid, compelling and simultaneously corrosive. India would embrace all the contrasts that make it alluring and enigmatic, enticing, and irritating. India would push us to our limits and test us in ways that we simply could not imagine as we arrived in Milwaukee to begin our training. But, at the end of the day, India also would leave us with a legacy and set of lessons that would never have been available to us had we gone down a different path in life.

Expectation Versus Reality

The mid-1960s were special for us, with a unique confluence of people and possibilities. It was also a special and unique time for Peace Corps. The Shriver vision for the program was expansive and far reaching. Some of the numbers that were thrown out internally were breathtaking, with 50,000 volunteers being envisioned for India alone.

Such ambitions were clearly ridiculous, more delusional than practical. But the numbers in that first decade were impressive nonetheless. Between 1962 (the first full year of Peace Corps operations) and 1966 (when we started training), the number of volunteers would increase more than five-fold. By 1966, over 15,500 volunteers would be serving in some 46 countries while some 42,000 Americans of all ages, but mostly the young, would submit applications for Peace Corps service.

The frantic search for numbers and significance became a classic example of reach exceeding one's grasp. It simply became too difficult to do quality programming while, at the same time, seeking significance and size. Unfortunately for us, India proved that point:

> *India was an example of how a first-rate program*
> *could be weighed down by White House pressures to*
> *expand. In 1966, India had more than 700 volunteers,*
> *the largest Peace Corps program in the world. In*
> *March, Indian Prime Minister Indira Gandhi visited*
> *Washington, and President Johnson decided to make a*
> *dramatic gesture of help at a time of impending famine*
> *in India. He promised to ship 6 to 7 million tons of*
> *food grain and, in a message to Congress, proposed*
> *sending U.S. Agricultural experts...*[xv]

Warren Wiggens, then Deputy Director of the Peace Corps, suggested that the president's promise could be partially ful-filled by increasing the number of volunteers dedicated to agricultural development being sent to India. The number he suggested was 1,000. In-country officials, such as Brent Asha-brenner, the country PC director who would soon be departing that position, argued that the existing infrastructure could not support an expansion of that magnitude and that disaster would surely follow.

Unfortunately, he was ignored and a subsequent internal evaluation report documented just how right Ashabrenner was:

> *In all, 700 new volunteers had been sent to India in six*
> *months. Wiggins had envisioned that a portion of them*
> *would be experienced specialists who would lead the*
> *others, but these experts could not be recruited. Almost*
> *all the Volunteers were generalists with a BA degree*
> *and no agricultural background. They were trained*
> *hurriedly and poorly. There was not enough staff in*
> *India to check out whether there were real jobs for*
> *them at every site. A bitter joke went around that the*
> *staff had placed the Volunteers with a Ouija board...*

> *A minority of the Volunteers managed to find some kind of work for themselves. But, as Ashabrenner wrote in his memoirs, 'The majority either resigned and came back to the United States or spent their two years in India with the frustration of knowing that they had not really been a help to the Indians.'*
>
> *The evaluators found that idle Volunteers would divert themselves with drug use, heavy drinking in public, escapist travel to areas like the beaches of Goa, and an obsession with purchasing extra things for themselves like monkeys and big refrigerators. They also had more bouts of illness than other volunteers.[xvi]*

This assessment makes many valid points, though it strikes us as a bit dramatic. There were no monkeys or refrigerators or obvious drug use for India 44, at least that we can recall. Moreover, each of us can identify contributions we made in our sites, some demanding remarkable ingenuity and effort. Nevertheless, there was the loneliness, the feelings of futility and irrelevance, and a pervasive sense that we were not prepared to make a substantive contribution. Arguably, though, that was not due to a failure of effort on the part of the PC staff with whom we worked. We simply were caught up in a web of overweening, even grandiose, ambitions.

As noted earlier, we came of age at a moment when that special feeling that all was possible had not dissolved into political cynicism. We had yet to sink into an almost pathological sense of self-absorption that too often (though not always) defines our nation's prevailing cultural milieu. We came together for training in Milwaukee armed with our ideals and our unbridled optimism. For the most part, we were smart, driven, idealistic and, oh so, unformed. And we would be going to a place that would demand much of us and would give us much in return, but only if we could be prepared for the rigors that lay ahead. We were, in effect, works-in-progress.

It was the task of the Peace Corps to transform us from kids imbued with little more than enthusiasm and purpose into young men and women who might actually survive and contribute in conditions that legitimately could be described as inhospitable. In retrospect, it is hard to imagine what might have been done differently. It probably was an impossible task given the nature of the challenge. The 44A group would be doing rural public health although very few had any formal training as nurses and some were transferred into that group so late in the training process that they had no time to learn the correct local language.

The 44B group, on the other hand, was to do agricultural development work even though its members were basically well-intentioned guys who, for the most part, had never even visited a farm before entering training and who had spent about half the available training time learning how to be something else—poultry experts. This would be a true exercise in exaggerated hopes over realistic expectations.

The training still turned out to be a memorable and transforming experience. There would be hours of language training, values seminars, skills development and technical preparation, cultural sensitivity activities, classes on Indian history and culture, physical training exercises, and group exercises of all sorts. There would be periods where we would be tested by living in an urban ghetto or an isolated Indian reservation. Our technical skills would be honed by time spent on a farm or working in an urban hospital. Our interpersonal skills were sharpened by forced interaction with an extraordinarily diverse array of peers whom we would never have met in our ordinary lives.

Overshadowing all that was the specter of deselection, the dreaded moment when you might be asked to go home. That ax seemed to fall without warning and arbitrarily, at least it seemed that way to us. We endured seemingly endless meetings with staff, with psychologists, and even with our peers against whom we felt we were always being compared and who, at times, were asked to assess our performance. It was both a growth-producing and a tension-filled exercise.

Michael Simonds kept a diary of those training days. Illustrative entries capture the flavor of what the experience was like:

June 22nd—Wednesday: First real day of classes. Two in Hindi, a large seminar on comparative studies, film-clips in technical studies where Ms. Moose (public health nurse who had spent many years in India) painted a dreary picture of it all. Then to P.E. We got lockers and had our physical tests. Ran a lot, did 31 sit-ups, jumped 7'4" and did 7 pull-ups. Bed fairly early but not before I read about all of the rare diseases in the world.

June 24th —Friday: Fullest day possible! Almost fell asleep in Hindi. Had a debate in comparative studies over language. Lunch, then built a chicken coop in technical studies. More Hindi and then a Peace Corps movie "The choice I Made." Good movie. Dinner, then a tremendous Values Seminar. Talked about it for over an hour with Bill and Nancy afterwards. Now they are singing folk songs again.

June 29th—Wednesday: Up at 6 AM. Language with Ga. Lecture in Comparative Studies on communication. Managed to finish and turn in my self-evaluation form. They murdered a chicken in poultry class. Swam for first time in P.E. Saw a "Twilight Zone Movie" in Values Class and had a fair discussion. Helped Greg feed the chickens.

July 2nd—Saturday: Up at 5AM, just in time for a meeting with Dennis (PC training director). Went to evaluations meeting before shaving. Had 3 hours of make-up language with Raki (wow!). Rather warm day. Went with Greg and George to the Bernstein concert. Washed my clothes after I got back and didn't get to bed until after 2:30 AM.

And so it would go, day after day, week after week. It was grueling and there were moments of fatigue, frustration, doubt, and surely tension. We also drank a lot, talked a lot, flirted a lot, opened up a lot, partied a lot and, in the end, grew a lot. We watched in silence, or with a hidden tear or two, as some of our peers left on their own or at the direction of the staff. Perhaps we whispered silent thanks that we were not the one this time around. Our numbers dwindled but not the feel of adventure and purpose.

At the same time, we sensed something special. We realized that we were about to embark on a great adventure, one not shared by many other Americans. True, many of our peers from that generation served in developing countries in one way or another. Virtually all, though, would live in artificial cocoons, surrounded by other Americans. They would live apart from the locals, separated by their relative affluence and privilege or they would wear uniforms and sport weapons that kept them apart from the native population, thereby becoming more like aliens who would generate more fear and respect than empathy and friendship.

We, on the other hand, would experience India first hand, on the ground, and absent the divides that separate us from the natives and, thereby, keep us from really experiencing the culture and the people. We would rub up against the grit and grime of the real India and see and feel the country in both its unadorned ugliness and its unsurpassed beauty. We would get to know the people and, thus, what made the country irritating and inscrutable as well as enthralling and unforgettable. For better or worse, we would see and feel India up close and personal. And because we would, our lives would never quite be the same again.

Shared Memories

In many respects, we touched Peace Corps at a high point in the program's history. The Kennedy inspiration was still fresh, the Shriver imprint still real, the numbers seeking to join and being sent overseas had reached their zenith. A mere decade later, the number of volunteers in the field would fall by more than half and the number of applications by some 75%. Moreover, the last PC volunteers in India would be gone.

Although the spirit and energy of the program might soon dissipate somewhat, what would never be taken from us as individuals would be our experiences, our memories, and all the lessons we gleaned from India and from each other. Sadly, we cannot go back to those times. As compelling as they were, they are now little more than footnotes to history. At the same time, we can do something to codify and memorialize the noble intentions of a remarkable generation of young Americans. If we do not recapture and express our experiences now, they surely will be lost for all times.

As in our first volume, what comes next are a set of reflections or creations based on those memories and lessons of our Peace Corps service. As with the first volume, each contribution is personal to the author, distinct in purpose and style. Each resonates to what the teller can draw upon to make some sense of a small portion of a long ago life...yet a life which determined their subsequent personal trajectories in such profound ways. Each contribution reflects what is important to the author and what he or she believes is important to share with others. Each contributor tells us something instructive about a special moment in time.

This process of sharing, we have found, helps sharpen what can appear dim and uncertain to the one who is trying to remember his or her past. Perhaps, more importantly, this sharing helps develop a communal recollection of a past time that risks being lost amid the detritus of our ordinary lives. This is our effort to recreate our own 'mystic chord of memories' and thus preserve a special part of ourselves as individuals and surely as a community.

So, join us, back in that special time with a rather unique group of young Americans still imbued with the energy and vision of an age that now seems quaint and surely innocent. Join us in Volume Two: *Return to the Other Side of the World: Further Reflections of India 44's Peace Corps Volunteers*.

CHAPTER 2

Imagination and Transformation

William Muhler

This is a story about one Peace Corps volunteer living in one village in India. Since there are about 550,000 villages in India, this surely is a small story in a big world. But this is also a story about imagination and transformation. Thousands of volunteers have served in India and tens of thousands around the world and each of their stories is unique. At the same time there are some important commonalities.

For those who have not had the opportunity to undertake this kind of journey, there may be no connection. There are, however, journeys in everyone's life, and the sharing of such narratives can increase one's understanding of struggle, self, and place in the world.

To think that a person could live in an Indian village on fifty dollars a month, work in a foreign language, and alter agricultural practices that had been unchanged for hundreds of years requires a certain kind of imagination. I say imagination and not ignorance or naïveté, although they may have been involved, because I believe that the volunteers who stuck it out for two years had some kind of unwarranted, and not always reciprocated, imagination. They had a belief or faith in themselves, in the Peace Corps, in the Government of India, and in the people with whom they worked.

Without this imagination, this seeing beyond the heat and the cold, the fevers and dysentery, the disappointments, the distance from home, and the boredom and loneliness, survival would have been difficult, if not impossible. But this imagination was also rewarded by incredibly rich experiences, accomplishments, friendships, insights and epiphanies, wondrous sights, culinary delights, and unexpected simple pleasures that emerged from the stress of daily existence.

This was not heroic imagination, but a simple stubborn hope for survival and success that kept people going through many dark days. It was formed from genetic, social, and cultural factors that are virtually impossible to sort out but which benefit from reflection and analysis. And of course, survival depended not only on adventurous imagination but also on personal tenacity and a commitment to selfless service. Each individual's recollections are different, but each narrative can heighten awareness of the variables involved ... the strengths, weaknesses, background stories, skills, motivations, and other attributes, that contributed to one of the most challenging and exciting periods of our lives.

When we arrived in India, we were informed that about one volunteer per month had been tackled by a few burly staff members, drugged by the Peace Corps doctor, escorted home, and put in a mental institution. Some volunteers were reported to have committed suicide. One guy jumped naked off a balcony into the U.S. Embassy swimming pool, much to the displeasure of our ambassador. India had very high volunteer attrition compared to many other countries, so we were warned to take care of ourselves or get help before something drastic happened.

In preparing to depart the U.S., Peace Corps allowed us to take one small government-issue steamer trunk and one backpack, so there was not much room for all the books and clothes and artifacts that we thought we would need for over two years. Many of us, I believe, like myself, felt as if we were leaving an old world and life-style and beginning a whole new phase of existence abandoning old habits, fears, anxieties, resentments, addictions, compulsions, and expectations. But no matter how tightly we packed our luggage, there seemed to always be plenty of room to take all of our old baggage with us. So how did we fare? Why did we stay? How were we changed? What did we become as the result of the trials and opportunities?

I'm saying that this is one volunteer's story but, in truth, for most of the time, my story involved two people. Our agricultural program recruited single men, and we were discouraged from getting married while in service. The administration at the time felt that a new marriage could require as big an adjustment as learning how to survive in a village, and putting the two together could be doubly stressful and often led to early termination or the breakup of the marriage or both.

I had left my girlfriend Dede behind to complete her degree at Berkeley. We had been going together for a year-and-a-half, but we had no plans to get married. However, after eating a thousand meals alone and after much correspondence, I began to realize that she might not recognize or understand me by the time I was done. Plus, she would miss out on the Peace Corps experience. She had accepted a job offer in Paris. So all I had to do was convince her that there was nothing in Paris that was not available in an Indian village. She somehow bought the wisdom of my arguments, signed up for a health and nutrition program and trained with single men and married couples under the stipulation that we would get married if she passed training.

She completed her training, and we got married in Delhi after I had been in country for a year. This meant that I had to have enough work after two years to justify an extension of a year so that she could complete her two-year term of service. I was never sure why the Peace Corps allowed us to get married. They took a risk, but by that time, I had a track record of stability in the village, and Dede had had village level work experience in Italy and Turkey prior to applying. Everything worked out well, but that is a separate story.

I'm thinking of these questions while sitting on the couch in my living room taking a break from rebuilding my three-vise workbench. In truth I had already taken a break from the construction work to clean out the gardening closet that had gone un-reorganized for over thirty-four years, but unable to see what was in there because the light bulb had gone out, and it took me three tries to find the right one. Then there was evidence of mice living on the top shelf, so I had to find a dust mask to

Bill and Dede's Wedding

keep from getting Hantavirus, and there was a bunch of toxic garden chemicals banned by the EPA decades ago, so it took a lot longer than I thought. The work seemed interminable with one digression after another, which kept enlarging and delaying each successive aspect of the project. No end was in sight.

Back in the living room, resting, I scanned the room in a clockwise direction. My eyes settled on the art works, books, family photos of children and grandchildren, and other knick-knacks that I had collected over a lifetime. Was this it...the sum of my life — rat droppings and knickknacks? How did I get here? What did it all mean?

When my kids were in grammar school, a fellow parent, who worked for the California State Franchise Tax Board, asked me what I did for a living. I paused to think for a while and then said that it was *as if* I had retired at the age of seventeen and devoted my life to intellectual pursuits, art, world travel, adventures in nature, mountaineering, family, and service to the community. He said, "Damn! How could you afford to retire at age seventeen?" I said that I couldn't, that it was all a big mistake, and that I had been poor the rest of my life. At that point he gave up on his inquiry, and walked away muttering to himself. If I had merely told him that I was a gardener, he would have been more easily satisfied, or at least could feign understanding.

In addition to trying to make sense out of my Peace Corps experience for my own well-being, I now have a more compelling interest in telling my story. I wish to explain my life to my grandchildren, so that perhaps they can avoid some pitfalls and possibly even benefit from my experiences. Recently, Dede has gotten interested in genealogy, and we have both found that it is very difficult to find information about our grandparents. So this is a beginning of a legacy project, and whatever I have become, while looking around my living room, it was clear that Peace Corps had been a big part of it.

To my left was a one foot square handmade piece of Iranian carpet. On the mantle was a block of ebony that I carved in Nigeria; over the mantle a black and white semi-abstract Chinese landscape brush painting; in the corner, a five foot redwood sculpture that I carved and inlaid with inch thick stained glass for a seminary class; on the book shelf, books on Rajasthani palaces, Japanese woodcarving, and landscape design; a two-inch thick *New International Atlas,* followed by an assembly of hand beaten Iranian copper kitchen ware; on the wall, an oil painting of a young Indian village couple sitting under a tree; on the far wall, a Nigerian Ayo board game with a carved lid depicting a man with a machete going after a cobra going after a chicken; finally, a tonsu-type chest from Korea. Every item has a story, but what did they add up to? Nothing in my childhood indicated that I would go to the places that I went to or do the things that I did, but to what end?

Sometimes when working near a sidewalk I would imagine a child saying to her mother:

> *Mommy! Mommy! Why is that man working so hard in*
> *the hot sun?*
> *Because my dear, he's been cursed by God!*

I never actually overheard this conversation, but digging in the dirt is not considered a high-status job in America. In Japan, on the other hand, if you are a good gardener, you tend to accrue points of spiritual merit that greatly enhance your chances of getting into nirvana or escaping the wheel of life, so I was probably born in the wrong country. I have been to several parties where someone will say, "Oh, cool! You're a landscaper. I did that for a summer for my uncle. I really liked it, but now I am a stockbroker."

Perhaps being an independent landscaper is somewhat like being a cowboy as described in the 1975 country music song, *Mammas, Don't Let Your Babies Grow Up to Be Cowboys.* I could picture mothers warning their children that if they don't work hard in school they will wind up in a ditch with a pick and pine-handled backhoe—a shovel.

I'm now sixty-seven, driving a sixteen-year-old pick-up, and still swinging a pick. Having been a landscaper for forty years, I told Dede that if I die before she does, like the old gypsy saying,

"Bury me standing up; I've spent most of my life on my knees." What went wrong or right? Whatever it was, it seemed the Peace Corps had been in the middle of it.

I think some people get the idea of joining the Peace Corps, sign up, and go. But for me, there was a long build up with many work and educational antecedents that culminated in my Peace Corps experience. Half asleep in my living room, I drifted off to the memory of a climb that Dede and I attempted in the Indian Himalayas. We were at 16,000 feet and only a thousand feet from the summit of a supposedly unclimbed peak. The next morning all we would have to do was traverse a horizontal ledge for a few hundred yards and then climb a long gradual ridge to the top. But big blocks of ice and rocks were constantly falling down the face of the mountain all along the ledge as the after-noon sun dislodged them.

The guide and I each had high altitude headaches, and there had just been an early pre-monsoon snow storm, so the chances of getting killed on the last pitch to the summit seemed high. We could leave early in the morning while the face was frozen, but what if we got stuck and came back late? So we aborted the climb and passed up about the only chance in my life to make a first ascent. Sometimes with the loss of that potential victory, I feel like just an ordinary guy with little to show for my life. Maybe I should have gone for it, but part of my growing up has been to discover that there are other important personal "first ascents" in one's life that have nothing to do with climbing mountains. But back to the history of how I got that far!

When I was twelve years old, my father put an ad in the neighborhood newspaper that said, "Boy will work." I was not happy about that. We lived in the Oakland hills in a very small house on a big piece of property and there were always chores to do on the weekends like mowing the lawn, raking up piles of pine needles, weeding, and burning the paper trash, so I was not looking forward to more labor even if it was paid.

A couple called who wanted their lawn mowed every week during the summer. It would take an hour to hike there, and I would get paid a dollar, which was not bad in those days. My parents insisted that half of that would go into a savings account and the rest I could keep and spend as I wished. The problem was that the job was over a mile away and on a hill on the other side of a canyon, so I had to hike several hundred vertical feet down, up a cliff on the other side, then three extra blocks to get around a snarling barking dog that was always loose on the street. It took an hour each way, and needless to say, it was uphill both directions. So three hours were blown every Saturday morning for an effective pay of 33¢ per hour, out of which I could play with 50¢.

On my last trip there, as I was about to make my three block detour (uphill) around the damn dog, the owner came out and told me to come over and pet the dog that was really very sweet and only wanted a head scratch, so I petted the dog and went on to collect my last dollar. As a retirement gift, I received a genuine light grey felt flat-topped Stetson cowboy hat that I wore with great pride for many years. The lawn job led to other gardening work and summer watering jobs when clients went on vacation. Sometimes after setting up some sprinklers, I would lie in a hammock and read Richard Halliburton's *Complete Book of Marvels* about his world travels. I was fascinated by his adventures, but never anticipated getting to the places he visited. Yet, I was infused with his lust for exploring the world and inspired by his idea that far-ranging travel contributed to self-knowledge, vocational discernment, and spiritual growth.

The next year, my family cut down a hundred foot Monterey Pine tree that threatened to flatten the house if it fell. My job was to split the three-foot rounds into firewood. My father taught me how to start the split with a five pound wedge and an eight pound sledge, and then finish the cut with an eight pound maul. As I became accomplished at this task, I felt that I had become a man, and that there were not many more important jobs in life. Later, a five-year-old neighbor kid came over and split a round, which took away some of my pride, but I still felt that I was on my way to becoming myself. I loved the sense of accomplishment, the pungent turpentine smell of the split wood, and the joy and satisfaction that I would be contributing to the warmth of the family next winter.

A few years later, visiting my friend Eric A., I heard the musical ring of a sledge on a wedge and looked next door to see a scrawny white haired seventy-year-old guy in a string tee shirt splitting wood. So I asked Eric who the man was, and he said that he was a Finn, and they were *sisu*. According to the 5 December 2011 version of Wikipedia:

> **Sisu** *is a Finnish term loosely translated into English as strength of will, determination, perseverance, and acting rationally in the face of adversity. However, the word is widely considered to lack a proper translation into any language.* **Sisu** *has been described as being integral to understanding Finnish culture. The literal meaning is equivalent in English to 'having guts," and the word derives from* **sisus**, *which means something inner or interior. However,* **sisu** *is defined by a long-term element in it; it is not momentary courage, but the ability to sustain an action against the odds. Deciding on a course of action and then sticking to it is* **sisu**. *It is similar to equanimity, except the forbearance of* **sisu** *has a grimmer quality of stress management than the latter.*

So I made a vow to myself to try and be able to split wood when I was seventy. I've got three years to go.

Also when I was fifteen, my high school chemistry teacher, Larry Williams, who was the first professional mountain climbing guide in California, invited any and all of his students to visit him at his climbing school in the Palisades near Lone Pine. I figured that half the class would jump at this opportunity, but only my friend Eric R. and I actually showed up. We were members of the local Sierra Club Rock Climbing Section, and had taken lessons in climbing on rock faces in Berkeley. I had bought a rope, slings, pitons, hammer, and an ice ax, so we were already somewhat ready for the trip.

We camped out for a week, at 5,000 feet, and hiked and practice climbed until Larry's assistant, John Sharsmith, agreed to take us on a real climb. We back-packed up to 11,000 feet, crossed the huge jumbled glacial moraine pushed up by the Palisade glacier, and spent the night in Larry's high camp at 11,400 feet. The next morning we crossed the glacier, jumped across the *bergschrund,* where the glacier pulled away from the mountain leaving a deep crevasse, and climbed up a steep gully to the top of Mt. Galley at about 13,500 feet. Never having been higher than 9,000 feet before, I felt this to be a big accomplishment. Rappelling down the gully, I knocked my watch off, but Larry found it on a later climb and brought it back to school. After a summer in the wind and rain at high altitude the watch wasn't working, but the message was that not all things lost are lost forever. Much of my life has been spent trying to recover lost time, lost skills, lost feelings, and crafting my life story is part of that process.

Somewhere around that time, Larry was making a solo night time descent from Mt. Galley, when he radioed down to John snuggled up in sleeping bag in the high camp tent saying that the wind was howling and it was freezing cold. John called back, "Larry! You're tough!" This became a family response whenever anyone complained about some mess that they had volunteered themselves into. Also on this trip, I met Allen Steck, a Himalayan climber who did the five day first ascent of the north face of Sentinel Dome in Yosemite Valley. He got me a job at the Ski Hut in Berkeley manufacturing mountaineering equipment. It was there I met other climbers and adventurers who had worked in Europe and Antarctica. Working and climbing with these role models was inspiring and further enhanced my desire to explore the world.

My college years were very difficult. I was not prepared academically or emotionally for the rigors of UC Berkeley. At that time, the official policy of the university was to flunk out 2,000 of the 4,000 entering freshmen by the end of the first year, and they almost got me.

I failed the English entrance exam because of some grammatical errors and had to take the "bonehead English" remedial course for no credit. I also failed the German exam and had to repeat second year German for no credit, and I got a "D" in that. I struggled to keep a two point "C" average and got a "B" in something that helped to balance a "D" in geography. After a year and a half as a freshman at eighteen, I decided to take a break. I had been able to keep my two point average because I got a gift of a "D" in German IV that should have been an "F." I set a UC Berkeley record for the number of mistakes on the final, 258, but the undeserved passing grade allowed me to be readmitted after dropping out without having to go elsewhere for more remedial work.

Just before dropping out, and not having done well in classes and having no idea what to major in or what kind of work I wanted to do, I took a vocational interest test. The results showed that I had the approach to life and problem-solving skills of artists and Marine drill sergeants, which not only seemed a strange combination, but also irrelevant because I had no apparent artistic inclinations or abilities whatsoever. And I never conceived of myself as a trainer, especially in the military. Nevertheless, the test may have turned out to be a little more prescient than I ever imagined. I later spent a summer as a houseparent for emotionally disturbed teenage boys which required the imposition of a little discipline from time to time. Eventually, I would teach at the undergraduate, graduate, and doctoral levels. I also worked in three Peace Corps training programs. My artistic interests developed slowly and actually became the core of my career as a landscaper.

By 1964, the lawn mowing money plus income from other summer jobs, weekend work, and ten-hour-a-week jobs while at Cal, had built up to $800. This small fortune allowed me to spend five months of spring and summer in Europe riding bikes with Eric A. My girlfriend from high school had dumped me, so for four months I did not even talk to a girl. Toward the end, I met a Finnish woman, Lena, in a youth hostel in Hamburg. She spoke almost no English, but was on her way to England. A month later, I tracked her down in Northern Finland not far from the Arctic Circle.

Eric and I spent a few weeks in Sweden visiting his relatives who were very hospitable, even giving us a free boat ride half way across the country through an ancient wilderness canal system. Overall, we had a great experience except that hitchhiking was almost impossible. We attributed that to the fact that the neutral Swedes had not suffered during the war. Most other Europeans had to hitch rides on trucks to get anywhere until their railroads could be rebuilt. By the end of my stay in Sweden, I felt somewhat put off by what seemed to be a uniform bourgeois conformity and comfort that seemed boring. On the final leg of the train ride to the Finnish border, as the train got closer and closer to the border, it got slower and slower and made more and more stops, thus increasing my desire to get into Finland.

As I walked across the frontier, in great need of a bathroom, the first building I saw had the sign, Tea House of the Veterans of the War. Thus, I had an immediate sense of the difference between the recent history of the Finns and the Swedes. Near the Tea House were groups of women doing pick and shovel work on the roads. Nowhere had I seen women do that kind of work. Finland had basically lost their war against the Russians even with unasked for German help. And according to the story I was told, the Swedes, not wanting to offend the Germans, had offered their troops free train passage to Finland. Later, as the Germans withdrew, for inexplicable reasons, they burned down much of northern Finland. On top of that, the Finns had to pay Russia large amounts of war "reparations" which further impoverished the country, so women were working on the roads.

I stayed with Lena's family for a week and heard many stories about the history and culture of the Finns, and the word *sisu* took on a new meaning. Lena had become fluent in English after a month in England, and was a great interpreter. She was a physical education teacher and lay theologian and had just ridden a one speed bike 175 miles across Lapland in two days. Eric and I were proud to ride 35 miles a day! The Finnish women's army corps had been so efficient in supporting the men fighters that the Russians demanded that the women disband as part of the peace treaty.

The whole European experience, the people, the historic sites, and the different cultures had sharpened my interest in travel. Surviving the flu in Greece, a cavity in Italy, and seasickness in a storm sleeping alone on deck passage on the North Sea all increased my confidence that I could survive on my own in strange places. I met a few travelers who had been to North Africa, and I treated those people with great respect. That was "real" travel, and I did not feel qualified for such an undertaking. Coincidently, I got back to New York on a converted World War II liberty ship at age 19, and Halliburton had crossed the Atlantic on a freighter when he was 19, so I was on my way to following his path. I came home penniless, but was able to sign up for a summer work camp with Operation Crossroads Africa. With a team of other Crossroaders, we spent the whole year raising funds for the cost of the project and went to Sierra Leone the next summer.

This fundraising did not include transportation across the country but I was able to get a ride with a friend to Indiana, and then hitchhike the rest of the way sporting my cowboy hat, belt, and buckle. On the back of the belt I had carved the word *palevume* which was a word that I had learned in an anthropology class. Apparently, in modern rural Greece, when you asked how someone was doing, the response would often be, *palevume,* or "we are wrestling," indicating the ongoing struggle of existence. When I visited Greece in 1964, it, along with Finland, was one of the poorest countries in Western Europe, and I could identify with some of that struggle.

As representatives of our country, we Crossroaders were not allowed to have beards especially at the beginning of the hippie era. Still, I had had a beard for a while and, not feeling particularly sociable, I suppose I used the beard to maintain a certain distance from others. At our staging area at Brown University, I sat at a table across from the Crossroads founder and director, the Presbyterian pastor James Robinson who eye-balled me and my beard, and I eye-balled him back, but he did not say anything. So, with several hundred volunteers, I was the only guy to get on the chartered plane with a beard. Crossroads was considered to be a precursor to the Peace Corps. Robinson had consulted with President Kennedy and Sargent Shriver on how to create the new government organization and later was appointed to a position on the Peace Corps Board.

Fearing that no one would talk to such an anti-social person as I was at the time, I volunteered to be the group "medic" so that I would have a useful reason to relate to the rest of the group. Provided with a guide book on tropical health issues and a medical kit, it was my job to make sure everyone got a malaria pill on Monday and to look after cuts and bruises, minor infections, boils, and intestinal problems. For a while, I considered going into medicine until I took our Department of Education van driver to the local clinic to get stitches in some deep cuts in his fingers and wrist. I had bandaged him up and had no problem with all the blood, but I was not prepared to hold him down on a concrete slab that served as an operating table as the real African medic stabbed needles with anesthetic into his wounds.

I almost fainted. I had always thought that the task of a doctor was to make people feel better, not to inflict more pain, but that can be part of the job. My parents had named me William, Bill for short, after a neighbor, Bill Mulgrew, who also lived on my street in Oakland. Bill was a bit of a local hero for having saved a man's life after a car accident by holding tight the ends of the victim's severed jugular vein. So I always felt that I had an obligation to live up to my namesake and at least be able to do first aid, which I continued to do throughout the work camp.

Having spent a summer as a carpenter's assistant, and apparently having a slightly more functional personality than our assigned group leader or the only other student with any construction experience, I was elected as the project foreman whose responsibility it was to get everyone to the job site in the morning, assign tasks, order materials, and supervise the work. I was totally surprised at this vote of confidence from my peers and even more shocked at how well we all worked together. Our American contingent of students consisted of half northern whites and half southern blacks, one of whom had never spoken to a single white person in her life, and until summer was almost over, she never did talk to a Caucasian.

In the end, she thanked us all for leaving her alone to work things out for herself and said that she was now ready to trust whites more and engage. Our project was going on during the transition period in the U.S. marking the end of the Civil Rights Movement and the beginning of the Black Power Movement, and emotions ran high. My nickname among the Sierra Leonean guys was "The Bluffer," probably because they thought that I was too serious and full of myself. In the end, however, I was the guy who got to dance at the local highlife parties in town with a girl in our group who was the grand-niece of a Fulani paramount chief.

While working on the construction project in Sierra Leone, I met a Peace Corps volunteer who had been there a year. I was impressed by his dedication to his work and his enjoyment of the local people. After having seen the needs of a newly independent country with limited natural resources and many health and nutrition problems, I could see how some forms of international cooperation might contribute to improving health, education, food production, and family incomes.

I also met some volunteers from the neighboring Republic of Guinea. Guinea had been the first region of French West Africa to gain independence from France, and under the leadership of the first President, Ahmed Sekou Toure, the new government decided to sever all ties with the old colonial power. In order to discourage other emerging nations from doing the same, the French took everything with them, including the power lines off of the telephone poles, and stripped the country bare. The economy was in complete ruin. When the Peace Corps volunteers arrived there was nothing to eat in the markets except communist Chinese tomato paste, so the volunteers had to make periodic trips into Sierra Leone to stock up on food. Thus I learned that some assignments were more difficult than others and that volunteers had some choice in their assignments.

Most Peace Corps training programs are about ten weeks long, but because of the perceived difficulties with the India placements, an experiment was made to see if doubling the training time might improve volunteer tenacity and effectiveness. So the summer before graduation provided the first phase of training in Milwaukee. At the end, I used my air ticket home to fly student standby back to Oakland via Miami for no extra charge and then got a three week air pass around the Caribbean stopping in Jamaica, Puerto Rico, Haiti, Santa Domingo, and the U.S. Virgin Islands, all for $117.

In Jamaica, I met some Peace Corps volunteers living on the beach and eating a lot of fish, shrimp, and tropical fruits and drinking good beer, stout, and malted soft drinks. I asked them how much they were paying the United States government for the right to be there, and they said that they were actually being paid, so again, I realized that some Peace Corps postings were more rigorous than others. I also realized that I was inclined toward the harsher tests.

During the Christmas break of my senior year, Peace Corps held a conference for us trainees in Houston, Texas. I took my round-trip ticket, re-routed it through Mexico City, and then flew home from Houston student stand-by. So I got a ten-day trip to Mexico for a net air fare difference of 75¢.

I enjoyed my summer in West Africa very much, but I was already a Far Eastern History major with a strong interest in Asian culture and history. So when I did sign up for the Peace Corps and was given three country choices, I chose India, Thailand, and Nepal as my desired destinations. I also believed that getting as far away from home as possible gave me the greatest opportunity to visit the most countries on the way home.

Being assigned to India allowed me to focus on the history of India, community development, and the political science of emerging nations during my senior year at Berkeley. This background helped me understand that India was on more than a path toward economic development but also on a quest for maturity as an independent democratic nation with a new identity. India had both gained and lost from centuries of Muslim and British rule, had suffered through the long independence struggle, and had lost hundreds of thousands of lives during the partition with Pakistan. India had a long history of droughts, floods, and famines, and had a huge and rapidly growing population of people with little formal education.

In addition, India had been insulted by the Chinese invasions of 1962 and a longer war with Pakistan. Hindi was being promoted as a national language, which was bitterly opposed by Dravidian-based language groups in the south. A huge family planning program had begun with mixed results, so India was searching for an identity within its own boundaries and among the community of nations.

India strongly resisted foreign investment in order to maintain its own autonomy, and India tended to foster closer political relationships with the Soviet Union than the U.S. Nevertheless, for a long time, it was dependent on American food aid until the high yielding varieties program of agriculture sponsored by the Ford and Rockefeller Foundations and USAID took hold.

When applying for the Peace Corps, I had asked my Indian History professor to write a recommendation. He was the son of missionaries, had spent much of his life in India, and was quite familiar with the situation there. His recommendation was supportive enough and he added that he considered me to be a person with mental toughness. Not being one of his stellar students, I could not figure out how he came to that conclusion, but I took it as a compliment and strove to live up to his expectations.

When I first arrived in our host state of Rajasthan, I saw women doing famine relief work all day in the late monsoon heat and humidity breaking stones with hammers by the side of the streets for road base. That was toughness that I could not imagine.

One of my greatest fears about joining the Peace Corps was my proven inability to learn a foreign language. If I could not learn the language, then I could not be a volunteer and might be drafted into the military. My father had volunteered for World War II, but had been rejected for his 20/200 eyesight. My uncorrected vision was 20/475 so I was pretty sure to be rejected also. But the army was happy to take me and declared me 1A and told me to report for induction. My college deferment was running out because it was taking me so long to graduate. I was not a pacifist, but I was definitely against the Vietnam War, and I did not think that I would have made a very good soldier. I had to call the Peace Corps office in Washington, DC several times to get the Army to postpone my induction until after my volunteer service. The Peace Corps officials got right on it, and I was saved.

Back to the language issue! German at least had some cognates in English and had a similar alphabet; Hindi had almost no cognates and a different script. However, when classes began, I was surprised to find myself in the second fastest learning group out of nine groups of five. How could this be? Motivation probably played a large part — learn Hindi or get involved in a misconceived war. The Hindi classes were also very well taught, almost all verbal, and with very practical survival kinds of vocabulary…not the existential anguish of Kafka.

While language ability would certainly be an asset in the Peace Corps, it alone did not seem to be a determining factor for success in the field. Of the fastest learning group, only two went to the field, and only one completed his service. Of the second tier, all five went to the field, all completed, and several extended their tours. This could all be coincidental, but at least my self-image as a language learner got turned around and years later would give me the confidence to tackle Hebrew and Greek in seminary, and later Spanish in a doctoral program. The Hebrew final had 606 questions and I correctly answered 602 of them.

Peace Corps training was an exciting period for me. I was challenged by the language, cross-cultural, and agricultural classes, and I especially enjoyed the Indian and American instructors, all of whom seemed very competent and dedicated to helping me survive and be useful. But I guess my old anti-social tendencies still clung to me. At a group reunion, several of my old buddies brought pictures from training including several group photos in which I seemed to be the only absent guy. Where was I? I must have been behind the barn practicing my soccer kicks against a wall or studying, but I rarely showed up in pictures. Many of the group seemed to see us as a platoon of soldiers ready to do battle with poverty and hunger, and like

Shakespeare's Henry V who, on the eve of the St. Crispin's Day battle, declared that:

We few, we happy few, we band of brothers;
For he today that sheds his blood with me
Shall be my brother...

I did enjoy our comradeship and, ultimately, we did shed blood together, literally and figuratively. I took one guy to the hospital for stitches in his head (no fainting this time) and visited another guy with a concussion. It turns out I had to help hold him down while he was in a delirious rage. We all would get physically sick and homesick, and group support became very important. But, all in all, I was still more of a loner than most of the other guys.

We finished our training in the city of Udaipur and in nearby villages. With about a week to go, I was sent to the town of Kankroli a few miles from my proposed village site where I met a public health Peace Corps volunteer just completing his service in the local clinic. When I arrived, he was having a farewell party with his co-workers in the clinic where almost all of his colleagues spoke English. The guys were having a wild and crazy time, eating, drinking, and sucking the marrow out of goat bones. They really seemed to be enjoying themselves, joking, laughing, and telling stories. I knew that I would never have a party like that.

First of all, I did not have that kind of personality. Secondly, there is a big difference between a village and an urban, western-style medical clinic. This intuition would be confirmed as I discovered later that there were only three men in the village who spoke English; two high school teachers and the village leader, and none of them were party people. Also, because of the comparatively slow pace of life in an Indian village, there was not a whole lot to talk about unless you were deeply involved in family, caste, and political issues.

These were all risky areas that required sophisticated vocabulary and great tact, and in fact we were discouraged from

Dede and Bill with Mohi village leader

getting too involved in ways that could get us caught in the middle of a local squabble, thus jeopardizing our main mission. I always felt that there was a tension between the areas of work and socializing.

I soon realized that I leaned more toward projects than people. I had a deep need to feel useful and to justify my presence and existence, but I quickly came to realize that personal connections were equally important and an essential part of any project. It was also a pleasurable and satisfying part of living in India. For years afterwards though, I wished that I could have done more to engage with people at deeper levels. Nevertheless, over time, in retrospect, I came to realize that there were many meaningful moments and relationships.

Our training village provided other opportunities for defining our role as volunteers. We made friends with some of the low level government workers who operated a toll gate at the entrance to Udaipur. They challenged us to a volley ball game, and we never scored a point. Then they took us on in chess and beat everyone in the house including defeating some of us with pawn attacks, the most humiliating kind of loss. So we were forced to concede that we had brought to India neither great physical nor mental prowess, just the willingness to accompany the farmers in their as yet unrealized quest for greater productivity.

In many ways I was very fortunate to get the village that I did. I had a spacious apartment on the second floor, so no one could look into the windows and no one could get into the compound without the permission of my host family. My cook was pretty good and very loyal. I had running water, electricity, and eventually, a western style toilet. The village leader had spent time outside the village working for the Maharaja of Jodhpur, so he was wise to the ways of the outside world. I asked him why he wanted a volunteer in the village, and he said that he thought that his sons would benefit from being exposed to a person from another culture. He was very free with his time with me and taught me much about the dynamics of the village and the government development projects. My boss and supervisor, the Block Development Officer, was an inspirational community leader, very hard working and caring, and quite willing to support me on any project I wanted to undertake. With this foundation, I was able to get involved in a wide variety of agricultural projects that kept me engaged with the local farmers and helped keep my mind active.

Our only major assigned task on going to our job sites was to work with the local Village Level Worker whose job it was to implement the government development program. This involved the introduction of high yielding varieties of wheat and corn wherever appropriate. So our only real responsibility was to develop a demonstration plot with the new wheat in the next planting season but that was a long time off. I contacted my supposed co-worker, who did not live in my village, and found out that he did not have much to do either, so I decided to work out my own program as best I could.

Mine was the only village with a special job to be done right away. I was to measure the water levels in all of the surrounding wells. This was great for me, because once I overcame my fear of leaving my house, which took about a week, I had to hike all around the place, meet the farmers, and measure the wells. It did not take long, but it got me out and about and I became known to the locals as an official of the government. From then on I became a kind of consultant, conferring on such issues as electric pump design, fertilization, tree pruning, plant diseases, and insect control. I was terrorized about planting the first wheat crop since I had little confidence in my ability to get the crop to grow, so I passed for the season.

The new seed was Sonora 64, which had been developed in Mexico. When planted and properly raised, it grew like crazy. At the end of the season, however, it turned out that the gluten content, good for tortillas, did not work for *chapatis*, the Indian form of flat bread. Therefore, the market value was low, and many farmers lost money on the deal. It turned out that several volunteers got burned for having advocated the new seed.

It was easy to underestimate the value of the experiment because it was difficult to see the historical significance. Indian agricultural practices had been relatively unchanged for hundreds of years, and farmers were very, very conservative. Innovation diffusion theory at the time argued that a farmer would have to hear about any new, even minor, agronomic practice at least nineteen times before considering making a change. Our job as volunteers was to instigate change in any way possible, so even if the first ever new crop was not very successful, at least some people began to see the possibility of a better future through new practices. Of course, some of those practices were not environmentally friendly. Still, some immediate increase in production was desperately needed, and many of the environmental problems were resolved later.

The next year I got hold of some new triple gene wheat that promised to be a better fit for the Indian palate. This variety was developed in India and had short stiff stems that did not lodge, tillered like crazy producing twice as many heads per seed as the traditional wheat varieties, and had heads that were twice as long. If I could get this seed to grow, it would be a breakthrough. The conventional wisdom was that only a large farmer could afford to take a risk on a new crop, so I went to my village leader, who seemed to be a very progressive guy, and suggested that he try the new seed. He refused, saying that it would be considered disrespectful to his father to experiment with something untested. With that rejection, I did not know what to do.

There were dozens of other farmers, but I was not sure that I could trust them to use the new set of practices precisely, and I could not afford a failure. One young man in the village, the son of a blacksmith, was a handyman who worked on houses doing carpentry, electrical, and plumbing work. He had a high school education and always wore western clothes. I did not consider him to be a farmer, but I found out that he and his father had one tiny plot of land. When I complained that I could not find anybody to try the new seeds, he jumped at the opportunity. I am not sure what his motivation was, but I suspected that he wanted to show the other villagers what an innovative person he was. I told him that he would have to do exactly as I said and that I would monitor each irrigation cycle, weeding, and fertilization. He agreed, and we produced a bumper crop. I am not sure what the impact was on the overall village, but hundreds of years of tradition had been broken, and the door was open to many new kinds of innovations.

Through a USAID contact in Udaipur, I was able to borrow a transit level that proved invaluable. There were no paved roads in the village, but one group of families wanted to pave half a block. I was able to establish all of the grades necessary for good drainage, and the system worked. Having established my credentials as a surveyor, a group of farmers who had received a grant to build a diversion dam wanted me to survey the elevation of the river bed, the proposed height of the dam, and the slope to the fields. Although I did not have much confidence in my ability to calculate such complexity, the numbers worked out, the dam and the channels were built, and the water ran downhill. Another farmer put in a new well, and I laid out the course of the channel to his fields around a hill, a project that also went well.

Using a Peace Corps school-to-school program, I was able to get $1,000 for supplies to expand our local grammar school. I asked the village leader to head up the project because he was the only person I trusted with the money. He refused saying that even if he were scrupulously honest and accounted for every penny, he would be accused by his political enemies of some kind of corruption. He suggested that I give the job to the head money lender, his arch rival.

Money lenders in India do not traditionally have a good reputation. I did not know this fellow very well, but I suspected that he was a bit of a slippery character. I asked, "Isn't he the biggest crook in the village?" Without answering directly, the village leader said that it didn't matter. Everybody in the village would be giving *him* what my father called "the scrutinizing scrut," so he would have to be totally transparent and honest on this deal.

I was terrified of getting involved in any kind of corruption and not being able to send a picture of the completed school room back to the American high school kids who had put up the money. I also had no idea how to build an Indian style building, so I just had to sit back and watch and wonder. The money lender seemed to be very pleased to have been given the honor of working on the project and accepted the job. My funds were only to be spent on materials and the villagers were to provide volunteer labor. I did not know how the labor was going to be recruited or supervised, but I went ahead and launched the project. Nothing happened for a week.

Then one day some men showed up and dug a circular ditch and lined it with stones. A few days later some bullock carts showed up with a huge grind stone and a wooden beam and limestone from some quarry. The villagers cooked the limestone and then mashed it up with the grind stone in the ditch as the stone was pulled around by a bullock. Later, bullock carts arrived with stones, a foundation was dug, and the walls began to go up. Every time some materials showed up, the money lender would come to my house with little scraps of paper in a wide variety of colors with some numbers and words in Hindi written on them and hand them over with great ceremony and pride. I made a show of writing everything down in a book, thanked him, and waited for the next installment.

One day a truck arrived with huge steel "I" beams. A few days later, another truck came with the large slabs of hand-cut stone that were to form the roof. Each slab probably weighed close to half a ton, so I waited eagerly to see how they were going to get them up on the top of the building. I had never seen a crane of any kind in the district, so I wondered what kind of magic was going to be employed to get the slabs up. When most of the "I" beams were installed on top of the walls, the last two were left leaning up against the twelve foot wall. A slab was placed at the bottom of this ramp with a rope looped from the top of the beams under the slab and then back up over the slab to some workers at the top of the wall. As they pulled on the rope, the slab flipped over and started walking up the beams. Once on top, it was pried around until it was installed on the permanent beams. So the building was finished within budget and without injuries. It was fascinating to see ancient technologies and village cooperation combine to enhance the community. Years later, with government support, the school would expand to include a junior high and, ultimately, a high school.

My final project was to try and get a tractor into the village to demonstrate the advantages of mechanized agriculture. It took over a year of planning and researching the rainfall, well water production, canal irrigation systems, soil types, plot sizes, and crop acreages, and so on to justify the project, and all of the data had to come from Hindi sources. Not surprisingly, my reading ability improved a lot. The tractor didn't actually arrive in the village until after I left, but USAID and the CARE organization finally got it together and delivered.

The tractor was paid for with PL480 rupees. PL480 referred to the U.S. Public Law which stipulated that India must pay for U.S. food aid. They could, however, use Indian rupees which would be kept in the country to be spent on development projects. One snag was that while the tractor was built in India, the high carbon steel plowshare was imported from Czechoslovakia which was communist, and no PL480 rupees were supposed to support communism. It took a few trips to New Delhi to sort that out, but ultimately the problem was overcome.

Dede's projects were also a joy to watch develop. She worked mostly with pre-teenage girls who would meet at our house after

Dede's girls' club, Mohi Village, 1969

school as a kind of girls' club. This was the only chance for girls of different castes to meet outside of school before they would be married. Their projects included helping a little boy recover from rickets, working on a poultry-raising demonstration, learning that infertile eggs are more or less a vegetarian food, and vegetable production plots.

Certainly not all of my projects were successful. There were dead trees, blown out irrigation pipes, bad advice on crops, failed concrete channel forms, and of course many mispronounced words that caused, if not confusion, at least opportunities for mirth. And thirty-five years later, on a return visit with my son, I was reminded of every screw-up and garbled word — but all in good fun.

One project in the village involved encouraging a large farmer to dig up a bunch of flowering plants in order to expand and "rationalize" the shape of his wheat field. What did beauty have to do with productivity? Only years later did I realize what an incredible sin this was and that Dante's buddies in hell were probably stoking the fires under the boiling pitch waiting for me. Perhaps that is partly why I have dedicated my life to being a landscaper, planting as many flowering plants as possible. Of course, this does not directly help the village, but creating beauty anywhere can help civilize the world.

America has great power to do good or evil and there are far too many smart, highly educated, and well-paid people working actively to make the world as ugly and dysfunctional as possible. I subscribe to the nineteenth century Romantic idea that aesthetics are essential to creating visions of a more just, sustainable, and beautiful world. Science and reason alone are not enough to get us there. So in my design/build gardens, I try to incorporate the latest energy and water-saving technologies, new plant introductions, high levels of skill and craft, and design elements garnered from travelling around the world and experiencing the great gardens of many civilizations.

When I went back to the village a few years ago, I had the intention of replanting some of the bushes that I had ripped out, but there had been years of drought and water had to be trucked into the village. There really was no room for beauty at that time. So some things that I did wrong can't be fixed, and I have to live with that.

One of the great advantages of the Peace Corps was paid vacations. We accrued two days of leave per month, and you got paid a few dollars for each day of leave. My idea of five days of leave would be to take off on Friday, spend a weekend somewhere then begin the five days of official leave, another weekend and then come back on Monday. My Peace Corps supervisor was 250 miles away, and my Block Development Officer supported the projects that I started and even took me on a trip with his family, so no one questioned my leave plans.

The Peace Corps was never conceived of as a high-tech program or a development program alone. It has always had a strong cross-cultural component. Volunteers often get confused about the Peace Corps goals which can lead to a lot of ambiguous reflections about one's accomplishments in the field. Were we community developers channeling outside resources or community organizers utilizing the almost non-existent local resources? Were we agents of change, or educators, or both?

Were we outsiders or what the anthropologists call "hinge" people who act as intermediaries between the city and the country? Each returned volunteer has to make peace with him or herself in the area of accomplishment, and there are no easy answers.

Nevertheless, it was clear that volunteers were expected to travel and learn more about the country and neighboring countries as well as enjoy the natural and cultural sites.

Future training programs, such as one that I directed in Iran, included an enjoyment component. Trainees were advised to find, engage in, and report on enjoyable activities outside of work. The new emphasis was for the trainees to be able to demonstrate the ability to discover new ways to be happy in an alien environment. Having a vital avocational life was considered essential to being effective at work. And while those goals were not explicit in our training, I feel pretty sure that most of us were ultimately able to have many pleasurable experiences in the village, and all of us took advantage of vacations and had many rewarding times on the road and in the big cities.

Along with occasional conferences and health-related trips, a volunteer could squeeze in close to 60 days a year of travel time. For me, these trips included Afghanistan, Sri Lanka, Mumbai, Benares, tiger-infested parks in South India, the back waters of Cochin, the temples of Chennai, the Himalayas, New Delhi, the Taj Mahal, and many other wonders.

A whole book could be written on the art, architecture, crafts, restaurants, movies, musical performances, poetry fests, and other delights that accompanied these trips. There is something to be said for a country and culture that has been evolving slowly over 50,000 years in the same spot. Its people learn how to value every foot of space and, whenever possible, to create the maximum amount of beauty using the materials, tools, and skills that have been refined for millennia. The experiences of my earlier life had prepared me for the project-oriented aspects of the job, but not the aesthetic ones. But with time, the white-wash designs painted on the dung plastered village walls, the decorations on the cows, the jewelry and saris on the women, the smiles on village children, and the ornate temples, the forts, gardens, and palaces became the stuff of powerful nostalgic dreams for decades to come.

Along with the travel joys, many of us discovered new sources of awe and wonder at the micro day-to-day level. Having been heavily dependent on a wide variety of cheeses available in Berkeley, I was reduced to one cheese in India. But I learned to relish a wide variety of Indian foods and sweets that more than compensated for my loss of a career as an extreme cheese eater. I loved classical music but I did not have much access to any in India. I did come to like Indian movies for their vitality and escapism. The huge billowing monsoon clouds after nine months of clear blue skies were a marvel to behold and the tropical fruits and "care" packages from home became life-sustaining treasures.

India was not perfect. I watched children stone a dog to death. Family members stole each other's land and money, and doctors misdiagnosed diseases. There were riots and wars, abuse of prisoners, communal conflict, robbery, and the mistreatment of women and the lower castes. But all of this, the glorious as well as the dispiriting, greatly expanded my emotional and intellectual imagination and inspired me to get a master's degree and a PhD in religious studies, during which I researched causes of social discord and its remedies.

The overall experience in India also moved me to travel more, spending a year travelling with Dede throughout Southeast Asia, the Far East, the Soviet Union, the Middle East, and North Africa. It motivated me to work a few years in Nigeria and Iran, to study the martial arts, to sculpt wood and stone in spiritual images, to climb many mountains, to stay married to an extraordinarily smart, hardworking, beautiful woman, to have two wonderful kids, and two stellar grandkids, and to collect things for my living room.

But I have more than the memories. I have the lingering imprint on my heart of the care and support of my fellow volunteers, the Peace Corps staff members, the Indian government officials, and the villagers who brought me eggs and vegetables, told me stories, invited me to weddings, feasts, rituals, festivals, and funerals, shared their wisdom, put up with my mistakes, made me the honorary brother of the cutest girl in the village, fed me, healed me, and inspired me with their courage and graciousness. So do I have something to pass on to my children and grandchildren? I think so but it is for them to read these stories and decide for themselves.

So did this period in India have the makeup of the classic journey of self-discovery? Was there reluctance to go? Trials and tribulations? Epiphanies and revelations? Failures and triumphs? A reluctance to come home? A return with a boon — stories, discoveries, insights, and wisdom — that really interested nobody? Yes to all that, but there was also a growth in confidence, an understanding that family and intact social structure can provide more happiness and satisfaction than material wealth, that being oneself and attempting to move toward a more ideal self can be more important than career or social status. And yes, that pursuing intellectual interests, art, world travel, adventures in nature, mountaineering, and service to the community could supersede financial success.

CHAPTER 3

How We Met: "He Said, She Said, And The Rest Is History..."

Carolyn T. Watanabe & Peter S. Adler

Editors' note: While Carolyn is a member of India 44, Peter is a member of India 40 who had the good sense to marry a gal from our PC group

The Gospel According to Peter

It REALLY was a dark and stormy night in Mumbai, then known by its British name...Bombay. Memories flood backwards and forwards in time... Bombay in the middle of its annual monsoon with rain, wind, and squalls. Bombay trains and buses packed with people, inside, outside, on top, everyone wet. So much rain gushes that a film of mold grows on wooden tables overnight. Bombay ladies in fancy saris scuttle along sodden streets under big umbrellas stiffly held at angles by servants. Bombay beggars living on the sidewalk; Bombay beggar kids pooping in the street beside the wheels of double-decker buses and over-stuffed lorries that are endlessly coming and going; Bombay thieves picking pockets in the market and Bombay bureaucrats stamping documents in triplicate while displaying their white-shirted sartorial splendor.

My group, India 40, all guys in their early 20s working in school construction, chicken raising, and rat killing, had rolled into town for the scheduled 6-month "séance" at Peace

Corps headquarters. You know, the usual drill of briefings, de-briefings, re-briefings, blood checks, teeth checks, stool checks, mental health checks, safety checks and, of course, the usual warnings, scoldings, and spankings for various infractions, actual and anticipated.

After a day of putting up with a lot of "eat your spinach" talk about representing the United States of America, one of the sec-retaries in the Peace Corps office mentioned that a new group of volunteers, India 44, had just arrived. No e-mails, tweets, Facebook, or linked-in notices back in those days, just someone in the office who quietly told us it was "PARTY" time. And then we learned more. India 44 is a public health group. All women! Some of them even posted to sites near some of us. "PARTY!" Everyone invited. "PARTY!"

Cool. So three of us, Dick Harris, Ted Riley, and I, decide to go and check them out. We are staying at Tom and Joan Traut-man's house over on Peddar Road. In the face of severe Bombay prohibition laws, Tom, our Peace Corps boss and the only per-son who ever paid any attention to our pitiful and truly hard-luck group, managed to stock a respectable cooler full of beer. The secret, he told us, was a loophole in the Maharashtra regulatory maze that allowed foreigners to buy thirty beers a month if they registered themselves as foreign alcoholics. He suggested we do it whilst in Bombay…which we subsequently did. To tide us over, however, we drank a few of Tom's beers, had some nice goat curry, before wandering over to the India 44 party.

Knock, knock, knock…Come in! Get this, twenty lovely ladies, a few guys, but not quite enough alcohol. Even without the beer, what could be better? We introduce ourselves, they introduce themselves. There is Kathy, Diane, Marilyn, Pat, Mary Jo, Nancy, another Diane, Susie, a third Diane, Lynne, Cheryl, Mary, Luella, and an oriental chick sitting on a foot-locker whose name I don't quite catch. We ask: who is going to be stationed down our way in Ratnagiri District in the Konkan region between Bombay and Goa and maybe near our towns of Khed and Mangaon? Marilyn Topp and Pat Gorski say "us." Nice ladies. Ted says, "howdy, podners," and I chime in with "

Riley, Adler, Harris

…let's go find some beer." Harris says to the gals: "Now, let us know if there is anything we can do to help after you settle in." I add: "Me too. See you down in Ratnagiri District"

Now telescope yourself forward thirteen months. India is a giant petri dish. There are diseases in our villages that haven't been named yet. Ted, Dick, and I are back and forth to Bombay on one bit of business or another, an uncomfortable 8-hour bus ride to go 150 miles. One critical task amongst all this voyaging are visits to the Peace Corps doctors to be treated for ear, eye, nose, and throat infections acquired whilst swimming in the scummy green waters of the river running through Khed, the small town we are sequestered to by Peace Corps headquarters.

Women of India 44A

Whilst the doctors had us in their clutches treating us for a wide assortment of worms, germs, and bugs ingested from bus station food and village water, we decide, in a moment of pure self-indulgence and homesickness, to have three nice suits made at a little tailor shop not far from the Peace Corps office. Colors and fabrics are selected. I like the idea of tan, something a world-weary expatriate type like Bogart in *Casablanca* might wear. We get measured and fitted. Suits are ordered. Mohan the tailor says "Come back in a month white boys. We'll do a last fitting and off you will go looking first-class."

Next, a flurry of letters to some of the India 44 ladies we had met at the party when they had just landed in the country and we were materializing at their party as hardened veterans with six whole months under our belts. Remember also, this is all before twitter, RSS feeds, iPhones, iPads, and Androids. It was communication the old fashioned way: handwritten letters delivered by the ever-efficient Indian Postal Service. To inaugurate our spiffy new suits (the first one in my life) the three of us decide to arrange civilized dates in Bombay with some of those nice ladies we met from India 44...you remember those nice public health ladies.

I send a letter to Kathy Kelleher. Kathy says she isn't able to be in Bombay. This leads to a fusillade of letters to others in her group. I tell Kathy via mail, "Hey, you remember that cute little Chinese girl sitting on her footlocker at the party? I'd like to get fixed up with her." Back comes a letter from Kathy: "She's Japanese, buster, and her name is Carolyn Watanabe, and she didn't much like you or any of those other mutts from your group."

More letters back and forth with Carolyn! Date? Suits and everything? How about it? Out of the question! How about you and your roommate Nancy go out with me and Ted? Not in this life, buster. A bout of dysentery sounds more appealing! Just what are you drinking or smoking? And so on.

A string of more letters follows. I don't accept defeat easily, and over a few more Indian aerograms (that go by ox cart), I sense a slight defrosting...perhaps the precursor of climate change. Eventually, our exchange of letters reaches a quiet crescendo. My letters are increasingly whiny, pleading little notes saying I am so sorry for any misunderstandings and if I pay your train fare to Bombay and get you and Nancy a hotel room, how about we go have a nice dinner. AND, it's all a misunderstanding ("what we have here is a cultural communication failure"). I also promise to never act bad again for the rest of my life. Or as a famous economist once said: "Sir, if your horse dies in the middle of the stream, we suggest you dismount."

So, more letters follow with even more egregious beseeching and supplication along with some excessive wheedling, persuading, cajoling, and humbling petitions for mercy. Watanabe is a very tough negotiator and perhaps an excellent judge of character. But eventually she is worn down. Ultimately, much

Carolyn Watanabe ("The extortionist")

haggling mixed with tributes offered in response to her complex and persistent efforts at extortion win the day. We make a date. We go out. Flowers are found. Dinner is served. Dancing ensues. We discover that we both like tomato juice with salt, pepper, hot sauce, and lime.

We learn our family histories. I am from Chicago, first son of Jewish immigrants. She is from Hawaii, first daughter of Japanese immigrants. Her father is a doctor, her mother a nurse. My parents are also docs...a general practitioner and a pediatrician. Her folks met in the Tule Lake Relocation Center. Mine escaped the camps in Europe. And so on. I envision her in the midst of sun, seashells, surf, and tall drinks with little umbrellas and fat spears of pineapple. She is gorgeous. She is smart, kind, easy to

India 40 departure

be with. She laughs at my jokes, which nobody else does. I am totally smitten. The night is magic, the prom I never went to in high school. Love blossoms. I am delirious with love and lust.

So history unfolds just as it was meant to be. Over the coming months, there are a few more dates in Bombay. Letters keep being exchanged between her site and mine via the glacially-paced Indian Postal Service. Vows are made. Promises are offered. If life doesn't intervene in some unexpected and aberrant way, we will get married the following summer in Hawaii. I will go home, start graduate school, and try to avoid conscription. She will join me in grad school. She wants to be a special education teacher. After that, who knows? But we are determined to be together

Then, in December of 1968, all of us in India 40—the hardest of the hard-luck groups ever to come to India, 20 pounds lighter and no longer pink and fat, now wizened and grizzled in the ways of the world—get dressed up in our nice tailor-made suits and head home on Air India flights to new chapters in our lives and to a USA full of furious anti-Vietnam war protesters and hippies. And yet, we still had big hopes for making things better in small ways.

The Gospel According to Carolyn

Not so fast Adler! Here's how it REALLY was.

My group had just returned to Bombay after six weeks of in-country training. We were being given our last medical clearances and picking up our trunks before heading out to our assigned sites. A group of us were in one of our hotel rooms thinking about how to spend our last night together. A few of my group had run into volunteers who were in town on their semi-annual medical check-ups. Not surprisingly, we were interested in talking with them to hear first-hand about life in the villages. Some of us were opting to stay in their rooms to finish packing. I was inclined towards some last minute shopping because my trunk of stuff from the U.S. had been totaled (a whole other story).

A knock on the door interrupted our discourse and in swept a bunch of hooligans wanting to know which volunteers were to be stationed in the Konkan region. Two of the girls shot up their hands and got the once-over; two of the fellows turned around and walked out leaving one of their own to regale us with life in his village. This was Dick Harris. The two others were his site mate, Peter Adler, and Ted Riley who lived 60 miles up the road. I was in the corner in the shadow of the room contemplating the demise of my trunk and all the precious cargo I had sent ahead watching this scene play out. I'm thinking "how rude and obnoxious" these guys are, except for Dick, who had charmed us with his Boston accent, courtly manners, and stories of life in the village.

Fast forward a year later. Nancy Simuel, my site mate, and I get a letter from Kathy Kelleher stating that the same guys who had all but up their noses at us now wanted to go out on the town with us simply because they had suits tailor-made for themselves. I'm thinking: "you can put suits on pigs and they are still pigs." A date with Peter Adler? Not in this life. Nancy, however, was going into Bombay around that time to finalize plans for our year-end conference. I told her she should go out with those guys if she was so inclined. As fate would have it, the night before Nancy was to leave for Bombay, a filling in my molar fell

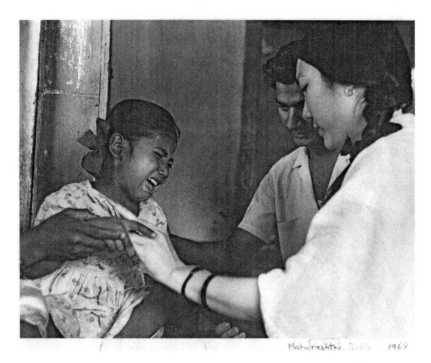

Maharashtra, India   1968

Carolyn at Village clinic

out so I accompanied Nancy, still hoping to avoid those India 40 blokes. That hope turned out to be wishful thinking as Peter ran into me in the Peace Corps office and once again extended an invitation to celebrate the Festival of the Suits.

....and actually, it was fun ... first impressions were fading. Soon enough, though, another SDI ("Sudden Death Infraction") landed on Peter and his idiot friends. After our year-end conference, several of us decided to take some "French leave" and had enlisted Kathy Kelleher to purchase train tickets back to our village. Not wanting to alert Peace Corps headquarters that we were on illegal leave, we asked Kathy to drop the tickets off at the front desk of the Red Shield Hotel, a popular hostel where out-of-town volunteers often stayed.

We got to the hostel late at night and after a horrific standoff between the taxi driver and Nancy (another long story), no tickets. The next morning we head to the train terminus and Victoria

India 40 and 44, Thanksgiving in Khed, 1968

Station on the outside chance our reservations were made and our names are on the train cabin window. Thank goodness they were but we now had to put up a second full payment with the assurance that we could, upon producing the original tickets, get our money back.

Next, an exchange of letters with Kathy! What happened to the tickets? Oh my, she says, I gave them to Adler and those other hooligans from Konkan with explicit directions to leave them at the desk of the Red Shield. We write to Peter, Dick, and Ted asking "what happened to the tickets?" and would you please return them so we can get reimbursed. Back comes a letter from Peter. Well, he says, they were in his pocket when, spur of the moment, they decided to visit another volunteer up country. While off with his comrades, he discovered the tickets in his pocket. Knowing nothing could be done, they made many toasts to the ladies of India 44 and drank themselves into what I assume was a state of oblivion.

Then, a slew of letters and lots of back-and-forth asking for the tickets and finally being told they had been disposed of accidentally. Finally, a half-hearted offer of reconciliation with an offer to repay us for an amount that didn't come close to the first class fares we had paid for. During this time, Nancy and I formed a new organization called WOW (Wipe Out Whites) and demanded payment in full. Finally, a settlement of sorts! We— Nancy, me, Marilyn, Pat and others -- agree to attend a Farewell-to-India party in Khed so we could collect our money first hand.

Being in November, the party became a Thanksgiving Day feast. Peter and Dick killed all their chickens and roasted them up. Tom and Joan Trautmann and their two boys came down in a Peace Corps jeep with a couple of turkeys he had found and several coolers of beer and wine. Then, a whirlwind courtship which is still being tested out 40 years later!

So far, so good.....

Carolyn, Nancy, and Mary Jo in Athens, 1969

Nancy, Carolyn, Peter, Indian Embassy

Epilogue

We really did fall in love. Peter finished his tour in India and went home after a few weeks of travel in Israel, bought a VW bug, drove to Columbia, Missouri, and started graduate school in the Department of Community Development.

Carolyn finished her tour in May, 1969 and traveled in Europe with Nancy, Pat, and Mary Jo. Peter and Carolyn got married in Hawaii that summer, finished grad school eighteen months later, she on a Kennedy Fellowship, he on a research assistantship. They worked in El Salvador, then in Boston for a spell. They missed the Islands and moved back to Hawaii, which they decided was a nicer place to raise a new race of kids than any of the other places they had seen. They have more or less stayed in Hawaii since.

Three grown kids later, Peter and Carolyn are still testing the arrangement out. Peter still has an odd beer now and then. Carolyn still extorts him. They are still in love.

CHAPTER 4

Digging Up the Peace Corpse and Other Tales of War

Tom McDermott

Editors' Note:
Arriving on the subcontinent a mere 20 years after India's independence, we witnessed a country still piecing itself together from a host of princely states and European colonies. Like several other newly independent countries, India had witnessed a violent birth that resulted in millions being displaced, maimed, or murdered. Immersed in day-to-day life in our villages, we were unaware of just how difficult had been this path to unity and nationhood.

For some of us it took an encounter in another country to make us realize how precious and fragile is the unity out of diversity enjoyed by India—or by any multi-ethnic country, including our own.

Yugoslavia gained its independence about 30 years earlier than India. It too was formed by unifying disparate ethnic, religious, and linguistic groups who shared little beyond a long history of strife. After many years of peace and economic progress, Yugoslavia surprised most of its European neighbors when it began to fall apart in 1991. By 1992 one of old Yugoslavia's six constituent republics, Bosnia, was consumed in a bitter civil war.

Based on his work in Bosnia during the horrendous ethnic strife there, Tom McDermott (the 'American') reminds us just how much insanity and depravity lies within all our hearts. Perhaps the lesson of Tom's story is that peace and national unity are never guaranteed. Rather, they are gifts that need to be continuously nourished.

Anniversaries

Is it advancing age? Or is it the empty spaces retirement creates in life? Whatever the reason, year after year these anniversaries seem to crowd in.

First come invitations for your 40th (and soon 50th) high school reunion. Then reunions of your college and grad school years appear. Pleas from the Alumni Association follow asking that you contribute some of your paltry pension to the university's endowment fund. I mean, folks, come on—are you really going to offer some poor freshman a reduced tuition if I cough up an equivalent amount of cash?

For those of us who went on to work in diplomacy, development, or the military, there is the added weight of anniversaries marking various world crises—Vietnam, Bangladesh, Biafra, Somalia. Okay, fair enough—we do want world leaders and the public to remember the terrible messes they and their predecessors created. And yes, we do want to honor the hardships suffered by those who lived and died there.

It is comforting to imagine that by so marking the manmade disasters of the past, we might learn to avoid similar mistakes in the future. Yet, we know full well that we are not likely to learn our lessons. Sadly, our children and grandchildren can expect in the future to look back on many other wars not yet imagined.

Do you recall when you were younger and you tended to accept those invitations quickly? "How great it will be to meet those guys again and trade stories. Remember the time when we...." Well, age may not impart wisdom, but experience does teach you to adopt less foolhardy tactics. After a few of these events, you learn to accept invitations gracefully, but then to develop some ailment at the last minute. "I really wish I could attend, but..."

That is a little how I felt with the recent (April 2012) 20th anniversary of the outbreak of war in Sarajevo. The U.S. media hardly mentioned the date but for European media the anniversary was a big item. The BBC offered a week-long series of memoires by correspondents, deeply moving stories of individual bravery amongst civilians caught in the madness of war.

I was stirred by many of those recollections, because they were so close to my own. Yet, I felt no urge to go back to Sarajevo to dig up the recent past.

No, in my view, Bosnia has too often dug up its past. It is hard enough to get Old Man War to go to sleep, but once he does, it is best to leave the old guy alone. May he rest in peace—forever!

Yet, as happens at reunions, one person's story opens the way to stories told by the next. Several of my own tales thus came forth in recent weeks—ones I might have traded with others had I joined the anniversary ceremonies. Of course, like all stories told at reunions, the details have no doubt been embellished by time.

Sarajevo, Sarajevo—cultured European city with such poise; city proud of its long history of Muslim, Jewish, Catholic, and Orthodox tolerance; city where 40% of the families were composed of couples intermarried from among the four groups; city where a Serb nationalist killed the Austrian Archduke and thereby set off World War I; city where Muslims protected Jews through Nazi occupation in World War II; city of the 1984 Winter Olympics; city where Bosnia finally fell apart; city even today held together only through a fragile peace agreement.

What happened? No easy explanation, but perhaps the answer lies in other questions:

After decades of one-party Communist rule what happens when you finally have "a free democratic vote?" For whom do you vote? If a Catholic Croat, you vote for a Croat party and hope for union with nearby Croatia; if an Orthodox Serb, you vote for a Serb party and hope for union with Serbia; if you are a just a "Bosnian" - Muslim, Jew, Atheist or Agnostic, you vote for a Bosnian party and seek a future not dominated by either of the neighboring countries.

"You know that we call it the grandmothers' war," the refined lady and former professor of history said.

"Grandmothers'?," the American said. "Why grandmothers— he could understand 'grandfathers' but why 'grandmothers'?"

"Because, you see—we were young, rich, well-educated Europeans. We were beyond Communism and socialism, beyond all those 'isms', beyond even religion and ethnicity—beyond our history. No, World War II had ended all that. We were modern people, like you in America."

"Yes, I can see that," he said.

"No, you don't see anything," she said. "You Americans can't see, can't understand, because you don't understand your own history— just as we once refused to understand our history. No, it was our grandmothers who saw and understood history, not us.

Every Sunday our grandmothers would insist we come to Sunday lunch. We were busy people and wanted to go elsewhere, but we had no choice when it came to Sunday lunch. We had to be there. Every Sunday she would lecture us about what 'they'—whoever 'they' might be—had done to us the last time around, and what 'they' would do again if 'they' ever got the chance.

We laughed at her, and called her a silly old woman. But in the end, she was right and we were wrong. All that education is for nothing. In the end it comes down to your ethnic roots. Muslims will be Muslims, Croats will be Croats, and we Serbs will always be Serbs. That is what we call 'ethnic reconfirmation'—our history reconfirms who we are, who we have always been, and who we always must be."

They thought that he didn't know, but he did. They had amputated his leg during the night. No one had told him anything, but it wasn't hard for him to see the empty space beneath the sheet where his leg should have been. Nor was it hard to recall the bloody stump that had been there when they pulled him up into the truck.

The boy lay in the ward of what had been turned into a military hospital. All around him lay wounded soldiers. Only months before the huge room had been the dining room of a ski lodge in the Bosnian Serb capital of Pale.

He was 15, maybe 16—he wasn't sure. The American by his bedside was asking through a translator for his story. How had he come to be here? Was he being well treated? Did he need help to cross the line?

He was Muslim like his father, although his mother was a Serb. He and his family farmed a small piece of a hillside above Sarajevo. His village was mostly Serb, so when the war began many of the Muslim minority fled down the hill to the relative safety of the city. At first everything seemed okay because the village was largely isolated from the city. Soon, however, rumors floated back to the village of massacres in the city below. At night they could hear the shooting. Before long the Serb artillery began firing down on the city from the high cliffs above them. It went on through the day and night. They could look down and see buildings collapse before their eyes.

At some point, his older brother slipped away—he assumed to join the fight on the Muslim side, but he wasn't sure. His father went off one day to find food for the family, but never returned. The family then consisted of his mother, a younger sister, and himself. Water became more and more of a problem. Piped water had stopped flowing, and the family's old well was nearly dry. One morning he took a bucket to a neighbor's house further down the hill. The neighbor was a Serb, but a good friend of the family. Instead of the familiar face, however, the boy found a squad of soldiers in the house. They were Serbs, but not from his village. His neighbor had disappeared.

They called him a Muslim spy. They beat and tortured him, burning his chest and genitals with cigarettes. He had no information to give them, so they sent him on to another unit down in the Serb held part of the city. That unit needed laborers, so they sent the boy along with other captives to the outskirts of the airport, where they were constructing a massive line of trenches just beyond the runways.

Each day they dug and then dug some more, pushing forward the long snaking trenches. It was summer, and the sun was hot. They were given little food or water. They were kept naked during sweltering day and chilly night. The guards told them that it was easier that way to know who to shoot, if someone tried to run.

This really was not necessary, he thought, as the prisoners knew very well that behind them lay other trenches with snipers looking for any movement, while in front of them lay a massive mine field. Beyond was "no man's land."

On the other side were the Muslim lines. Somewhere over to the south of the airport lay the Croat lines, and inside the airport were the UN forces. NATO planes came and went all through the day. The wheels of landing aircraft seemed so close that one could almost reach up and touch them—yet they were a world away.

Some days there was so much mortar fire that after a while you didn't hear it. But you did see it—at least when it came close. That day it came close indeed. Heavy firing started to hit the positions all around them. The Serb soldier guarding them unwisely put his head up to call to his mates sheltering in the trench behind them. The soldier died instantly when a grenade went off near his head. More grenades came down, this time in the trench itself, killing one of his two fellow laborers. The other was badly injured. The boy, remarkably, was untouched.

The injured laborer was much older than the boy—a former school teacher and a Catholic Croat. He was bleeding badly. The boy stripped the uniform off the dead soldier and tried to fashion a tourniquet. No guard came that night, meaning no food and no water arrived. By morning the former school teacher had bled to death.

By the second night, it was clear to the boy that he had been forgotten and was now alone in a strip of no-man's land. That night he managed to crawl back to the trench behind them. Amidst his dead former captors he found some bits of food and a canteen of water. He was about to start crawling back further when the firing started again. Suddenly, everything went blank.

When he woke, it was early morning. He was lying out in the open between two trenches. He was unable to move. He could see that his right leg had been shattered. There was smoke but no sound of firing. He thought that he might be deaf until he heard the sound of a heavy vehicle. He assumed it was a Serb tank.

Then through the smoke he saw two soldiers move cautiously towards him, weapons held up in firing position. Once again, he prepared to die. He was surprised when one spoke softly to him, but in a language he had not heard before. It took some time to understand that the soldiers were not Serb or Muslim, but French UN troops.

They put him on a stretcher and loaded him into the back of an APC (armored personnel carrier). A translator asked him— Serb, Croat, or Muslim? He didn't understand the question at first. Then the translator asked, "Which side are you on? If you are Muslim, we can take you to Sarajevo; if Catholic to Mostar, or if Serb to Pale . Where do you want to go?"

Without thinking, he said, "Pale."

The American now asked, "But why not Sarajevo? Why, after suffering so much at the hands of the Serbs, did you choose to go to the Serb side?"

The boy thought for a moment and said, "I wanted to be home, or close to home. My home is not Sarajevo. " Then he drifted back to a morphine-induced sleep.

The team—one American and two Bosnians—drove slowly up the long valley. Their original destination had been a health center, where they were to check on deliveries of drugs and other medical supplies. A firefight between Croat and Muslim forces had broken out unexpectedly that morning and swept swiftly up the valley from east to west. They thought at first that the fighting was now far enough ahead to move safely. It was not in fact safe, but they were reckless enough to push on anyway.

They finally stopped when they heard firing ahead. It was a small town where many houses had been destroyed. Some were still burning. The driver stopped by a tree under which a mother and two children were sheltering. The team had nothing to offer, aside from some water and the contents of a quickly exhausted first-aid kit.

The woman wanted to go back to her house to search for clothes and foodstuffs. She had no idea where they would go next, but wherever it was the family would need food and clothes. The American went with her to help carry things down to the roadside, while the driver stayed with her children.

In the house the American had a sudden vision of his own home. Was it the well-equipped kitchen, complete with microwave oven, or was it the TV in the living room, or the dining room table set as though the family had received guests for dinner the night before?

For a moment, he was not in some foreign land, but in his own. "This could have been my house," he thought.

The odd feeling continued after visiting the nearby school. It looked like the American's own school. Neighbors were busy trying to put together a temporary shelter in the school gym, turning the bleachers into a sleeping area. It was like some U.S. community hit by a flood or tornado—not a country at war.

When the American got back to Sarajevo that night, he wrote a few lines in his notes:

"What an arrogant generation we are, we Europeans and Americans born after World War II! Our armies fought in the lands of others—not in our own. We believed that civil war was something of the third world; not our world.

"This arrogance grew further among those of us who worked in international development. We looked on armed conflict as some madness that grew out of poverty and lack of education—problems we naïvely thought we could solve or at least alleviate.

"Yet, here I am in a rich European country where the population is well-educated and well-fed—yet locked in a war worse than anything I have seen in Africa or Asia. It seems war lies in all of us—rich and poor alike. How fragile is unity in any country, including our own!" he wrote.

Enemy soldiers were often hard to spot. Civilians were easier targets. Snipers would wait for them to cross intersections to find bread or carry home a jerry-can of water.

And the best bait to draw out civilians was one of their kids. Wing one—shoot for the leg or arm—just enough to leave the child screaming in the intersection. Brave passersby would go out to try to pull the child to safety. The snipers then had a rich target field of adult civilians.

Yes, children were always a favorite target for the snipers.

Where snipers were active, travel became impossible. Whole sections of the city became isolated, as effectively as if a wall had been erected. The wall was particularly real for the children. Parents might be forced to take the risk of a trip to the market or to a water point, but they kept their children indoors.

The girl was nine years old. She lived with her mother in one of the eastern enclaves that had been cut off from the rest of the city by snipers and shelling since the early days of the war. She often tried, but now found it hard to picture her father. There were photos of him in the living room of their apartment, but nowadays the girl was not allowed to go in there. Any room with windows was too dangerous to move in. The windows had been blown out long ago, and were now covered by plastic sheeting. Even if it hadn't been so dangerous, with no heating in the building, it was impossible in winter to be inside the apartment for long.

In a fortunate bit of Communist-era planning, city officials had once ruled that nearly every apartment building must include a shelter in case nuclear war broke out. In the early days, the assumption was that the war would be with the Americans; later the Russians. In any case, the shelter was intended for a few days of protection from fall-out, not for survival over years of war.

So, like their neighbors, the girl and her mother camped in the dark hallways of the building. Body heat of so many people and the heat of small cooking stoves made those corridors feel almost cozy on winter nights.

There was no electricity, no water, and therefore no working plumbing. Everyone had to share common latrines in the basement shelter. The stench of the overflowing toilets was awful but people got used to it.

What the girl most missed, aside from her bed and her bathroom, was her school. She loved her books and her friends. She longed to be back at school again.

Her school had been hit by a shell the year before. Fortunately no one was inside when the shell hit and the roof collapsed. The community had decided at first that it was too dangerous to reopen the school. Instead, they tried to hold classes in the stairwells of each building.

After some time, however, classes became impossible. Adults constantly cut through the class as they moved up and down the stairs to fetch water or reach the toilets. What's more, you can coop children up in a stairwell only for so long. Thereafter, they find ways to escape outside—to play, to scavenge, or just to breathe.

Eventually the community decided to set up classes in a nearby abandoned workshop. There was no heating, aside from an old pot-bellied stove someone had donated. In winter each child had to bring something to burn in the stove—often one of their toys or pieces of clothing.

The girl was happy to be back at school—even if this was nothing like the school she remembered. There were fewer pupils, so everyone sat together in one big class. This was nice,

Children in school

as the older children helped the younger. When one student was slow, others would help. When firing started, there was always someone to hug.

It was hard though for her and the others to bring things to burn. At first, she would bring an item of clothing. Her family had been relatively well-to-do, so she had plenty of clothes. She knew, though, that the day would come when her stock of clothes would run out, and she would have to do like the others—start bringing toys.

It was okay for the boys, since they could go to scavenge in the abandoned apartments of nearby buildings. She could not. Even worse, she did not have many toys. She had only her precious dolls. She prayed that summer would come before the day when she would have to choose between her dolls and her school. In her nightmares, she could see the teacher toss her favorite doll into that stove. No, when that day came, she decided, she would simply run away.

Foreigners often came to the school. They would drive up in their big white armored cars, wearing helmets and heavy protective vests. Somehow they could cross through the maze of snipers from parts of the city she could no longer remember. Those places were just a couple blocks away, but they might as well have been on the other side of the moon.

Like the rest of the community, the girl knew that the foreigners provided basic (really basic) food, fuel for cooking, and drinking water. For the school they also provided notebooks, pencils, and crayons. Yet for all "the stuff" provided, it seemed strange that the foreigners couldn't or wouldn't do anything about the snipers and the shelling that walled them into this little prison. Older people often joked that the Serbs were the prison guards and the UN were the prison janitors.

One of the new classes supported by the foreigners was a kind of art class—mostly drawing. The idea was that drawing could help you deal with your war-related fears. Drawing also provided a way to identify children who were particularly traumatized and needed one-on-one sessions with psychologists. Of course, all the kids were traumatized one way or another, but psychologists could only work with a few.

The girl knew nothing of the theory, but she enjoyed the chance to draw. On this day the class was asked to draw "your worst fear"—a topic that came up every couple of weeks. The idea was that you drew pictures of what you feared the most, what would make you wake up screaming in the night. When you finished your drawing, you would share it with two or three friends and talk about it. Finally, you would wrap your drawing up with those of the others and put them in a small box. You buried the box in a hole in the wall or in the ground beside the school. Weeks later you would dig up the box and talk about what had changed or not changed.

Most of the kids in these sessions would draw tanks entering the city, or planes dropping bombs, or soldiers pointing guns at children. The little girl, however, just drew a rectangle that day…nothing else! No airplanes, no bombs, no soldiers.

So the American asked through the translator what her picture was about—why a rectangle? She didn't answer. Instead, she just drew a stick figure in the box. "Aha," he thought. "The psychologist needs to talk to this girl. Maybe she sees herself in the grave."

The American then asked cautiously who was that in the box—was it herself? Suddenly the girl started talking. "No, of course not," she said. "This is my doll, Ivana. I will not let them burn her in the stove. I will hide her in a box where no one will ever find her until this stupid war is over. Then I will dig her up and we will both live happily again."

The sergeant looked skeptically at the young lieutenant, who went on blabbing with the American in a weird mixture of German and English. "These f….ng kids," he thought to himself. "They aren't soldiers. They're just civilians with a university degree. They join up because they have no choice, and yet here they are bossing us regulars as if they were generals."

The sergeant after all was a "regular"—twelve-year service in the Yugoslav Army, and now he found himself suddenly in the Army of the Bosnian Serb Republic—a real soldier in a real war, but in an army commanded by a bunch of "f….ng civilians."

The lieutenant, on the other hand, was—or had been, at least until a few months earlier—an architect. From the point of view of the army, this qualification made him an engineer. Soon after joining the army, he had found himself assigned to an artillery unit high on the hills overlooking his beloved Sarajevo. It quickly became all too much for him—the constant roar of the guns—the never-ending demands for firing "solutions," i.e. trajectories aimed at destroying buildings down below. It was the easiest possible kind of artillery work—you could actually look right down and see what you were shelling, could hear the impacts, see the dust come up, and watch the people try to flee. The snipers would pick off many.

Some of those buildings were ones he had worked on designing or re-designing. Some were priceless old buildings with histories back to the Austrian days. Others were soulless concrete blocks of the 1950's. Whatever they were, they were buildings where he had lived and worked, and where many of his neighbors still lived.

He broke down after a couple weeks into the job. He simply was not cut out for this kind of work. The army reluctantly reassigned him to an intelligence unit down near the front lines at the airport. Unlike most soldiers, he knew some languages—decent Russian and German, and a smattering of English and French. His job was to chat up the foreigners crossing in and out of the city, to find out whatever they would tell him about the other side.

Most of the foreigners were UN peacekeeping troops—French, Ukrainian, Egyptian, or Norwegian. These were soldiers serving in their regular units, but wearing blue UN helmets and nominally under UN command. The majority though were members of the French Foreign Legion.

It was the Legion with its wide assortment of nationalities which provided favorite pickings for Serb intelligence. The Slavs among the Legionnaires provided the easiest sources of information; first because of their ethnic sympathy with the Serbs, and secondly because communication was so easy. The Legionnaires were only allowed to speak to each other in French, but in private the ethnic Russians and other east Europeans would speak in Russian, a language most Serbs understood well.

The French commanders understood this weakness, and so wherever possible limited contact between their men and the Serb forces. But there were always opportunities—fighting would start somewhere along the line, leaving a UN unit stranded sometimes for hours, occasionally overnight. At such moments the local brandy and cigarettes came out. Those were the moments when you wanted an "intel" guy in the card game, ready to chat.

Lately, however, a new group of foreigners had begun to turn up—civilians working for the UN humanitarian agencies. The Serbs assumed that most of these people were intelligence agents out to gather information. Whatever they were, these foreigners were more difficult to approach. They seldom lingered, but instead rushed off to meetings in the Bosnian Serb capital at Pale or on to Belgrade.

Now at last, however, they had one of these civilians close at hand. He had come down from Pale, expecting to take the "5 p.m. shuttle"—a French APC that crossed the front lines carrying UN personnel back and forth three times each day. There had been some heavy shelling that day, and the 5 p.m. shuttle, the last of the day, did not come across as planned to the Serb position. It was too late in the day to go back to Pale, so the civilian had no choice but to stay the night and wait for the morning shuttle at 8 a.m.

The colonel was pissed. In fact, he was furious. He did not want "any f....ng UN spy" hanging around his position for the night. It was even worse when the colonel found out that the "spy" was an American. On the other hand, the lieutenant responsible for intelligence was delighted at the rare opportunity to chat—first because this was a civilian and second because he was an American. Who knew? Maybe the lieutenant could actually learn something useful from this guy and thereby redeem himself in the eyes of his higher-ups. At minimum, it gave a chance to talk with someone out of uniform—someone like what he considered himself to be—an educated man.

The colonel ordered the lieutenant to keep "the American spy" as far as possible from any action. So the lieutenant took the American back to the remains of what was once a small restaurant. It was now a bunker where troops ate and slept between their watches on the line. There the lieutenant and the American sat with the sergeant and a group of other off-duty sentries. The soldiers would come and go through the night, but while they had the chance, they ate, smoked, drank, played cards, and slept.

The lieutenant was disappointed when the American said he didn't smoke and didn't play cards. These were two usual routes to open up a conversation. On the other hand, there was the ever reliable route of slivovitz (local brandy). Foreigners knew that in Bosnia an offer of slivovitz could not be refused without causing grave offense. In this case, avoiding offense didn't seem to be the guy's concern. Indeed, he was grateful for the offer.

The American, however, did limit himself to two drinks—just enough to guarantee a night's sleep. Even so, he had discovered that with or without the slivovitz, he had a talent to sleep through anything, including the drumming of heavy shell fire. There was a strange comfort in sleep in the midst of danger. But, of course, those couple of drinks never hurt.

So the lieutenant and his target ate, drank, and chatted, while the others played cards. The lieutenant found the American easy to open up—where did he come from, who did he work for, what had he studied, where did he work before coming. The American seemed to gush out his life story—so much so that the lieutenant wondered if he could ever get it all into his notes later that night. Moreover, the lieutenant found that he himself was opening up, telling his life story to the American.

Even if he did not understand the language, the sergeant now really started to worry. The lieutenant seemed to be telling the American more than the American was telling him. What kind of interrogation was this?

Moreover, when it came to militarily useful information, the American was a dead end. He talked about children, vaccinations, health centers, schools, psychologists. However, he seemed to have no idea about troops, supplies, or weapons. This was very different than "chatting" with soldiers, who usually could talk about almost nothing else.

Yet there was one thing in the American's background that caught the lieutenant's attention. When asked how he had come to be assigned in Bosnia, the American explained that he had been working in India for the UN, but had previously worked there in something called the "Peace Corps."

Now every Bosnian knows the word "corps," though they invariably pronounce it "corpse." The word "corpse," however, was usually preceded by terms like, "First Armored," "artillery," "medical," or "signal." Bosnians also knew the English word "peace." But how did a word for peace go together with a word for war? And what in the world was a "peace corpse?"

The American tried to explain something about farmers and water wells in villages, but it made little sense. The American's

German was not very good. He had learned the language years before in school. At first the lieutenant thought he must have misunderstood. So he asked again, "Which army corpse?" When the American repeated his answer, the lieutenant asked the others if any had ever heard of a "peace corpse." No one had a clue, but the term had a nice ring to it—here on the front line of a very nasty war.

They started to tease the American. "Hey, Peace Corpse—colonel no like you… says you can walk back to Sarajevo, tonight!" The American was not at all sure that they were kidding, but had learned enough to know that at such times it was best just to say goodnight and go to sleep—which is exactly what he did.

Maybe for the soldiers it was that ludicrous combination of the word "corpse" with the word "peace." Whatever the reason, the name stuck, and whenever the American crossed at that check-point someone was bound to call, "Hey, Peace Corpse, you back again?"

Soon none of the original card-players was around, but the name had firmly stuck among their successors. By now they used the term not just for the American, but for any other "humanitarian" who would cross.

These do-gooders were the weird ones, idiots without guns, naïve enough to go off to someone else's war. Others called them "war junkies" or "conflict tourists," but here at this particular check-point they were just the "peace corpse."

So, if I had shown up at the events marking that grim Sarajevo anniversary, I might have told a few stories of little interest to the politicians and journalists there. More likely I would have wanted to slip away from the ceremonies to wander the city and ask impossible questions—"What do today's grandmothers tell their grandchildren?" "Whatever happened to that Muslim boy in the Serb hospital?" "Did the little girl manage to keep her doll?" And whether any of those former soldiers still remembers "the Peace Corpse?"

CHAPTER 5

Too Many Shades of Grey

Mike Simonds

Editor's Note:
This chapter, along with the two that follow, reflects an
epiphany that struck several contributors during the
preparation of these two volumes. These three authors,
in one fashion or another came across documentation
of their Peace Corps service after completing their
contributions for Volume One. Michael Simonds and
Gareth Loy discovered long-lost diaries that they had
written during their PC tenure. For Tom Corbett, the
source materials were letters he had written to his then
girlfriend back in the U.S. In each case, the writings
from four decades ago were a revelation. Long-held
memories were found to be, in some instances, a bit
misleading. In other cases, new memories, long lost
in the mists of time, were restored. Retrieving these
sources gave the authors a second opportunity to get
their stories right, or at least a bit more complete.

Guess what! All of the stories I have told about my time in
India over the last forty years are wrong in some major
respect. This is something I discovered with no small amount
of surprise, and, to say the least, this small epiphany is very
disconcerting.

While I was in the Peace Corps, I kept a daily diary that
recorded the events of each and every one of those 730 days as

well as a 300 page journal that recorded my reactions to those events. I retained over the years a fair amount of personal correspondence and some miscellaneous subject notebooks as well. For most of the last four decades, these documents sat tucked safely away in my basement.

Over the years, I had a repertoire of stories about India that I told and retold whenever the occasion arose. Not that this was a daily occurrence. But whenever a news event or someone else's travel story provided a proper lead in, I could count on an appropriate anecdote.

The fortieth reunion of our Peace Corps group in 2009 inspired me to contribute a chapter to a book of memories that resulted from that event.[i] Eventually, I decided I needed to dig out my old diaries to add some detail to the stories I wanted to relate. This was when I discovered the truth, that there were major problems with the way I remembered just about every one of those stories.

The point here is not that memories fade over time. That's a relatively trivial observation. It's hard enough remembering what I did last Wednesday, let alone forty years ago in India. What fascinated me was how my memory could take a series of events and rearrange them in a new narrative, sometimes with a very different perspective than would have been the case with the actual story of those events.

This was the case with one of my most important memories of what I now believe I should call it my 'Myth' of Peace Corps India.

Background

As related in the original book, and in other chapters here, the India 44B group was composed of a bunch of recent college graduates assigned to agriculture development in the Indian state of Rajasthan. With few exceptions, we were city boys with little experience with any type of agriculture, and the training we received was rudimentary at best.

From the very beginning, I had doubts about my ability to succeed in this assignment. After all, I was being asked to convince people of a different culture to change their ways of making a livelihood in an area where I had no background, and to do so by working in a language in which I had only minimal fluency. I just couldn't imagine how that was going to work, but the Peace Corps told us it happened all the time, and who was I to question their wisdom and experience.

I was assigned to a small town called Fatehnagar. Fortunately, I have a description of the town in a letter I wrote in support of an application to the Peace Corps School Partnership Program.

> *Fatehnagar is a small but growing town of about 3,000 people in the North Indian State of Rajasthan. It is, for India, a relatively young town growing up as something of a local business and trading center around a station on the main rail link between the cities of Udaipur and Chitorgar. Already the town has 15 small factories including two cotton and eleven peanut oil press mills. Its advantageous situation on both road and rail links speak well for its growth potential.*
>
> *Since my own field of work here is in agriculture I am more familiar with this aspect of the community. The fields around Fatehnagar grow wheat and corn, some vegetables and the cash crops of cotton, peanuts, and tobacco. That is to say they grow these crops when the monsoon is good, the whole district being dependent on the rain fed wells as the only source of irrigation water. In the past four years the rainfall has been below average, significantly reducing the amount of land under cultivation.*

My good friend Bill Whitesell was assigned to Sanwar, a much more traditional Indian village about a half-an-hour bike ride from Fatehnagar. For about a year he lived in a rundown castle of the local Raja, a sad little figure who had lost all his power and influence with the coming of independence, and was about as relevant during our stay as his 1930's Rolls Royce

Streets of Fatehnagar

Rajah's castle

Bullocks with plow

that sat on blocks in front of the castle, serving as a makeshift chicken coop.

Our area of responsibility over-lapped, and was usually referred to in Peace Corps communications as Fatehnagar/Sanwar. In the second year of our stay, Bill moved into Fatehnagar and got his own place right around the block from mine.

The farmers we worked with used the same methods of planting that had been in place for centuries if not millennia. This meant that they were using wooden plows pulled by teams of bullocks. I don't remember seeing a tractor anywhere outside of the government agricultural institute. So, in that sense, the environment we were asked to work in would have been alien even to those Americans more familiar with the world of modern agriculture. But for us, it was just one more element in the challenge facing us in our assigned area.

The Myth

Shortly after our one-year anniversary in India, we were called to New Delhi for a medical conference. Mixed in with blood, urine, and stool tests were the inevitable group discussions of the Peace Corps mission in India. Somewhere towards the end of these sessions, I was called in for a private session with the Peace Corps brass.

Bill O'Connor, the area Director, put two very direct questions to me:

Did I really believe that there was enough work in the Fatehnagar/Sanwar area to occupy two Peace Corps Volunteers?

If not, would I be willing to accept a transfer to a new site?

My answer to both questions was "No."

These questions struck deep at my growing sense of failure. Fortunately, I had stumbled onto a school-to-school project that gave me some feeling of accomplishment. In the area of agriculture, our primary focus, however, I felt I had slipped into a routine of going through the motions, with little hope that anything I was doing would amount to much.

The first question actually hit on a sore point. As I mentioned above, Bill Whitesell and I had been given over-lapping service areas. Having Bill that close by was critical to preserving my sanity. I'll never know how volunteers stationed alone managed to make it through their tours without another American close by. Having a companion enabled you to share things when dealing with the emotional toll of living a fishbowl existence where one's every move was subject to public scrutiny and comment.

But while Bill's presence was critical to my survival, we never managed to get on the same page when it came to work. Often it seemed that we were tripping over each other out in the field. And since Bill had mastered the language better than I had, and was naturally more out-going, he had established himself more effectively than I had. The brass had not called him in to ask if he wanted to relocate.

The idea of transferring to a new site at this point in time was a non-starter. From a practical point of view there was only one growing season left in our tour. Even if I had been much more effective in the area of agriculture extension work, there would not have been enough time to get established before the winter crop. And the idea of starting over alone in a new site filled me with apprehension. Gee, now I could fail in a second site!

No, I could not justify two volunteers in Fatehnagar/Sanwar. No, I would not accept a new site. And no, I would not let them off the hook by resigning. If they wanted to send me home, that was okay. But I was going to stick it out where I was through the end of my tour if it was left up to me.

In the end, that was what happened. Nothing else was ever said about this meeting. My assumption was that the brass figured that it was less paperwork to let me finish out my tour rather than go through the red tape of sending me home.

But that outcome did nothing to lessen the impact of that meeting on me. It put a bright spotlight on my own sense of failure. And while I'm sure that Bill would have been the last person to claim that his activity in the fields around our site was a major accomplishment in the success of the Green Revolution (the introduction of high-yield seeds into the local farming community), the very fact that he seemed much more engaged and active than I was made this seem like more of a personal failure than anything I could blame on poor training or support.

I was so upset by this meeting that I resolved that I would turn over a new leaf on my return to Fatehnagar, rediscover the motivation that had brought me to the Peace Corps in the first place, and give this agriculture business a second shot. I felt I had a window of opportunity here that I wanted to exploit.

Bill's girlfriend, Carol, had actually traveled all the way from America to visit him, and the two of them were going off to tour India for several weeks. For that period of time, I would have no competition while trying to reestablish myself among the farmers in the Fatehnagar/Sanwar area.

As soon as I returned to my site, I put my resolve into practice with a two-week blitz of frantic activity. One of my first acts was to meet with the Headmaster of the local High School and ask him to recommend a Hindi tutor for me. It seemed to me that improving my fluency beyond my basic survival level would be critical to my success. As it turned out that this was one of the best decisions I made all the time I was in India.

I also remember getting a list of the farmers who were experimenting with the new high yielding variety of wheat and tearing around to their fields on my bike, picking up soil samples, and connecting or reconnecting with the farmers themselves.

It wasn't long, however, before the deadening inertia that was rural India once again made itself felt and I remembered why I'd had so much trouble getting started a year earlier. The climax came sometime toward the end of the two weeks of my recommitment to the Green Revolution in Fatehnagar. I was on my way to meet with one of the more progressive of the local farmers, and had to catch up with him as he was out supervising the seasonal planting in one of his fields.

During our chat in his field he told me that he was thinking of diversifying his crops and wondered about experimenting with potatoes in the future. He asked whether I thought that was a good idea. I confessed that I didn't know much about potatoes, but promised to research it for him.

As I was leaving his field, I remember thinking how hopeless this was. All we had for reference was this general *Handbook of Agriculture,* which I knew would be both too general and too specific to tell me much about whether potatoes really made sense in this particular area with its unique combination of soil and climate. It was also clear that all decisions about whether to experiment in this way included major risks for even relatively successful farmers such as this one. There was a huge downside if they were naïve enough to accept advice from someone as ill-informed as I was in agriculture. It was one thing to give advice, quite another to give advice when the stakes were so high.

This insight was wonderfully reinforced by a pathetic visual image I then presented to the farmer. Walking through a newly plowed field with its deep furrows and large clumps of soil was not a native talent for a city boy, and I stumbled several times making my way back to my bike. In the background, I could hear the laughter as the Indians contemplated the spectacle of the "American Agricultural Expert" who could not make his way across a plowed field.

Back in my room that evening, I recorded my new insight in my journal. I was not spending my days reading through the Peace Corps Book Locker because I was lazy, or because I didn't care about feeding India. I was doing it because when it came to agriculture I didn't know what the F#@k I was doing, and I was more of a danger than a resource to these people.

I then gave a very specific instruction to the future me... never to second guess myself when I was back in the States. I knew I would have a tendency to do exactly that. Looking back on my time in India, I would constantly wonder if I could have accomplished more if I'd only tried this or that, or worked a little harder. I considered myself incredibly lucky that I had faced those doubts while still in country so I could actually give it another try and be forced by the reality of India to understand the real limitations under which we labored.

This lesson was critical to me over the forty years since my return. It was an antidote for the guilt that I was to see in so many of the members of our group after their return. In fact I remember sharing it with a small group during one of our early reunions at Bill Whitesell's place in Greenwich. That must have been about ten years after our return.

This memory was so critical to me that the shock of discovering that it was not true was truly monumental.

The Real Story

Most of the opening of the myth seems to be right on target. That famous meeting with the Peace Corps brass took place on September 27th, 1968. And my reaction to it was exactly as I remembered.

Returning to Fatehnagar I did, in fact, find a Hindi tutor. And I did begin a whirlwind of agriculturally based activity. And I did encounter the famous Indian inertia, which began to drag down my initial enthusiasm. For example, on October 4th I made the day trip to the block headquarters in Mavli to meet with the Agricultural Extension Office (AEO) only to wait in the office for four hours before someone on his staff remembered that he was on leave. I returned on October 7th and this time spent five hours in his office before someone remembered that he was in Udaipur that day. Two days, completely shot, with the added bonus of having severe stomach cramps on the bike trip home where I was extremely fortunate to make it back to my place in time.

Where the real story differs from the myth is with its outcome. After several weeks of bumps and false starts, I ended up with some of the most successful and effective projects of my entire stay in India.

And my most successful project by far?

WHAT?

Yep, POTATOES!

It turns out that almost exactly a month after that meeting in Delhi, a Peace Corps Officer showed up at my site with 25 kilos of wheat and 85 kilos of potato seed. I spent the next several weeks meeting with farmers, explaining the advantage of planting potatoes, and convincing them to try the seed I had available.

There are many times when something in my journals will jog my memory and the images will all come flooding back to me. This is <u>NOT</u> one of those times. Even after reading those entries, I still have <u>NO</u> memory whatsoever of this project. If someone, Bill for example, were to have interrupted my myth story to remind me of my potato project, I would have vehemently argued that he was wrong. I would have been ready to swear under oath that I was never involved in potatoes in any way during my tour.

But there it is, in black and white. And not just one or two entries, this was a major undertaking. It went on for weeks. I even reported my argument with the Indian Agricultural Extension agent who told me that I should not provide potato seed to one farmer because "He is not a nice person. We should not help people like that!" And I also recorded a dream I had one night of being hemmed in by sacks of potato seed that formed a wall around my bed.

Not only did I manage to dispense all of the 85 kilos that I had received, the project was so successful that I found myself debating who to give the last packets of seeds to, where would they do the most good?

There is, of course, a whole new science that attempts to deal with "repressed memories," but that is when our minds try to block out painful experiences so that we don't have to deal with them. Here my mind was burying a successful project in order to refashion a narrative to explain a failure to have any successful projects!

The problem here, is not so much "repressed memories" as what psychology calls, quite simply "False Memories":

> ***False memory*** *refers to cases in which people remember events differently from the way they happened or, in the most dramatic case, remember events that never happened at all. False memories can be very vivid and held with high confidence, and it can be difficult to convince someone that the* <u>*memory*</u> *in question is wrong.*[ii]

Okay, and where do these false memories come from?

> *Humans are biased to extract meaning from events, and this may lead to confusions about what was inferred versus what actually happened.*[iii]

I am fairly certain that the events of my original story did happen, although obviously not in the order I remember them. It does seem to me that this was a case of my subconscious trying to "extract meaning from events," as described above.

Reviewing the details of "The Myth," it does seem that the activities I was describing (racing around fields, collecting soil samples) was more like my first few weeks of trying to establish myself in my site, than the second effort a year later. When I got the results of those soil samples back, I didn't know what to do with them. I had naïvely expected them to give results in terms a layperson could understand, and what I got was a list of chemicals with percentages attached. We had no training whatsoever in how to interpret them, so they were quite useless to me.

I'm sure that my experience stumbling around in a field while thinking despairing thoughts about how to learn about potatoes actually happened, but that too must have been during my first year. I can't find it specifically mentioned in my diaries, but that's not surprising. I had many humiliating experiences tramping around in the fields, trying to hide my basic ignorance of what I was doing, and this probably didn't stand out at the time. It was just the one that stuck with me afterwards.

The fact that I cannot find my "Don't Second Guess Yourself" entry in my journal is a bit more surprising. After hours of searching I have not been able to turn it up. Now that doesn't mean that it's not buried somewhere. A lot of my journal is early post-adolescent introspection so it is pretty tough going working my way through it forty years later. So it could be lurking in some obscure corner amid some otherwise banal musings. But it is nowhere that I would have expected to find it.

If it does not exist, then I think it may be a simple logical fallacy. This was a profound thought. I always wrote down profound thoughts. Therefore, I must have written this down.

None of this speculation, however, goes to the basic question. Why would my unconscious construct a false memory to explain my failure, replacing completely memories of relative success? That doesn't seem logical at all.

There may be a clue in one of the developments that did come out of this Mythical time.

Hemet Singh was the tutor who was recommended to me by the high school headmaster. Engaging him was one of the best decisions I made in India. Not only did my Hindi improve, I actually learned to read Devanagri script at about a third grade level.

But there was a more important development with Hemet, one of incredible synchronicity.

My Senior Thesis in college had been an analysis of *The Twice Born* by G. Morris Carstairs. This was an anthropological study of a Rajput Village. I brought the book and my thesis to India with me. Who knew when his insights might come in handy?

98

By some incredible coincidence Hemet Singh was from the village that had been the subject of this study. I don't remember exactly how we stumbled upon this fact, but it was one about which he was very proud. He had a photo of himself with Carstairs, which was a prized possession.

He'd never read the book that Carstairs had produced, so I loaned it to him. He was very appreciative of getting the chance to review the outcome of the study, and in return offered to take me on a visit to his village so I could see the actual site.

Sometime during that visit with his family in the *Twice Born* village they asked me about my assignment. It turned out that they were very interested in doing a demonstration plot for my hybrid wheat. The next thing I knew, we were out marking out the fields to use to compare the yield with my seed against the local variety.

That's when we hit a snag. Apparently I hadn't made it clear when I was describing the demonstration plot concept that the new hybrid wheat required timely doses of fertilizer (the local variety was pretty much a weed that would grow no matter how badly you treated it). At any rate, they pleaded poverty and it looked like the demonstration plot would be a no-go after all.

Now, one of the principles of our extension work was that we were not to use our personal funds when starting one of these demo plots. The very reasonable idea was that the farmers had to make some investment (we were providing the seed) so that they would take ownership of the experiment. But now, following that directive would mean that all the set-up work would go for naught.

It seemed to me that I had a perfectly good compromise that would salvage the situation. So I made a deal with Hemet. I would pay for the fertilizer initially, with the understanding that his family would reimburse me if, and only if, the new high yielding variety produced at least a minimum of 150% of the local crop. I rationalized this as only a bending of the rules, since under any reasonable circumstance we should substantially exceed this outcome.

On those terms we went ahead with the project. His family provided me with what they assured me was one of their best fields. I made sure it was set up next to a precisely measured local field for a good comparison, and we were off to the races.

I made the trip back to this village on at least two separate occasions to check up on the progress of the demonstration, but I was not able to make it when the field was harvested. Soon afterwards Hemet came to report on the outcome.

Dropping by my place one afternoon, Hemet could scarcely contain himself as he exploded with superlatives. This hybrid variety was incredible. They'd never seen anything like it. They were not going to sell any of the seed, but rather keep it to plant as many fields as possible the following season. No one in his family could believe how great this stuff was.

I reminded him that this was as I had predicted, so I wasn't surprised.

"No, you don't understand," he protested. "This was on our worst field! Nothing ever grows there!" Obviously he had forgotten his assurance that they were providing one of their best fields.

There was literally no stopping Hemet as he soared to new levels of excitement. That is, until he got to the bad news part of his report.

Unfortunately, despite the apparent success of the project, it had not quite managed to hit the 150% level of yield we had agreed upon as the goal, so according to our arrangement they would not be able to reimburse me any of the expense.

What? Exactly how did we manage to get there, from the epic crop yield described just seconds earlier?

Rabbits!

Yep, Rabbits.

It seemed that rabbits had gotten into the demonstration plot and eaten just enough of the hybrid wheat to cause the yield to drop below the agreed upon target. Hemet then added that those darn rabbits were the reason they rarely bothered planting that field at all.

There was little use in arguing the point. I should have been there when the fields were harvested, and not trusted my

A successful demonstration plot

partners to report honestly on the result. But I had come to like Hemet, and our tutoring sessions had gotten to be a high point of my time in India, so this was really a double disappointment.

I went back and forth about this in my journal. This demonstration plot was, in fact, a great success. The whole idea was that once you got a farmer excited about the hybrid crop they would spread that enthusiasm throughout the whole village. This is what we were there for, right?

Still there was a sour taste left by the episode. It wasn't the approximately $20 that I lost in this transaction. A personal relationship was damaged by what seemed to me to be very petty behavior by someone I was almost ready to call a friend.

In a similar situation when let down in one of my school projects I wrote a quote in my journal from Hemingway *"But I don't know. Seems like when they get started they don't leave a guy nothing"* ("My Old Man" Ernest Hemingway). Or, as Bill Whitesell once said to me *"India never lets you do anything and come out clean"* (from memory).

So maybe the answer is here. Even when we did manage to accomplish something in our assigned areas, it always fell short, in some significant way, from the Peace Corps ideal of what should come from an effective "Agent of Change." There was always something that kept us from ever taking away an unvarnished feeling of accomplishment.

Maybe my unconscious mind just had too much trouble with all the shades of grey that haunted the Indian Peace Corps experience. It was simpler, it was cleaner, to have a logical myth that explained failure, rather than trying to preserve the mosaic of achievements, false starts, betrayals, and frustrations.

And a myth was nothing if it was not simple, logical and clean…everything that the experience of India was not.

CHAPTER 6

Gullible's Travels Revisited: My Journal, India 44, 1967

Gareth Loy

Forward

When I wrote "A Passage to Udaipur" for the first volume of India 44's reflections, I told the story of my sojourn in the Peace Corps as an autobiography. When I later went back and compared it to the daily journal I kept through the experience, I found that my autobiography was missing an important perspective.

I missed the immediacy that the journal captured so well. I had no crystal ball when I was writing it, no idea that these experiences would someday cohere into a story. The story hadn't been lived yet! I was just trying to capture the poetry of the moment.

And I missed the wild dreaming, the blind alleys, misplaced enthusiasms, magical thinking, misguided longings, ardent foolishness, and hopeful impossibilities!

That is to say, the journal revealed my innocence in a way that the autobiography could not. "Gullible's Travails" was the original title I gave to this journal. Yes, it was a pun on Jonathan Swift's classic parody.

But there was real substance in that playful title; I was painfully aware of my inexperience and of how parochial my life had been. I also knew that the only cure was to throw myself as courageously as I could at the opportunities life presented and watch what happened.

... which explains how I ended up in the Peace Corps.

And what a momentous opportunity it was! Rereading the journal, I experienced again the perplexing ambiguity of each moment, the stubborn opacity of the future, the unexpected highs and the bone-crushing lows. I felt again the strong feelings that welled up in me as I encountered that magical nexus of choice and fate that I—we—experience with every breath.

So I invite you to be my companion on a journey into innocence, to wander through the landscape of India with this naïve soul on his quest for self.

Gullible's Travels Revisited

June 20, 1967

Today I am confronted with the bewildering fact of being 22. Part of my confusion is that I am seemingly doing something about it, since tomorrow I leave home to seek my fortune in India with the Peace Corps. My friends from high school are coming by to wish me well. I haven't seen most of them in years. They looked older but the inner spirit hadn't changed. One still has impeccable manners, another constantly cracking jokes... wonder what I am still doing? Apart from the music, that is.

I got Yellow Fever today. The shot, not the disease. Didn't hurt at all. Tonight I packed and cursed and cursed and packed, finishing about midnight. Total weight: 100 lbs. The word is anxiety.

June 21

Woke up sleepy, but my stomach knotted up immediately, which got me out of bed straightaway. Dad drove me to the bus to get to the airport in L.A.; said goodbye. Anxiety continued until, curiously, I got on the airplane, then everything seemed to settle out, though I'd never been on a jet before. It was amazing to feel the massive tug of inertia when the plane changed directions.

June 26 Madison, Wisconsin

The anxiety of going but not yet being gone is over and has been transformed into enthusiasm. Asher raised the last doubts to me Friday night walking around the streets near our training site. I think he's going to deselect. But being here at the start of training has convinced me: I am in the right place doing the right thing. Today, the first day of our field experience, we planted gardens, a harrowing experience.

June 27

Went to an experimental farm today for a lecture on soils from a researcher in wheat. I was afraid I would start snoring, I couldn't stay awake. I asked him to summarize his findings. It boiled down to: there sure are a lot of diseases of wheat and kinds of soil. Great.

July 3

Just got back from the dentist where I had my wisdom teeth removed. I feel about as well as I could, given the circumstances. I suppose it is better here than having them out at the hands of a dentist in rural India. If anyone asks about my battle scars from the Peace Corps, I'll point to my mouth.

We are living in canvas tents lined up in the back 40 of the Henry Seed Farm. Language lessons, culture of India, more language lessons, and some hands-on farming experience. The matron of the farm, Mother Henry, is like a character out of a movie, very blunt, assertive, and plain-spoken. I like her, she reminds me of my step-grandma Nina. There's a girl on the farm, Judy, who is visiting the Henry's, she's not in the program. She's young but very interesting. I like spending time with her. She likes it too, I think.

July 4

So today we sang Merry Christmas to the USA. Several people went to town to celebrate; the rest of us stayed in camp and had a good time: we made a fire, poured benzene over it and dumped ammonium nitrate fertilizer on it and watched it flash and spark. We put bottles in it to melt. At one point I grabbed a stick burning at one end and ran out into the field and threw it into the air, watching the sparks as it hit the earth. And way off in the distance we could see the fireworks in the city blip faintly against the overwhelming crystal star patterns overhead.

July 21

Our time on the Henry Seed Farm is over. I am packing, hassling with packing, getting shots, language tests, supplies, headaches. We are leaving for New York Monday, for India the 29th, arriving the 31st, a 36 hour trip.

July 24 New York.

I'm not sure how to say this, but suddenly, now that I am leaving the US, I have become hot with girls. And I don't think it's because I've changed. A couple of times in the last few days, when girls hear that I'm leaving for India in the Peace Corps, it's like they open up to me. Like, really open up. I ended up in a shower naked with one of them. Another ended up in my bed late the night before we flew to London. Ultimately, nothing happened, of course. But it makes me crazy. Why, when it's impossible to start a relationship, do they open to me? Is that the reason, because I'm unavailable after tomorrow? That's really fucked up.

The most amazing experience in New York was the meditation room in the United Nations building. As soon as I entered I was thrust into a deep state, a very powerful combination of emotion and calm. I thought about my dedication to the Peace Corps. As I left, I read the dedication on the wall: "This room is dedicated to peace and those who are dedicating their lives to peace."

London was next. It was only when we were out of the airport in downtown London, seeing the smiling faces, that it ceased to be a dream. The Peace Corps is treating us very well. The thing that impressed me from New York to New Delhi was all the service, food, drinks, comfort. Rather like the Aztecs used to elect one of their number to be a god for a year and then sacrifice…

July 29

Arrived in New Delhi. We almost didn't make it. The cowling fell off an engine. The pilot had opened the door and let us stand around next to the cockpit when the plane lurched and all the lights on the console lit up red. He casually flipped some switches and kept flying. We were over India by this time, still very high, and I imagined this enormous piece of metal crashing to the ground out of a clear blue sky next to some farmer standing in his field.

When I stepped from the airplane I was clubbed by the humid heat: 85 degrees, 100% humidity. We were whisked through customs with no problems. The officials looked like roosters strutting around in their costumes.

Sitting on the bus to leave the airport, Sheryl came over and slapped my arm that was in the windowsill and said, "Well, Gareth, I'll see you," and walked away. The reaction among the

Indian International Center

onlooking Indians was excited and startled. The "loose American women" theory got about fifteen new converts.

We stayed at the Indian International Center, a hotel that gives out free Coke, air conditioning in each room, etc. The Peace Corps pays 45 rupees a day for this luxury. That afternoon they handed us each 450 Rs. and gave us a lecture on something I've already forgotten.

We proceeded immediately out to see Delhi, and ended up at the Red Fort, which was closed, so we just walked around the streets. It was rather traumatic. The cultural differences are visceral and shocking. My body came to India Friday but my mind only showed up today. Everyone in India was looking AT ME. Not because of what I was doing but because of who I was: this 6-foot 5-inch white giant. I tower over them, and their mouths fall open as their eyes travel up to meet mine. The lepers on the streets are completely horrendous, I can't look at them. I'm told they cultivate their disease to beg more effectively. People

High noon in Salumbar

urinate and defecate in the streets. Cripples are everywhere. Gaunt dirty-white cows stand in the road and cause huge traffic jams and nobody chases them away. Dirt. Dry. These terrifying 3-wheeled glorified motorcycle carts barge around corners and each other narrowly missing us, horns blaring. Gangs of children crush us begging for money. Of course if you give them any the crowd just gets bigger and more insistent.

August 4

Udaipur. We arrived yesterday morning after a 24-hour train ride from Delhi. I was very stirred up by Delhi. It was too much of everything and I was just reacting at nerve level to the days we were there. The atmosphere in Udaipur is much more congenial. Here I have a chance of being something besides a tourist. In fact, I am so happy with this location that yesterday I spent the day rushing around town on my bicycle to see the sights. Yesterday I saw the Telab Mahal (Lake Palace Hotel), the Gulab Bhag (Flower Garden), and the city wall. While downtown I picked up a 220 v. transformer and plug and now have my tape recorder working well.

I am sitting on a charpoi (a wood frame with flax rope woven as a mattress) in a dormitory room of the Vidya Bhawan Rural Institute where we are headquartered. It has a grass courtyard. It looks western, but there are subtle things that tell me it is India: smells I never encountered before bring my thoughts back to my situation faster than anything. Students walk by speaking Hindi. Oh, the birds! And the new stars at night in the southern sky! Mealtime always brings surprises, most of them pleasant. And occasionally a Volunteer shouts from an adjoining room, "India?! What the hell am I doing in India?!"

This evening we had a lecture by our doctor about all the horrible diseases we should be very afraid of catching. Lovely. At dinner we had some local officials come speak to us, an experience that has to be witnessed to be believed... Then, calmly sitting in my room with Don Carter, we were suddenly deluged by about a hundred students. Noisy, excitable, sometimes unintelligible, they practiced their English on us as we practiced our

Hindi on them. *I played my guitar for them, and they stayed very late. I am very tired.*

My first bout of diarrhea abated and I'm enjoying good digestion while it lasts.

August 7

Yesterday they took us to a field nearby where a pair of bullocks were harnessed to an old-fashioned wood plow. I got a chance to make a furrow. The bullocks went when I told them to go and stopped when I told them to stop. Amazing.

In two days this American colony I am living in will be dispersed and we will go to live in temporary villages, three to a group. So far at this site things have become increasingly secure to the point where I've made an adequate biological adjustment to the food and surroundings. So at times I even forget I'm in India. I'm finding the Indians very approachable. Everything I do right now is crucial or basic to my total response to India. But nothing I am doing is accomplishing anything... yet!

August 11, Lacowli village.

Wow. Two days ago I was a safe, secure pucca sahib, sitting in Ian Brody's pad, drinking Indian gin and talking music and politics, and other good western topics. The next morning we arrived in our temporary sites in small villages outside of Udaipur. Culture shock! The experience for me was the realization that I was completely out of my natural environment, totally submerged in a situation in which all I could count on was my own two hands and my Hindi. The local children are a plague of locusts, shouting in our windows, crowding around, following us everywhere... We got quite paranoid. Two others are here with me, Don Carter, who is going to deselect himself, and Don Nordin, who is, like me, retaining his cool a little better.

After we got settled in I jumped on my bicycle and rode back to Udaipur to attend a concert. Ian Brody is going back home shortly and he has made friends with Ram Lal Mathur, music master at Viddia Bhavan school where Ian taught. So he arranged a recording session with Mr. Mathur for last night to take some tapes home. Ian had invited me, so I went. When I arrived back at Udaipur I was a nervous wreck. I sat at Ian's place and smoked a bidi (a type of Indian cigarette) to calm my nerves. In the next couple of hours I went with Ian and Jo (staff) to see the art master. He showed us his works, some of which were very impressive, then in the evening we went to the school. By that time I was calmed down. The concert started an hour later (Indian time). My recording abilities came in handy, as I adjusted everyone's setup to get a good signal between the sitar and tabla. Sri Mathur asked for a copy of my recording and asked how long I would be staying. This was a stroke of luck as I had hoped to talk with him about sitar lessons. So I arranged to meet with him again in three weeks, the length of our stay in the temporary villages.

But there's more! I stayed that night at Ian's house (didn't want to risk breaking my neck on the road back to Lacowli after dark) and in the morning before I left, Sri Mathur (who lived next door) came over and asked if I would come and play the tape at his house so his wife could hear. Of course I would! So while the tape was spinning, we sat on his veranda and drank tea. He very proudly showed me pictures he had taken of his master, Ustad Ali Akbar Khan. So it looks like my chances are good for lessons, plus a friend of high character; a very important thing for my sanity over the next two years.

I rode back to Lacowli and spent another traumatic day. Don Nordin lost his wallet with 400 Rs. in it. The rest of the day was spent answering villagers' inquiries about it, and tisk-tisking. Yesterday Don Carter gave the milk walla (seller) our brass pot to get milk. The man has not returned. I must laugh, we have been played for suckers with a very old trick. Don Carter will definitely deselect himself.

Notwithstanding the trauma, I am expanding and refining my perceptions. This kind of stress is good to let me know what kinds of situations I can handle and what I need to work on more. I am so far away from the center of my ordinary life that I appear strange to myself. I have no way of knowing what impact (if any) I am having on the villagers, or they on me. Yet.

111

August 12

I've never seen anyone as blatantly paranoid as a new volunteer in a new village. While trying to get to sleep, sounds of dogs scrapping outside my door sound more like burglars trying to get in. I stop and think about it and decide the sound is coming from inside the house. My heart starts thumping. Then Nordin turns over in the next charpoi and my imagination really gets going. The flashlight is the only thing that will calm me down. Nothing. But the noises outside persist and keep me awake.

Today was the most productive day so far in India. I was awakened at 8:00 am by a young voice in the window wanting to bring us some water. The morning was just as hard as yesterday; it was 10:00 am before I had the dishes washed and the milk boiled so I could have cereal and milk. Carter's jaw was swelling up—probably a residual infection from getting his wisdom teeth out, so he was even more miserable than yesterday. Some staff came out to visit yesterday, and he told them his decision. So today more staff will arrive. Don N. and I left at noon for Udaipur to lay in supplies. We met the staff on the road to Lacowli, then proceeded to Vidya Bhavan where we managed to score a hot lunch. The staff finally decided that the lousy wick kerosene stoves they gave us are simply unusable, a decision we had made on our own the first time we tried to boil water on them. So we were very pleased.

Carol, wife of one of the staff, accompanied us downtown and was invaluable helping us navigate the food stalls to buy vegetables and spices. We ran all over Udaipur buying great quantities of essential, useful, and useless things, poking our noses in stores, trying out our Hindi, and spending enormous sums of money, at least 50 Rs. ($6.60) We bought cups and saucers, eight liters of kerosene (in Hindi it is called "liquid of the earth"), burlap to cover our latrine, spices, vegetables, rice, sweet biscuits, chutney, bottles to hold kerosene, etc., etc. On our way back out we stopped by Vidya Bhavan to pick up our stove and found Don Carter there. He was staying at least two more weeks, probably at the main base at Vidya Bhavan.

Back in Lacowli at sundown, Don N. and I worked swiftly together and made beans and chapattis for dinner with our new *stove. We swigged it down with good hot tea and topped it off with an after-dinner bidi to smoke. Since then, I've been trying to get to sleep with little success, as the first paragraph outlines. I guess I'll try again now...*

August 13

Awakened by the dudh walla (milk vendor). Went to cook breakfast and again it took two hours. The monsoon rains have come on strong, and the rain really came down. The houses were so beautiful, the fires burning inside them, smoke rising through the brick roofs. I saw the "tank" today, which is a lake dammed at one end, just down the road. It's big, not too cold. Nobody fishes, no boats, very peaceful. It rained and rained.

Don Carter came back today, his spirits higher, but his depression still going strong. In the evening our neighbor, the tax collector, and only Muslim in the town, invited us over to his house for dinner. Only he did so with a very conspiratorial air, bringing us one at a time to his house after dark. Very mysterious until we were assembled there, whereupon he fed us meat! The first I have had in a long time. From its toughness it was evident that it was a fairly antique goat that the gosht walla (meat vendor) brought to town yesterday. This was served with chapattis and a local brew of wine, which tasted like tequila—very good. This was actually our first social visit in the village.

August 14

The dudh walla woke us up again. Today I went with Don N. to take a "shower" at the lake. It comprises stripping to your underwear, climbing up on the dam and jumping 20 feet into the water. You get out, soap yourself up, and then climb up again and jump! When you come out you are clean! The scenery is like a paradise, and there are usually no people around that early.

When we got back, some staff came out in a jeep. We took them on a short hike to the top of the hill that stands between the village and the lake. You can see to Udaipur and all the outlying hills and villages. When the staff left, I ended up at the school next door eating with the principal and the two school teachers.

They have invited us tomorrow to attend the Independence Day ceremony at 7:00 am. It should be one hell of an experience.

August 15

It was! Everyone important in the village was there sitting in the schoolyard. The VIPs sat in front of the flag pole in the main square with the grade-school kids lined up in rows on the ground facing us. There were (mercifully) short speeches from a podium, then some songs sung by the kids, then some incense was burned. A gentle monsoon rain began to fall, so we all moved to the veranda of the schoolhouse. When tea was served, we and the sarpanch (council representative for the village) got it first, and in crockery. The elders sitting around, talking, had a very powerful feeling on me. Anything to be done in the village went through their discretion. And there I was among them, an "agent of change," whatever that means, trying to imagine where the levers of power were and how they operated.

Then we left for Udaipur. In the afternoon, we had group discussions, pouring out our troubles, insights, aha moments, and meager successes. All of the complaints sounded about like you'd expect: those damned bratty kids, exhaustion, getting sick, hours spent cooking, etc. In the evening Vidya Bhavan staged a talent show. A large hall was jammed with noisy and inconsiderate people. But when I took out my guitar, it really got their attention.

August 16

Bad diarrhea day. Back to Udaipur for some medicine. I ran around all over town buying supplies.

I must admit I really love being a pukka American sahib. We are hybrids being self-grafted into another culture with a positive goal for change. The goals spring from high up the world government mountain, and change and shift meaning as they filter down: world peace, health for all, human self-confidence, nourishing food for all, better quality markets, more family income. And for me? A two-year opportunity to boost my ego by trying to get something positive done.

August 21

The biggest challenge living in this village is working together functionally. Fried eggs and cereal for breakfast, then I washed out the kitchen. A language instructor came and taught us Mewari, the local dialect, which to her is a "dirty language" of "bastardized Hindi." I wasn't too keen on it either, since all it does is confuse my already marginal Hindi. After she left, Don C. (who is still deselecting) and I went into the village to take pictures. Kids began swarming around, bugging us, of course. I wonder when this will ever stop? Don N. went to Udaipur for some meeting I'd not heard about.

Last weekend the friend of Govind who I was supposed to look up came up and found me. I'm to go to his house this Saturday to meet his friend who can teach me Indian instruments.

August 24

Yesterday Don, Don, and I went to a Mewari mela (festival) in the mountains (jungali) in back of Lacowli. We were not only the only English speakers there, but also the only Hindi speakers. I shot quite a bit of film. I should have had color because I've never seen so much of it in one place. I drank bhang tea with the Mayor and Superintendent of Education, sipping out of proper British cups and saucers. I sat and watched the troubadours dance and give plays, sitting in a circle; the women and men strictly segregated. One man wore a mask of bright colors, the others had sun and moon sewn on the backs of their shirts. In another section, some men, high on bhang sat next to an altar to Vishnu and played instruments, tabla, hand cymbals, tambourines, and sang. I wanted to get close-ups of their faces on the camera so I joined them. I was gladly invited. They handed me a tambourine to play and I beat along to the rhythm, a big broad smile on my face.

Coming home we lost our way and ended up pounding over rocks on a cow path for five miles before reaching Lacowli.

Today, Aruna, staff from Delhi came to Lacowli to teach us Hindi. I woke up just as she arrived. She is very easy to talk Hindi to, unlike most other teachers. Just as she left, the trou-

badours arrived in town. Sitting here on my charpoi I can hear their chants in the background. Don N. is painting our door and Don Carter is going over to Sinalpur to buy us some bidis.

The mela provides a vivid contrast to the Independence Day celebration. In this village, Independence Day was very low-key. All the figureheads of the village attended and the ceremony was solemn enough. The mela, on the other hand, was a big, wild, emotional release for everyone involved.

August 27

Weekends like this one are what make it all worthwhile. Friday afternoon, I had a good meal with Don C. at Berry's, a local restaurant in Udaipur. Western food! Then we went out to the Udaipur Archeological Museum and got a tour of the sites and of the local temples with a description of the statuary and bass-reliefs. We were swept away by the exquisiteness and aesthetic impact of the temples. I got very stimulated by what we saw and stayed up late drawing jewelry, temples, and landscapes of India.

Before he left, Ian had introduced me to his tailor, who made me two sets of khadis: long, filmy white shirts and pantaloons. The shirt billows out behind my bicycle as I ride along. I complement this with a maroon beret and my wire frame glasses. Yes, I'm quite a sight.

Saturday we registered with the police. It took all morning for a simple operation. In the afternoon I went with Jerry Weiss and Mike Simonds to Hiara Nayan's house where we met Sri Dagar, the sitar player Govind had suggested for a teacher. We listened to him play for a long time. Then he asked

Gareth in native dress

*me to play my guitar, which I had brought. He was very pleased.
I was very impressed with his playing. So we made an appoint-
ment to visit his school on Sunday.*

August 29

*Sunday, 10:00am, I went with Jerry Weiss to Sri Dagar's
school. I took my tape recorder. I got a full performance of
many different instruments they teach there. Water-filled bowls
arranged diatonically were played in some Hungarian minor
key by a boy striking them with chopsticks. A child played an
Indian banjo, which is eight unison-tuned strings on a sounding
board with levers like old-fashioned typewriter buttons on their
ends that the performer could press across the strings to stop
them at various diatonic lengths. And there was a magnificent
tabla solo performed by the tabla teacher, Ustad Hafiz Mian.
He was Nathu Lal's teacher, one of the very best in India. I got
excellent recordings of all these performances. Everyone had a
wonderful time. I understand from Ian that Sri Dagar is from a
distinguished musical family of Rajasthan. I arranged to have
sitar lessons with him at his school, though I have no idea how
this is going to work if my site is very remote.*

*I got back from this very pleasing experience to VBRI
around noon and was about to lie down when the staff ran in
and said, "Gareth, it's time to go, you're on!" It turns out that
I had been put on the bill to play at a reception that was being
given for the volunteers by the mayor of Udaipur, so I grabbed
my guitar and jumped in a jeep. We arrived at what looked like
a large fairgrounds with a stage overlooking a large dusty field.
The field was filled with residents of Udaipur, men, women, and
children all together. First on the bill was an introduction by
the mayor. He only droned on a bit, then some official from the
Peace Corps spoke. Then the mayor turned the proceedings over
to a troupe of local musicians and dancers who played some
very festive music and danced a colorful dance. It did not look
like Bharat Natyam, but the music had a similar feel.*

*Then it was our turn. Gary Gruber played a Bach solo par-
tita on his violin. I accompanied Dave Bauer singing "The Hills*

Muscians at a mela

Are Alive" from The Sound of Music. We are both barefoot with red marks on our foreheads that they'd put on us at the beginning... I guess as a sign of honor for being their guests.

Then I sang Raghupati Ragav Raja Ram on my 12-string guitar. It was amazing. First, their jaws dropped open and their eyes bugged out. They looked at each other and at me. Then, as it sank in that here's this American singing in Hindi, they got very excited and started singing along...all of them. There were a lot of people in that field. They loved it! I was thrilled! At the end they placed garlands around our necks, and when they came to me there was a good round of applause, which was quite a compliment. After the program a large group of people surrounded me and talked me into playing it again, which I did very earnestly.

Sunday night we rode back to Lacowli. The sunset over the Western Ghats filled the sky with colored lights. A sense of peace descended as I rode along on my bike.

August 30

Aruna came back to continue our Hindi lessons today. She told me the significance of what I had sung yesterday. She said that this song was the unofficial national anthem of India because Mahatma Ghandi had written one of the verses. She translated it as, "The Hindu God and the Muslim God are the same, they both give peace to everyone."

I'd learned the song from a "Weavers at Carnegie Hall" album my parents had bought in the mid 1950's. Pete Seeger sang Raghupati with his giant 12-string guitar. I thought it was very cool, so when I bought a 12-string guitar myself, I learned the guitar part. When I joined the Peace Corps, I went back and learned to sing the song phonetically from the record. The words were in Sanskrit, so I had no idea what they meant, I just really liked the song. Anyway, Aruna's story would explain why this song ended up in Pete Seeger's repertoire. And it would certainly explain the reaction it got from an Indian audience for a white guy to come from America and sing it to them!

August 31

A very full day of many contrasting events. At 8:00 am the jeep came for us at Lacowli. We packed everything in and took off on our bicycles over a new route. Don C. and I ended up carrying our bikes over vegetable gardens and following cow paths to get to VBRI in Udaipur. As we rode through the city, a man broke out singing Raghupati in the street as we rode past! So I'm famous in Udaipur.

As soon as we arrived, Don C. was told that he would leave today. So in a flurry he sold everything and packed. In the afternoon, we went downtown. Don bought some silk for his girlfriend when he gets back. We had lunch at a good downtown restaurant, hit the silver bazaar, and came back. Don left shortly after. It was very hard to say goodbye, but there was absolutely nothing I could do.

Some staff wives picked me up in a jeep and we went cruising around Udaipur. We ended up at a lecture on Hungarian folk music. The guy was saying that the Gypsies in Europe came from India.

This evening Mike Goldberg sat with me, reading my poems out loud to me, commenting on them. It was very sweet.

Gareth and guitar, 2009

The sun shines daily
But leaves the night so deeply
That the moon changes.

September 1st

What a hell of a way to begin September. At 7:00 am sharp,
they rolled us out to a breakfast of two pancakes. Then off to a

tea and crumpets reception at Udaipur University, listening to Mickey Mouse speeches. Then we went on a worthless field trip, 120 km to see compost pits and a really bad demonstration plot. Today was really lost though because, through it all, I had a bad stomach. It was all I could do to sit on a bus, bouncing up and down, without puking. I lost my appetite at dinner. I haven't had a bath in a week. I feel like crapping all over God's big, beautiful earth.

September 7th

Bacillary dysentery, fever of 105, stayed in bed for a week, feeling blah, thinking blah, shitting blah.

Monday, before I was too sick, I had my first sitar lesson. I was having a great time! Blowing my mind, wow! It's just as exciting as I had hoped, and that's something.

People still recognize me as the guy who sang Raghupati. I guess that's not too surprising, considering I'm this enormous white guy in their midst. Not too hard to spot me. But it's nice. No matter what else happens here, I've already accomplished something.

September 8

Woke up today to see Dave Bauer packing his stuff. I asked why, he said he's going home: family problems... That means out of my room, Roger Edwards, myself, Don Carter, and Dave Bauer, we're losing 50%, plus they are the only two guys to go home from our project. I'd just love to be going home now. But I'd also like to be going home after completing two years successfully (that is, without going crazy).

On an elementary level, the problem breaks down to a conflict between me and my karma: a personal wish to become a musician, and a strong feeling that India is where I should be. But I chafe at the problem. I calm myself and try to be rational, trying to use one power in my life against another, so that I am relatively free in the middle, I hope.

One reason, very important, that keeps me here, is that so many good things have happened as a result of being in the

Peace Corps so far, not to mention all the things that the Peace Corps has given me: a job, security, a future, travel, etc. In other words, this seems to be the line of least resistance and most positive emphasis, no matter how much anxiety and frustration it embodies.

September 9

After lunch, Bill O'Connor, head of P.C. Regional in Delhi, asked to talk to me. As we walked along, he explained how it is that the staff feels "unsure of whether you will find a role for yourself in agriculture." He said it was becoming clear to them that my first love was my music and that it was occupying my interest to the degree that my role as a 'Village Level Food Producer' was in danger. And that, judging on these considerations, I should find myself another project.

I think they are going to deselect me. I got really sick tonight, heaving, fever. Had such vivid dreams that it seemed like hallucinating.

September 10

I'm writing this on the airplane leaving Udaipur. I was instructed to pack last night. I sold most of my things, including the tape recorder. My mind reels at the speed with which all this has been pushed through. I am angry at the way it was shoved down my throat. This, after having gone through a year-and-a-half of training, and then in an instant it is all over, just on the threshold of an assignment, just as I am all psyched up to do this. The confused emotions built up in me last night until I broke down and wept.

I thought perhaps in India I would be safe from my destiny, but it only provoked it. My attempt to retreat from the center of my life has failed, and I am thrust back into it with a force and clarity that I have never felt before.

And I feel really, really sick.

Late this afternoon I discussed the entire subject with Bill and Aruna—the two who exercise deselection power. How could they do this? After the Peace Corps had invested all this money and time in me, and I had in turn given the Peace Corps my life? How could they just throw away my good intentions, my hard work, my dedication? Did that count for nothing? School has already begun, I have no money, no job to go back to. I am bonded with my fellow volunteers, who are my only friends and my community, and they are sending me into involuntary exile. I have to face my family as a failure before I was even given a chance to succeed. This will haunt me for the rest of my life.

They replied that they wanted to make it clear to me that it was easy to see my motivation and desire to be in the Peace Corps and that this was not what they were concerned about. Nor was it a personality conflict. They didn't want volunteers in the field who would just end up bitter because of the isolation. Aruna said she could see me in maybe an urban project where I could do my job and still have access to a cultural center. She felt it would be a waste of my abilities and my life for me to be so isolated in a village.

When she said this, I smiled. Deep down inside I was worried about this too. Somehow, however, I don't think it is something I could have ever decided for myself; I was so charged up about the Peace Corps. Anyway, they made it plain that I have no power in this situation; their word is final.

September 26

Woke up with tremendous pain in my stomach on the 20th. I staggered over to the Peace Corps office and they sent me straight to the hospital. The pain subsided two days later, but because of weakness and weight loss I stayed until the 25th. Indian hospitals are really an unforgettable experience. Blood tests show an abnormal involvement with the kidney. Mono? But not conclusive. I've had a good pint of blood removed from my arm for blood tests, no telling where it will end. I'm just seeing more and more doctors.

Since getting out of the Holy Family hospital my health has again declined; same old gland and stomach pains. They send me in taxis all over Delhi to hematologists.

I befriended some WTs (World Travelers) staying at my hotel. Americans, they've traveled across Europe, through Turkey, Afghanistan, Pakistan, and now India. I wonder how they pay for it? They are in the room next door to mine.

September 29

Looking in my wallet today I realized that all of my money was missing. About 300 Rs. Gone! Shit! Not even enough for a taxi to get over to the P.C. office. The manager called the house detective who came and investigated the "scene of the crime" in my hotel room. Nothing came of it. I then walked over to the P.C. offices to beg for more money.

October 4

Yesterday I received a telegram from the Peace Corps, Washington "Department of Special Problems" informing me that as of September 20th, my Draft Board had reclassified me 1-A. So I'm going straight home now, not to Washington DC. Oh well. I think now's the time to try to get my C.O. status and start working, pay some debts, keep some bureaucracies happy.

The horrible thought is that I may be finishing the pages of this journal in Boot Camp. As far as the Army is concerned, that's my next stop, and Vietnam shortly thereafter. Only my very own efforts within a narrow field of possibilities will intervene. I may be crushed by impartiality. I see guys fleeing to Canada and I wonder. I may be anywhere next year. Maybe even London.

October 5

Two days ago I did not receive a telegram from the Peace Corps, some other guy did, and it was mistakenly delivered to me!! Just like in the movies!! I took it over to PC Regional offices and found out the mistake there. Oh, I am so happy!

October 12

My diagnosis is infectious mononucleosis, amnebiasis (amoebic dysentery) and bacillary dysentery. So I have a lot of pills. This final diagnosis means the end of my medical hold status and if I stay in Delhi longer it will be on my own (nonexistent) money. Maybe I'll ask a staff friend to sleep on his floor for a while. Maybe not. I don't know. I really don't know. If I agree to go now, they'll pay for it, otherwise...? I'd like to stay, but...

One of the WTs told me that there was a place he was looking for that he'd been told about, that if you can find it, the day you show up there will be a message there waiting for you with your name on it, like they expected you. You show up with any question you want, you don't tell them what it is, but they go back and find your letter and hand it to you, and there's the answer to your question! Kind of reminds me of the I Ching. Maybe this is the Hindu version of that? Hope he finds it.

October 15

Before I went into the hospital I bought a sitar. Since then I've been practicing it a lot. I met a guy who is teaching me. He comes to my hotel every day. I'm leaving for home tomorrow.

This evening the WTs and I went to the Oberoi hotel for dinner to celebrate my departure. A Swedish girl was with us. She got really drunk and wanted to go swimming in the hotel pool and tried to convince the rest of us to just jump in with our clothes on. She grabbed one of the guys and pulled him in with a giant splash. I ran to help them out but she wouldn't come out. She kept swimming around until the hotel staff very nervously informed her that the pool was closed. She got out but then jumped right in again.

A very matronly American woman came over and sternly demanded: "Are you people with the Peace Corps?" Fortunately, I was able to deny it. "Well, why don't you get this girl out of a respectable place like this?" At which point, the girl jumped out of the pool and got in a shouting match with the woman about who should mind who's business.

The scene ended with us walking through the posh lobby of the hotel, the girl and the guy dripping wet and scraggly. The hotel personnel got quite a kick out of it all and were nodding and smiling as we dribbled by. A fittingly surreal end to my surreal Peace Corps experience.

October 19

I'm sitting at my Dad's desk in his study in Diamond Bar, California. There is no dust in the air, the cry of the fruit sellers does not penetrate the walls, no dogs barking, no cows force motorists to honk them out of the way, even the whine of jet engines and the popping sound in my ears as we change altitude is a day-and-a-half behind me. The cultural reentry has been brutal. And I'd only been out of the country four months. But I see the culture of America with new—jaundiced—eyes. Just as one does not register that the sky is blue, I had not ever been able to look at the culture I grew up in like this before. It has lost its inevitability. What if India was my home and I came to America? What a strange place it would seem.

I am in an amazing frame of mind. Amazing to me mostly because my thoughts so easily jump high into the air, and so simply allow true irony to stand out, and so potently shine light on my formerly muddled thoughts. I feel truly that I am walking by the light of vision as well as by the sight of vision.

But nothing is more amazing to me than the path I have been following. Last month was a big circus in which I sat back in my seat of illusion while nurses and doctors poked and prodded me, musicians made me weep with joy, friends showed up out of nowhere, people stole my money, shopkeepers and taxi drivers took the rest, the Peace Corps gave me more, doctors stuck 59 needles in my arm, and finally my very soul rose into the air, grabbed the rings and did its own trapeze show. Of course, the master illusionist is me.

And what is driving this? Love, that's what. My need for love must be met or I will surely wither and die. My highest hope is that I will be fulfilled spiritually by the future, which lies squarely in the hands of Fate. I pray I will be carried to my true vocation, and that I will find true friends.

November 28

Where is Gareth? He's lying before a fireplace enjoying its warmth. The room is dark, though the light from the kitchen shines gently while he writes this. A beautiful girl, Vicky, is sit-

*ting beside him, her boy-child sleeping on the floor. She is writ-
ing a poem on a deep subject that doesn't satisfy her yet.*

*Gareth has just extended his job at the West Hollywood
Presbyterian church, hoping this will be the C.O. job he needs,
if his Draft Board agrees. He is living with Vicky and her son
Tony in a house the church owns, enjoying it very much. Vicky is
the child of a church member, extracting herself from an abusive
relationship by hiding out here with her son. He is very drawn
to Vicky for reasons and passions he hardly understands, but
accepts with gladness.*

*He is just emerging from a crucible of intense suffering.
He is trying very hard to be himself in ways that he is just now
learning about. Being himself has led him to this point, and he
stands in wonder of the exactions of life. But his perseverance is
increasing, so that he may rest assured that his future trips will
all be blessed ones.*

CHAPTER 7

Further Reflections on a Prior Life

Tom Corbett

Success is going from failure to failure without losing your enthusiasm.

Abraham Lincoln

In our first volume of reflections, I wrote a chapter called "Reflections on a Prior Life." It was, more or less, a standard trip down memory lane…a sometimes humorous, sometimes sad, sometimes uplifting, and too often embarrassing narrative of what I did and what I experienced during my tenure in India 44. That set of reflections covered a lot of the conventional ground from how my early upbringing led me to the Peace Corps, to the PC experience itself and how my life unfolded upon my return. I am sure the best part for most readers was the relief they felt when my rather lengthy story was finally at an end.

So, as we began discussing a sequel to the first volume, my initial reaction was that I have already said all I want to say and, surely, all that anyone might possibly want to read.

Life, though, has a way of playing strange tricks on you. In my prior chapter, I mentioned the college girlfriend (Lee) I left behind to go to India. I spoke, with a touch of sadness, about the letter I received about halfway through my India stay telling me she would not be waiting for my return. Rather, she was to marry a Harvard post-doc she met while working at a research lab there. Even at the time, it seemed to me to be a very sensible decision on her part…choosing an established academic over a directionless Peace Corps volunteer living on the other side of the world; a guy with few demonstrable prospects who routinely expressed striking ambivalence about such minor matters as marriage and commitment.

With the resilience of youth, I stuffed whatever disappointment I may have felt wherever one puts those things and went on with my life. For the record, and much to everyone's amazement, I did overcome my commitment phobia and have been married to the same wonderful woman for four decades. The really amazing part of it all is that she has put up with me for so long. Go figure!

After our first group reunion in May of 2009, and after I had written my draft for the first volume of reflections, I finally joined a billion other largely friendless individuals on Facebook, thinking I would prefer virtual connections to the real things. To be honest, I find this social network tedious … at least most of the time. It strikes me as remarkable, if not inconceivable, that so many people have lives as boring and inconsequential as mine.

Nevertheless, while stumbling around the site one day not knowing what I was doing, I came across that gal who dumped me some 45 years ago. After some hesitation, I said 'what the hell' and sent a message. I mean, the worst she would probably say is…Tom who? Or maybe take out a restraining order. Much to my great surprise, however, she remembered who I was. And much to my total shock, she was thrilled to hear from me. You can never overestimate people's atrocious judgment.

The reconnection, however, was to be touched with sadness as Lee was to be diagnosed with a terminal case of cancer not all that long after we reconnected. Before her passing, we did have an opportunity to catch up and revisit old times including processing what might have been going through our heads as immature college kids. I remain quite grateful for that.

More to the point, though, she forwarded to me the letters I had sent her during my PC service which, to my utter amazement, she managed to hang onto all these years. Only a subset of those letters survived the subsequent four-plus decades and, of course, I only include illustrative excerpts in this work. But the surviving missives do manage to capture the flavor of who I was and what I was experiencing back then. More importantly, they remain the most unvarnished record, the only written record in fact, of my Peace Corps experience and I am very thankful she kept them safe.

Lee, graduation day, at Clark, 1966

Having said that, the majority of my letters to her are missing, lost by accident or on purpose. She may well have kept only what she deemed the more reflective letters, showing less interest in those that were more newsy and superficial, or perhaps she retained only those letters she thought might be useful in some later inquiry into what drove this young man completely over the edge. Hard to say, but such a hypothesis could, I believe, explain why I so often come across as a whiney, borderline neurotic with decidedly depressive tendencies.

Nevertheless, reading the missives that survived is illuminating, even if embarrassing. I shudder at the raw emotions spilling forth in the words of my youthful innocence and passion. At the same time, I am equally struck by the occasional insight and even a revelation or two embedded in those long-ago written sentiments.

Memory, it turns out, is an elastic phenomenon. It can be stretched and twisted to make a sensible narrative out of fleeting images and half-recollected events. Our pre-frontal cortex, the last part of our brain to evolve, apparently is the first to decay, which is surely true in my sad case. It becomes harder to accurately retrieve what we have stored away or to weave what we recollect into a narrative approaching what really may have happened.

Not that much of what I wrote while in India contradicts what I said in the chapter I prepared for the first volume. The bigger problems with my earlier reflections are mostly those of omission, where events and feelings and perceptions have been obscured by the passage of time or lost completely. On occasion, though, I was shocked to find that I had woven personal narratives that bore no relation to what actually happened.

At times, it felt as if I were reading the letters of another person entirely. And yet, at the end of the day, I could see myself, fully revealed and emotionally raw, pouring out my insides to the one person who mattered at that time.

Thus, I have a second chance to tell my story, or at least part of the story, this time grounded in my words from that time and place. I let my own words from long ago talk for me, surrounding them with some context and interpretation. Where my prior chapter mostly described what I did back then, this story line is more of an interior journey focusing on what I felt and how I responded to what was going on about me, or to me. Let us see where this takes us.

SUMMER OF 1966

As discussed in my earlier chapter, Reflections on a Prior Life, I grew up in an ethnic, working class neighborhood in Worcester, Massachusetts. For the uninformed, this was an absolutist world of right and wrong, good and evil, black and white. Prejudices were rampant, levied against those of the wrong color or religion or class or ethnic affiliation or whatever other way people might invent to divide up the world. It was a world, and a childhood, that hardly prepared me for the openness to others demanded of Peace Corps or of the service to others demanded by my conscience, never mind the professional career of tilting at the windmills of social justice I eventually pursued.

Yet, after a detour through a year-plus of study for the priesthood as a Catholic missionary, I found myself in a small, liberal, and decidedly secular college...Clark University. There, my neat and tidy world began to unravel, and my instinctive disposition to see things in a more nuanced and complex way emerged. Apparently, this metamorphosis continued when I entered Peace Corps training in the summer of 1966. From a letter to Lee I wrote that first summer of training:

> *I really don't know where to begin. The past three or four weeks have been filled with exciting experiences, not only in the sense of different or pleasing but rather in the sense of challenge and growth. That growth and challenge emanate from a very basic tension which is derived, I believe, from an elementary realization of what you are and what you want to be. The people (here) have forced me (and I them) to articulate and defend some of my most basic assumptions, my most basic sacred cows.*
>
> *In the articulation of that defense there inevitably emerges a more meaningful realization of yourself and your relationship to others. It is very difficult to put into words what I feel in my heart. The one thing of which I am certain, however, is that I will not experience this program unchanged. Whether I ever become a Peace Corps volunteer or not seems almost irrelevant. The important thing is that I feel I am changing and growing, in which direction it really does not matter.... I would have to assign the major responsibility (for this growth) to several staff who have encouraged and inspired an atmosphere of inquiry and questioning.*

As suggested in the first chapter of this volume, our training was a transformative experience. We were pushed by the staff, pushed by our peers, pushed by ourselves to better understand who we were and why we were there. Overhanging all was the specter of being deselected, being told that you had not made it. And yet, we usually kept our focus on the process of self-discovery that a motivated and motivating staff had pushed us toward. Of course, they could not magically turn a kid like me who possessed zero practical skills or knowledge into a poultry or agricultural specialist with a few weeks of training. But they could, and did, push me into becoming more aware of myself and the world around me.

I do recall feeling very insecure and almost sure that I would not be one of those selected to go overseas. In those days, I suffered from an almost paralyzing case of self-doubt... the dreaded imposter-complex. This fairly common affliction leads one to believe they will be discovered as a total fraud at any moment which, in my case, was not an entirely unrealistic proposition. There were even episodic panic attacks that would leave me struggling just to get by.

In truth, I suspect no real evidence existed to support this dark, negative self-image other than the black cloud that most Irish carry with them, nor do I suspect others readily saw my debilitating internal doubts. We Irish cannot believe that good things might happen to us, unless by accident or as an evil taunt by some malevolent deity, and we remain equally convinced that any good that might come our way will be counterbalanced by something bad. As the late U. S. Senator Daniel Patrick Moynihan, a classic Irish politician, once quipped, "There is no point in being Irish if you don't know that the world is someday going to break your heart."[i]

I was shocked, therefore, when I was picked to represent the training group in a special way:

Among the more trite things that have happened to me since the last letter is that I have become a television star. One representative from each of the five groups training here was chosen to take part in a 15-minute panel discussion on one of the local shows. It was really a blast but I have taken a lot of grief ever since.

So much of what we did in training is now a blur. I recall images and some events, like the Hindi classes and the values classes, and the chicken coop, and some of the people. But so much of what must have been important to me at the time has been lost. Most of the memories that remain are so small, like my first Hindi class. I walked in late and the Indian instructor asked me something in Hindi (no English was allowed). I instantly deduced that the most likely first question would be a query regarding my name and responded thus to his surprise. Believe me, it was all downhill from there.

The bigger events elude me for some reason. For example, I have no recollection of the 'progressive party' and our small rebellion against some PC training protocols that I wrote about below:

> *Last Saturday, we had what we called a progressive party. There were five locations starting with the director's house (Dennis Conta) and ending at a reserved room at a local bar. Each site represented one of the five basic Indian caste divisions, e.g., Brahman, Warriors, Merchants, Working Class, and Untouchables. You were supposed to dress and drink accordingly, i.e., only mixed drinks at the Brahman or Maharaja's party and beer at the untouchable party. It was really quite an affair. I wound up carrying the fellow who rooms across the hall from me back to the dorm.*
>
> *I might add that in addition to the work and play this training group has made quite an impression in Washington. Some of the more liberal of us (I have been identified as a member of the new left) fought against part of the assessment program, the peer evaluations, and forced Washington to make some concessions, although it wasn't really a victory. Reportedly, this was the first group in Peace Corps history to even attempt to buck the power structure, never mind dent it.*

*Among some of the other members of the new left
are a thin red-headed existentialist from Berkeley, an
ultra-radical liberal fellow from Colorado University, a
very tall, thin, blond guitarist from UCLA, a quiet but
interesting fellow called Asher, and a brilliant, Italian
kid from UCLA. They all really make for one hell of an
exchange of ideas.*

I am struck by two thoughts on the above passage, the importance of people in our young lives and the unique passion of
youth. As described in the introductory chapter, we trainees were
a diverse and special lot. Self-selection played an important role,
no doubt. Not everyone chooses to forfeit a head start on their
careers or seek out two years of personal deprivation just for the
hell of it. Nor did the Peace Corps accept all that applied, particularly in that era. In 1966 over 42,000 applied whereas only a frac-
tion of those were selected. Those starting out on day one already
were a rather talented and heterogeneous lot.

Referencing the synergy attached to interacting with some
of the other trainees brings back a truth about life. There is
something special about the innocence and passion of youth.
Everything is fresh and exciting, especially ideas, feelings, and
relationships. I cannot now imagine the number of small epiphanies I had at Clark and in Peace Corps training as I broke out
of the narrow Catholic, working class cocoon in which I was
raised.

The aura of that time and stage of life was brought home a
year or so ago when I got together with two old college class-
mates (now married), one of whom had served as a PC volunteer
in Iran before heading back to graduate school at Clark. It turns
out he was instrumental in my own decision to sign on. They
both had long careers in academia but we still reminisced just
how special the years at Clark were. What we most recalled
were the long and passionate talks about ideas and causes, about
visions of what might be, and about what we could contribute to
some better world. The Peace Corps training proved for me an
exciting extension of that transformative period of my life where

our stubborn idealism pushed us to confront the Peace Corps establishment itself.

SUMMER OF 1967

The correspondence next picks up a year later, in the summer of 1967. There is a somewhat different tone here, more serious, more aware that we are about to embark on a very challenging adventure. The next excerpts were written from a farm in Waunakee, Wisconsin, just north of the state capitol of Madison, where we were desperately trying to become agricultural experts in just a few short weeks.

> *Right now, three of us are sitting in our tent wondering what will happen when we turn off the light and the thousand mosquitoes hovering nearby for warmth suddenly discover that our flesh is very desirable. Peace Corps is just one series of such major crises but accompanying them are just as many laughs, and laughter is a good thing.*
>
> *It is peaceful here. We are on a farm about 20 miles north of Madison, WI. Most of the day is spent studying language and technical skills. We've spent quite a bit of time laboring in the field. And I am in grave danger of acquiring some actual muscle. In the evenings, we play cards, listen to folk music, run around kicking a soccer ball, or simply engage in conversation.*
>
> *While the days are full, there is not the hectic pace nor pressure of deselection of last summer. There is, in a sense, a greater seriousness and purpose due to our imminent departure for India. Don't get me wrong, however, this group is still as insane as ever. The days are just full of laughs, stemming largely from our hopelessness. I guess the real question is not whether we will be ready for India but whether India will be ready for us.*

There is a lot more to say but I'd better stop now. I want to make sure this gets into tomorrow's mail. Then I'll wait for your return letter which will probably never come.

One can almost sense a growing realization that this was really going to happen. We are really going overseas and, oh my God, we have no idea what we are doing. And there is already a sense of fatalism about my relationship with Lee. Somewhere inside, I just knew that, in leaving for India, I would never see her again.

Michael (a fellow trainee I was particularly close to) is really wigging out now. His girl has not written for about a week now. Her husband has probably returned from Vietnam and, needless to say, the situation is tense all the way around. It is another case of the shifting sands of human emotions, the liquidity and vacuity of which never cease to amaze me. The course of human involvement typically seems to run from the improbable to the absurd. The grasping, hoping, seeking become inevitable frustrations and unfulfilled anticipations. Today's bliss and ecstasy are tomorrow's despair and emptiness. In order to maintain your purpose and direction, you have to love and believe in it. And out of the deepest despair of its reality evolves the highest respect for its necessity and appreciation of its existence.

Partially, one may say that love is illusion, or some form of selective reality, and further, that distance perpetuates these illusions. But the emotional character of love is only the superficial surface. Its real nature lies in the contract made between two people. It is the arrangement between separate individuals to share common excitement and joys and accept each other's burdens and fears. It is the merger of their identities as well as their bodies, an investment of themselves and their trust in the other. It is perhaps the most incredibly difficult goal to accomplish and yet the easiest thing to convince yourself that you are doing. It is something that cannot be manufactured but rather must simply exist. Yet, it cannot be taken for granted but rather nurtured and cultivated with all the strength that can be mustered. As you know, this kind of investment has been particularly difficult for me. The exposure and investment of ourselves to other human beings is a noble aspiration, perhaps ultimately unrealizable yet seemingly the only reality worth pursuing.

In rereading this letter, I have realized that it is extremely ambiguous and unintelligible. It is just so incredibly difficult to verbalize emotions in general, never mind probing one's own thoughts and feelings. Beyond that, these kinds of thoughts are alien to my analytical, pessimistic nature. Perhaps there is some kind of metamorphosis, a maturing which is taking place, and I am neither able to describe it nor analyze its direction.

There is something I want to say now, that I must say or perhaps forever hesitate. I do want to marry you. This is an incredible confession for me and I know it will freak you out. Before you retreat into a shell of self-security, let me assure you that I don't believe it will ever happen. Circumstances, two years, and certain common weaknesses will, in all probability, prevent it. But let me also assure you that I mean it and that if you ever, at any time, feel strong enough to make that arrangement, that contract of identities, let me know.

Reading these passages four decades after they were put to paper shocked me (and Lee who also had not read them in many, many years). Could this really be the cynical, detached Tom Corbett of my memory waxing on and on about love and relationships? One explanation leaps to mind. Perhaps I was busy and had hired someone to write these letters for me. But if I really did

Tom musing over the Thames enroute to India

express such thoughts or, more importantly, embrace such sentiments, then surely some kind soul could have been persuaded to put me out of my misery. Yet, here I was apparently talking about marriage of all things!!! What the hell was I thinking?

My parents, good people that they were, would never be described as an ideal couple. In fact, I cannot recall too many civil words between them, and certainly no affection. That, however, seemed rather typical of marriages in my working class neighborhood where economic tensions and life's struggles promptly eroded any early romantic attachments. As kids, for amusement on long summer evenings, we often sat on the front stoop of our 'three-deckers' while listening to the screaming matches emanating from the surrounding flats. Unlike my wife's childhood experiences (she never heard either her parents or any of her neighbors argue while growing up, really!), I had few positive role models for marriage.

My long-held narrative of what happened back then was that I had never mentioned marriage until midway through my India tenure and that her 'Dear Tom' letter and my formal 'proposal' letter of sorts passed each other in the postal airways. But there I was, in black and white, raising the topic of marriage as early as the last days of my training before heading overseas. Fortunately for her, she was smart as a whip, later earning a Ph.D. in something like Molecular Virology, and enjoying a long career as a research scientist in academia. She was certainly smart enough to ignore my 'offer' and move on when the opportunity arose. Still, this was an instructive lesson in how we can reframe our own histories.

Shortly after, off to India it was…

INDIA 1967

The first surviving note from India came in the form of words scratched on the back of a picture I sent to Lee at the very end of our training. The guys of 44B are standing at the edge of a field looking on while getting instruction from someone from the Udaipur Agricultural College.

> *Though the university staff was excellent, the only thing I can grow now are calluses. With a little bit of luck and some good old B.S., I suppose I'll be able to fake it for two years (actually 21 months, we terminate about June 23, 1969). But prepared or not, we leave for our sites tomorrow, Sept, 17, 1967.*
>
> *Yesterday, 18 of us were sworn in as volunteers and, in the evening, we had a big cultural evening attended by about 400 people. Tonight, (the 16th of September), we are having a final blast at the Lake Palace. I do believe we are all pretty anxious to get going. Training was a rather drawn out affair. So far, we have received so much and apparently been able to give so little. There is a great debt to pay, and I do hope we are able to do so.*
>
> *(Referring to the picture) I must admit, this looks like a pitiful crew, but that is only because it is.*

I have no memory of the swearing in or the 'big cultural event' I referenced. Just who were all those people celebrating our initiation as volunteers? But I do recall our final celebratory evening before heading to our sites. It was held at the rather famous Lake Palace, a quite romantic site sometimes used in tourist advertisements by the Indian government. A former palace of the local Prince, it is now a luxury hotel situated in the middle of a lake located in Udaipur. A number of scenes from the James Bond movie *Octopussy* were filmed there. Our final fete was a grand affair with good times and drink in this spectacular setting. In fact, the whole evening had the distinct feel of the condemned man's last meal before being led off to the 'chair' which, in my case, was the town of Salumbar.

The next note that survived the passage of time jumps ahead some three months…

> *One aspect of life here is time, time to think, time to reflect upon what I have already done and what I intend to do. There is time on the long walks between farms, on the quiet evenings at home, and even on the long bus rides to Udaipur. Life is relatively unfettered by the proliferation of distractions considered absolutely essential in Western life. As a result, it is rather impossible to prevent oneself from becoming more reflective, and perhaps a bit more aware.*
>
> *If you dwell upon your own behavior and that of others and further the relationship between the two long enough, then it becomes increasingly more difficult to maintain the superficial defenses by which we shore up the soft inner-self. Of course, the inner-self can be described, itself, as little more than a plethora of patterned roles arranged to respond to specific cues. But I yet tend to believe that beyond the potentially numerous responses which one organism is capable of and ordinarily does emit, there is a consistency or uniformity which usually appears when the individual faces stress.*

> *The upshot of all this is that I've faced another*
> *little bit of truth about myself with what I hope is a*
> *degree of honesty... When I reflect upon some of the*
> *letters I've sent, many of them seem designed to evoke*
> *pity or sympathy or admiration through the emphasis*
> *on the loneliness, deprivation, or accomplishments*
> *here in India. It has all been a rather semi-romantic*
> *escapade through some of my philosophical stream of*
> *consciousness meanderings.*

This passage touches upon one of the most significant dimensions of our India experience. We all had time, more time than we would at any other period in life. Everything passed by with immeasurable slowness…events, people, thoughts… much like the ambling of the water buffalo along the road. The glacial pace of life gave us so much time to think, to reflect, to ponder. At the same time, I had doubts about the veracity of my own communications, whether they might be slanted just a touch for effect. On that, one can never be absolutely certain.

I now think back to my subsequent professional life when, simultaneously, I helped run a major research entity at the University of Wisconsin, taught policy courses to undergraduates and graduate students, served as the Principal Investigator on numerous research projects, worried about raising money to keep things going and people employed, and traveled around the country giving talks or organizing conferences or consulting. During all that frantic activity there was no time to think or write (other than professional writing) or reflect on the meaning of things. Hell, finding time to take care of one's bodily functions was a stretch.

Even the college days before Peace Corps were full of stress. I worked all the time (even doing the 11-7 night shift as an orderly in a local hospital before heading off to classes) in order to pay for college. And I still found time to chase women and pursue social causes, although absent much success in either endeavor. In retrospect, those long days in India were indeed serene, a time out of time.

142

THE WINTER OF 1968

Winter in Rajasthan is an active period. The daily temperatures are finally tolerable although the nights can be quite chilly. But at least you felt alive and looked forward to what might be accomplished. At the same time, we confronted a lot of unstructured time given the absence of a TV or the other usual distractions. And with time on my hands, really for the first time since childhood, came an opportunity to return to a long-held dream...

The book you sent several months ago finally arrived the other day. I suspect I may enjoy it very much. In school I had a tendency to concentrate on psycho-social and political questions much to the exclusion of more artistic and literary works. Now that I have time to rectify that oversight, I don't have access to very good literature. I have a compulsion to pour through a number of diverse authors including Camus, Hemingway, Kierkegard, Dostoevsky, Proust, Fitzgerald, Joyce, Sartre, Updike, etc. as well as poets such as Cummings, Macleish, and Alden.

As I believe I mentioned previously, I'd really like to do some writing myself. I haven't done anything serious since my seminary days. The old need is welling up again. I can feel it but it takes a bit of courage to tackle something of this nature honestly.

I guess I've always wanted to write. As a young boy I even started two 'novels' which fortunately never progressed beyond the first chapter. Yet, until now this desire or need, while rather effectively buried beneath the insecurity of my own perhaps realistically appraised commonness, remained annoyingly there in a persistently conscious and restless latency. It occasionally emerged, briefly at the seminary where I somewhat immersed myself in contemporary philosophy while wrestling with the enigma of self-definition, and during my last semester at Clark where socio-political

*problems captured my attention. Yet, for the most
part Clark did little more than devitalize this 'poetic
expressive necessity' through a kind of scientific rigidity
and intellectual sterility... It had become gauche to
equivocate about concepts through the use of ambiguous
artistic expressiveness. And of course, it did not help that
I remained as ill-defined as ever and just as insecure.
Now this need is as compelling as ever and, what the
hell, there are plenty of lonely hours to fill.*

Later that year, I started my one and only fictional work to
date (my academic works don't count).

Occasionally, there were references to daily life. Below is a
description of an evening's activity long lost to my memory by
the passage of time and the misplacement of too many brain cells.

*Stoklas and I are going out to dinner tonight and
later on will play a little Pinto (a form of Blackjack)
with some of the boys. {Resuming the letter after the
evening's fun and games.} Back now. As usual, I lost.
The stakes are small, so my total losses amounted to
only about 2 rupees (about 30 cents). Orthodox Hindus,
of course, do not gamble, drink, nor eat meat (at least
among higher castes). The fellows we played cards with
last night were Borahs, a liberal Muslim sect, which
allows all the little vices that make Western society so
palatable...gambling, drinking, gluttony, etc. There is
really nothing like a little debauchery now and then.*

*Speaking of debauchery, Randall and I are
heading south in a few days. We are hitting the big
town, Bombay, and also plan to spend some time at a
beautiful little (former) colony called Goa. According
to the fantastic tales brought back by other volunteers,
Goa possesses such fabulous treasures as clean, sandy
beaches, tropical splendor, bars with cheap beer, sexy
girls in western dress, plus other amenities associated
with the corrupt life. Did I mention sexy girls in*

*western dress? While there, I intend to do nothing more
than drink a lot of beer and write.*

I now wonder just how often we might have played cards with
some of the locals. Funny, we lose so much with time though I do
have a number of pictures taken with folk from the town whose
identity is now long lost to me. In any case, it would appear we
were at least somewhat engaged in the ebb and flow of local life.

It is hard to imagine commenting on India without referencing its mysteries. There was so much that remained just beyond
our comprehension and so much that challenged our rational
understanding of the world. Part of what remained beyond us
might be attributed to a society that, in part at least, had not yet
transitioned into a contemporary, so-called rational society.

*As I write this letter, it is about 10 PM. The world is
silent except for the pained groan of the wind. And I am
alone. Randy has gone to Delhi. He has had some form
of physical breakdown. To be brief, he has worms, an
infected foot, dental problems, nausea spells, general
weakness, lesions on his arms, and several other
indefinable aches and pains. Chances are, however,
he'll survive.*

*...the nights can be somewhat spooky since we
are rather isolated. To compound the feeling, I've run
across some interesting tales concerning spirits, holy
men, and general extrasensory phenomena from rather
reliable sources (university-educated men). One story
is about the former princely ruler of a neighboring
district. Since this man was educated at Oxford in
England, he often entertained foreign friends in a
palace built expressly for that purpose, at least until
one of his visiting friends died in it. After that, no one
was allowed to spend the night, not even the prince. It
is reputedly reported that anyone who attempts to sleep
in the palace will be physically ejected by the spirit of*

the dead guest. Stories of communications with dead relatives, physical cures by holy men, and possession of bodies by spirits are legion. After a while, it makes one wonder.

Religion and spirituality liberally mixed with town life to provide entertainment for the locals and a respite from the tedium of everyday life. It provided us with welcome distractions as well. A colorful, religiously inspired event is described next...

Another aspect of Indian culture has been brought to light this week. It seems that a group of naked Sadhus (sort of like Saints to those of the Catholic persuasion) have come to town for a while. When they arrived, the whole town, it appeared, turned out to greet them. Even Cutchroo, our 16-year-old cook, took part. Dressed in an oversized white uniform and wearing a hat which hung down over his ears, he produced some kind of cacophony on a drum which some naïve soul had given him under the ridiculous impression that somehow music would be forthcoming.

Well, anyways, amid the heavenly strains (?) of the band, the choking dust, and the milling crowds, these skinny naked men arrived. I must admit, despite that, the town never looked better. Decorations were abundant. Across every street hung banners, streamers, pictures, and other assorted paraphernalia of assorted colors and shapes.

The spectacle was not over yet. Yesterday, one of the holy men pulled out, by his own hand, all of the hair on his body. This, I suspect, is a ritualistic form of self-abnegation and a general disregard for materialistic matters.

Another interesting point is their culinary habits. When it is time to eat, they proceed from their temple while thinking of some sign or signal such as a man holding a coconut under his left armpit or something. If

Festival time, 1967 or 1968

they see that sign, they will eat at the nearest house. If they don't, they will fast for another day (they eat only once a day). It really does seem like a tough way to make a living.

On at least one other occasion, I managed to trade words of wisdom with some visiting holy men...

Have just returned from Salumbar where I had the opportunity to visit and talk with the visiting Jain holy men. These meetings are, I suspect, the very kind of cross cultural contrasts which Peace Corps is famous for brokering... east and west, mysticism and rationalism, aestheticism and materialism. These confrontations are more awkward than enlightening. Yet, it is probably true that my somewhat affected interest in the Eastern world does create a modicum of good feeling.

147

More remarkably, I began to write about fitting in…a slow and awkward process at best. Still, we seemed to be developing real relationships and settling into a patterned existence. We were no longer a kind of freakish entertainment for the locals but part and parcel of the local landscape. All that felt good.

Beyond the realm of spirits and holy men lies the real world of genuine human relations. And right now, at least, I'm very happy with my own. The town, in general, is finally accepting us as part of the scenery (much to our relief). But more importantly, some genuine friendships are emerging, based not upon curiosity or status-seeking but rather something quite close to a genuine response to the other person. Our relations with Indians, to be sure, will always be somewhat stilted. The incredible dichotomy between cultures and the language problem (even with those that speak English to some degree) render no other possibility.

But more than ever before, there is a comfortableness and a certain ease. It might just be that, in certain cases, at least, we've come to recognize an essential humanness that we all possess. When that occurs, it can make one feel awfully nice inside. As I've often said, human beings are the most difficult things to work with but, in the final analysis, about the only things worth the effort.

And yet, there remained a dark side that I could never quite escape. Some of the darkness could legitimately be attributed to the situation in which we found ourselves. After all, we were expected to function in an almost impossible situation.

We were generalists being asked to make a practical contribution with very questionable technical skills, limited language skills, and without any real resources to bring to the table. Moreover, danger lurked everywhere, from rampant corruption (good seed replaced with bad seeds), to acts of God (no rain when needed), to simple failures to be understood or trusted. And the consequences of failure for local farmers living on the edge of survival could be devastating. There was plenty to worry about in the everyday reality of our situations.

But even while I feel a certain warmth and happiness now, one cannot ultimately escape the depressing realization that whatever tiny fractional bit of good may be accomplished here, it will inevitably be destroyed by forces over which we can have no impact. Both the genius and stupidity of man are beyond comprehension, both his humanness and depravity inexplicable. In the past, the relative powerlessness and isolation of man guaranteed that a delicate balance could be maintained between the extremes and that somehow the human species could perpetuate itself. But now we seem to have reached a point of incipient desperation, of incredible gaps between the species' technology and its wisdom, between its science and its conscience. We have allowed ourselves to become enmeshed in a morass of fear and frustration, increasingly thrashing about with incomprehensive violence, fighting for inappropriate, decayed symbols.

As illustrated in the above passage, I brought part of my darker side with me to India…it was already part of my interior self. I had come a long way from the good Catholic boy who obediently accepted the scripts of faith and country. The intellectual crucible of college forced me to question everything, to arrive at my own definition of truth and what was the good, a habit of questioning further fostered in Peace Corps. It is hard to explain the dislocation associated with the transformation I underwent as a young man, from a believer in givens to an asker of questions. As a child, you grow up in a world of certainties, one being that your country is on the side of unadulterated good. Some never lose that simple and naive faith. Some do….

*In Vietnam we sap our strength, prostitute our
sensibilities, and potentially precipitate a holocaust.
It seems to me that the sensible thing to do would be
to establish our commitments along a pragmatically
defensible perimeter, e.g., Australia, India, Taiwan,
the Philippines, and Japan. This would not only
'rationalize' our military posture but liberate the
dynamic energies of both the western and eastern
worlds to confront some of the critical questions of
our generation: food production, population control,
socioeconomic equality, and the quality of human
existence.*

*It will do absolutely no good if we destroy every
single communist in Asia while the rest of the world
is devoured by famine, disease, and pollution; while
society disintegrates under the tensions of social
inequality; and while civilization is crushed under
the mass of its own weight. At home our response to
the Negro (sic) revolution is to modernize our riot
forces with the latest, most sophisticated equipment
and techniques. Somehow, mace, guns, armored
trucks, and improved gas attacks do not appear to be
an appropriate reaction. But then again, there is no
reason why we should break with tradition and adopt a
thoughtful, humanitarian approach.*

Rage at the wider world, and America's role in that world,
would occasionally be tempered by the smaller, everyday things
I experienced in my site. Below, I touch upon the meaning of
human connections across great divides. Such connections
could be transformative, though, even in the face of the cultural
obstacles we confronted daily. At the same time, these connections could be exhausting.

*I truly doubt whether India, or even Salumbar,
is wiser for my stay here. But once in a great while
something good occurs on a personal level where I,*

150

*as an individual, using faulty Hindi or elementary
English, can teach or learn something from another
individual. There are moments of sharing and they
do make one feel rather warm and good inside. Of
course, there are the incidents of misunderstanding
as well, when distances between us and our rhythms
of existence create abrasiveness and impatience. The
incomprehensibility and intransigence of the Hindu
culture can often be trying, requiring a great deal of
the only quality that anyone needs who lives in another
culture...tolerance.*

*It may be, when I think on it, more than tolerance,
but rather a kind of cynical idealism....something which
allows you to expect or be affected by absolutely nothing
while, at the same time, retain the capacity for interest
and, should I say, involvement. Beyond all the analysis
weighs the burden of commitment, an incredible burden
which I am not sure is worth all the effort.*

Often in my letters I would touch upon a pace of life that I
found seductive and even instructive. At the same time, the daily
routine stretched my patience, as it probably did all of my fellow
volunteers. We were all driven, relatively ambitious, Westerners.
We were used to working hard, pushing ourselves. Now, we were
isolated, typically alone with ourselves and our thoughts. There
was loneliness to be sure, a theme that arises from time to time
in a number of these missives. But there also was this struggle
to adjust our internal clocks to our new world, a transformation
that did not come easily. For me, the water buffalo captured at
least part of my new environment perfectly.

*Life is really incredibly slow here. As I look out
my front door, rickety wooden carts inch their way
with painful reluctance along the dust-filled road. At
a further distance are a group of water buffalo, which
must rank as the ugliest and stupidest animals on
earth, who are doing what I suspect comes naturally...*

*waiting for death. Their lives, when I think on it, are
little more than a perpetual response to momentary
stimuli....food, water, noise, and other things that catch
their attention.*

*In reality, I admire their capacity to wallow in a
complete void and lack of awareness bred by centuries
of dependent servitude. Yet, perhaps my attraction to
these beasts stems more from their obvious analogy to
the human species. They have adopted many of man's
more intractable characteristics ... dullness, slowness,
dependence, and a complete lack of awareness. Yet,
they have maintained one inestimable advantage,
a debilitating self-indulgence that vitiates their
capacity or desire for senseless savagery and pointless
domination.*

Amidst all the endless days of heat and routine, there were
moments of triumph. We were, in fact, more ambitious than the
water buffalo I so admired and really did have a bunch of ideas
and projects, a few of which resulted in something actually
being accomplished.

One such project was the erection of a chicken coop on the
top of our government house as a way to encourage others to
engage in this cottage industry. As I recall, we built this edifice
entirely with our own hands as a few onlookers watched and
occasionally snickered. Those who know me have surely succumbed to a fit of uncontrollable laughter by now. Changing a
light bulb typically is a major achievement for a klutz like me.
Building a chicken coop, on the other hand, is beyond the pale
and a testament to how Peace Corps stretched me.

The miracle of the chicken coop project is described below....

*Well, the miracle of miracles has just occurred.
No, it is not the second coming. The fact is that we are
now the proud owners of egg laying chickens. That's
right! Randall has just suffered a case of apoplexy
screaming for me to come up to the roof. There, praise*

152

Our chicken coop project

*to God, was an egg which one of our chickens had
the audacity to lay.....You may say that that I am
perhaps exaggerating the importance of this event.
Well, perhaps it is true that we do so little right here
that we are grasping at straws. Besides, our veracity
and claims to expertise had come under question.
We had stated on numerous occasions that chickens
were capable of laying eggs without cohabitating with
their male counterparts (the Corbett-Stoklas course
in poultry raising was complete with appropriate
references to analogous human female functions). This
now vindicates our righteousness and enhances our
claims to omniscience.*

 *One last point which I just remembered, if you know
of any groups or individuals who might be interested in
contributing to the Salumbar library fund, let me know.*

We may be short of funds even after all local and peace
Corps sources are exhausted ... I am serious about this.
We may wind up, due to inflated costs and ambitions,
with a $1,000 deficit. If there are any possibilities, let
me know, and I will forward the necessary information.

I do have some memories of the library project but they are vague. In volume one, several 44B volunteers mentioned soliciting funds and arranging for local schools to be built. This was something tangible they could do and leave behind as evidence they had actually been there.

Salumbar did not need a school building. Still, Randy and I wanted to do something along those lines. Toward that end, we did manage to raise some money, referenced in the above letter, to upgrade a local library of sorts and to purchase additional materials (mostly books, I believe). The most successful initiative, at least as I can recall, involved soliciting help from a former Professor at Clark. He, in turn, got a group of his current students interested in the project and they did raise some money, exactly how and how much I cannot recall. It seemed a worthwhile effort though, and some in the Salumbar community seemed appreciative.

SUMMER OF 1968

Ok, April is not technically summer but this is the date of the next letter. In many important ways, though, it was summer to us. Inexorably, the daily temperature had been rising day after day, week after week. By April, the heat was overwhelming, surrounding us with a debilitating torpor that sapped our energy.

Welcome from the world's original blast furnace.
Summer is here and the Loo, the hot, dry summer winds
have begun to sweep across our developing desert.
The temperature averages about 110 degrees now, but
fortunately it is a dry, more tolerable kind of heat. The

only difficulty here is that as soon as you step out into the intense sunlight, the moisture is literally sucked right out of you, leaving your skin with the texture of a dried prune.

As you would imagine, we are not getting out very often. Since the harvests are in there really isn't much to do. As an index of our paucity of work, I've devoured four books and started a fifth (Ulysses) in the past five days. This is the worst time of year. Beyond the heat and the boredom, the incidence of diarrhea and dysentery rises sharply. And a host of unsavory beasts (cobras and scorpions) begin to appear. It is truly the time that tries men's souls, both Indian and American alike.

Regarding last letter, the damage to the crops was localized. Therefore, while a few farmers were almost totally wiped out, the majority escaped serious damage. So, perhaps there is progress after all but it is so, so painfully miniscule.

I cannot now recall what crisis resulted in the crop loss mentioned above, which I apparently described in more detail in one of the lost letters. One possibility is that a torrential rainstorm at the beginning (or perhaps even before the traditional onset) of the monsoon season ruined some of the crops. I do recall some downpours that resulted in flash floods. In fact, I still have a picture of the lake over the hill in back of our house overflowing the man-made dam. But the timing strikes me as off, so the culprit may be beyond recapturing at this point. But whatever happened caused me concern for the local farmers that I must have described in graphic terms. Likely, I despaired that a whole growing season's effort to convince local farmers of the benefits of the new, high yield variety of wheat seed had been in vain. Here, I was either setting the record straight, minimizing a negative reality, or trying to sound upbeat.

In another letter a few weeks later, I summarize the first year's agricultural effort and my state of mind.

Monsoon rains near Salumbar

It is another typical Rajasthani day here. The temperature under the aegis of a bitterly hot sun is creeping over the 110 degree mark and the sucking dry wind... is blowing off the hills and sweeping along the brittle, cracked earth. Like most of the other living creatures here, we simply crawl into some hole for protection until the sun sinks into a bloody demise toward the west. ...life is frustrating but it is exactly what I expected. It may very well be the difficulty of the experience that gives it value that makes us aware of both our limitations and strengths.

In many ways, though, life is quite satisfying here. There is a great deal of satisfaction in the relationships, the small successes in agriculture, and the increasing awareness of self and other people. And there is progress. Despite some late damage, farmers are impressed and much more of the new wheat will be planted next year along with newer and better seed

*varieties. A variety of maize (corn) which was used by
30 farmers this year will be sown by as many as 200
in the next season. Farmers are also going to try a new
variety of rice we have brought in. Things are moving,
and I am basically satisfied.*

Despite the hardships, the heat, the boredom, the loneliness, and some late crisis that I thought might have undermined our outreach efforts, I remained fairly upbeat. I had obviously been shaken by whatever had caused the late season crop loss. My estimate of what we would have called target group penetration (the proportion of targeted farmers who actually considered using the new seed varieties) amazes me all these years later. I am really struck by the discussion of maize and rice, which were not grown in the area to any extent as I recall. But, then again, so much has been lost to memory after four-plus decades.

Tom and his garden project

Randy and Tom, an evening at home

I do recall working closely with a number of farmers. I still have a few pictures of demonstration plots, some with a wonderful high-yield crop situated next to what would be produced by the local seed type ordinarily used. But I cannot recall the kind of success discussed above. Maybe it is a false modesty or maybe I exaggerated my impact, though that does not sound like me. In any case, it would be nice to think it was all true.

Of course, all was not serious musings or tales of tragedy and triumph regarding our work in Rajasthan. These letters often contained small bits of insight into our day-to-day life, some of which were quite humorous.

Below is a graphic description of one of our pathetic attempts to master our household environment.

Randall and I have been enduring the boredom
of these last days of April until we are able to take
off for the Himalayas on the 1ˢᵗ. Today the temp was
120 degrees, a couple degrees higher than I am

accustomed. But there are diversions to keep our corrupted minds occupied….we decided to finish off our favorite rat through the discriminate utilization of our rational faculties. We decided, after much thought, on the following plan.

When the rat entered our combined living room, study, and dining room, we would: A) close the door; B) position Randall on the cot within easy striking distance of the door; C) I would flush the rat from behind the combination desk and dining room table (the usual habitat of our prey); D) as the rat scurried to the safety of the other room, Randall would take careful aim and let fly his sneaker (especially secured for the occasion) with precision and accuracy, which would inevitably hit me on the toe; E) Randall would fall off the cot in a drunken stupor; F) we would say 'fuck it' and go back to our drinking.

And after an apparent pause in my letter writing to execute the well-considered plan…

We just blew it. We had the rat trapped in our combination entrance hall and work room. Randall was poised as usual with sneaker while I braved risks far beyond the call of duty to flush the bastard (the rat, not Randall) out from behind its protection. But at the critical moment, my drunken roommate decided he had to relight his half-smoked cigarette (I think he doused it when he took a drink while forgetting to remove the cigarette from his mouth). In his rather uncoordinated state, he only succeeded in burning the tip of his nose, which sent him into some ridiculously grotesque dance of pain. As he hopped around our combination entrance hall-work room, the rat scurried to the safety of our kitchen. Well, you have just witnessed (in a way) one of the great moments in Peace Corps history.

As I described in volume one, we eventually conquered the rodent kingdom by bringing in reinforcements, a cat we named Billie (pronounced beelee), a loose phonetic expression of the Hindi word for cat.

Sometime during this period the infamous 'Dear Tom' arrived!

That, at least, is my best recollection of the timing of things and I do know that Lee got married later that summer before heading for Atlanta where her husband was taking an academic position at Georgia Tech. The letter certainly did not come as a total surprise. Well, to be honest, it did not come as a surprise at all.

It likely arrived after our trip to a hill station in the Himalayas. As I described in volume one, Randy was talking away as I read the letter in silence, not hearing a word he was saying. After it finally soaked in, I silenced him with a nonverbal gesture, told him what had happened, and we proceeded to get very drunk.

After reconnecting, Lee shared that she had begun dating the man she eventually married as early as the fall of 1967...not all that long after I had departed. At the time, of course, I was unaware anything like that was happening. And yet, I always had this sense that our relationship was a train wreck simply waiting to happen.

Even in the few letters that have survived, I mercifully spare the reader from some of the more tedious expressions of personal feelings that, given their occasional emotional character, yet drive me to frissons of shame. I still argue that such words must have been written by someone else (that is my story and I am sticking with it). However, I will bore you with just a few personal sentiments written just before the end of the relationship...I surely was looking straight into the headlights of that train at this point.

The following passage likely comes from my final letter (or thereabouts) before receiving the infamous 'Dear Tom' missive.

...I heard the music from Zorba the Greek the other day. As usual, it sparked a flood of memories.... For

*one thing, it reminded me of Zorba's recommendation
that we all must possess a little bit of madness,
madness that has placed me here, madness that may
never allow us to see each other again, but more
importantly the madness by which we dare to hope. But
the ultimate madness of them all is the one by which we
desperately yearn to survive and, in the face of all this
increasing insanity, seek the kinds of futile happiness
that our illusive dreams pretend. Yet, maybe, just
maybe, we'll make it.*

*Still, I want to say something now, not out of
fear or lack of trust in you, but simply to clear up
any ambiguity. While I love you and do hope the
relationship will endure my service here, the reality of
the situation is that we will be separated two years, a
little over a year more. I also realize that my irascible
moodiness, chronic immaturity, and impractical
idealism hardly make me an ideal catch. If you have
any doubt, or change your mind, please feel completely
uninhibited to communicate this to me. Perhaps, given
my peculiar Irish pessimism, I anticipate it anyway.
And, of course, if you are insane enough to like me, you
are also allowed to tell me that as well.*

Perhaps a quick note on the 'Dear Tom' letter is in order. Lee and I had an opportunity to process the whole thing some forty-plus years after the actual 'dumping' took place. I found it ironic that the words Lee used to describe her memory of me from our college days are, frankly, totally embarrassing. She remembers me as being extremely handsome, funny, charming, caring, very smart, sensitive, quick-witted, passionate about causes, articulate, and 'a divine kisser, the best ever.' Oh, and she simply loved my self-deprecating personal style.

Now, what is a guy who prides himself on that self-deprecating sense of humor going to do with positive feedback like that? It is almost enough to make me like myself…almost. It is easier, however, to conclude that she is confusing me with some other boy but, quite frankly, she didn't really date much…to put it mildly.

Though she could not recall what she was thinking at that time, we agreed that my choosing Peace Corps and leaving the States had some kind of irretrievable effect on her, one that was not apparent to either of us at the time. She likely started closing down to me when I went off to Peace Corps training, and the door completely shut when I got on that plane for India.

Sadly, from everything she revealed after we reconnected, her marriage did not turn out well though it did endure for some two decades before she finally put an end to it. Perhaps her own family also sensed she was making a mistake right at the start. One of the only things I could recall from the 'Dear Tom' letter to me was an observation that her family would really miss me and how much they liked me. More remarkably, she noted after we reconnected in 2010 that her mother actually made a pitch for my so-called candidacy on the very night BEFORE she was to be married. Then again, I always did well with the mothers; I could usually fool them. The daughters…not so much, guess they were harder to fool.

Her second marriage, I am happy to note, turned out much better.

AFTER THE 'DEAR TOM' LETTER

Here again, my memory played tricks on me. I thought I wrote only one more letter immediately on getting the 'Dear Tom' note in order to say some of the most obvious things… you know, the 'I understand and don't worry about me and good luck and have a nice life' kind of sentiments. I am positive I wrote such a letter though it did not survive (too bad since I would be most interested in seeing if I was really as gracious and noble as my memory suggests). But what shocked me (again with the shock) was that, after some gap in time, she wrote again and we picked up our correspondence for the remainder of my tenure in India. Good thing, otherwise I would be ending this about now or maybe most readers are thinking this is a bad thing...something like 400 more pages of this drivel to endure.

> *...your ('Dear Tom') letter must have been an unpleasant experience, one which finally having been done would be difficult to repeat. Writing again was a marvelously brave thing for you to do. I'm not sure it was a wise thing but it did please me, immeasurably. Thanks.*
>
> *You mentioned that sometimes you break into tears without reason. Well, I must admit there are times when I become misty-eyed. It is not so much for what might have been but rather for what was. The years that have just passed were, at least for me, extremely pleasant ones. And the time we spent together was perhaps the most rewarding of all. There was a certain warmth and comfortableness there, and a sharing and excitement which now seem unique and may never again be duplicated. The days at Donoghues (a favorite local bar)...are past now and they will never return. But we are in no way to blame, for it had to be that way. The times and the people who fill those times do change, inexorably, and without apparent conscious direction and there is little, so damn pitifully little, we can really do about it. It, us, would have changed no matter whether I left or not. And I suspect that what we still may fondly be attached to is not what we were to each other or what we might have been to each other but rather the simple function of a time and place in our lives which is irreplaceable.*
>
> *In my Irish Catholic pessimism, there is no room for happiness.*

I can surmise what I was trying to do in that last (long) paragraph. I might well have sensed that she was already somewhat disenchanted with her marital choice although I later discovered the real unhappiness would not emerge in force for several years. In any case, I appear to be arguing that our strong college 'connection' was more a function of time and place than anything particular to us. Thus, it was not necessarily retrievable even if we wanted to try. That was a noble sentiment on my part, apparently designed to make her feel better about her decision. I look back on it now with a touch of amazement since, whether or not the sentiments were grounded in reality, they were coming from a man not generally known for his nobility or sense of self-sacrifice.

When I sent my cyber-message to her after so many years I half-wished that any return note would come from a fat, toothless, harpy who had sired a dozen or so kids, most of whom now resided in state penal institutions. Then I could look back on being dumped with an unambiguous sigh of relief…dodged a bullet on that one, for sure. That did not turn out to be the case at all. After a gap of some 43 years, we discovered that our easy ability to communicate and especially to make each other laugh seemed exactly the same.

In addition, she still had that same aura of goodness and optimism I recalled so fondly. Even as her health ebbed, and she experienced a couple of episodes of renal failure (and near death) during early chemo treatments, she kept saying how blessed she was and how much she treasured the life she had… the family and friends around her. That positive, upbeat view of life still puts me to shame. Hell, I bitch for days about duck hooking a golf shot into the damn pond.

Her Caringbridge site, a place where friends and relatives and acquaintances could go to check up on the status of someone very ill, typically dying, accumulated almost six thousand 'hits' before she passed on in the Spring of 2012. It is so clear from the character of the messages left for her that she had been an inspiration to the many who knew her. If I were to have a similar site, I am sure I could reach double figures but only if I liberally employed the services of Rent-A-Friend.

In several emails, Lee had observed something else that caught my attention. From what she sensed about me today, I had not evolved into a 'different' person over the years. Rather,

I had become a more complete version of the young man she had known so many years ago and to whom she was so drawn. In her mind, that was a very good thing, all those traits she so admired back then now appeared fully developed and expressed. To be frank, I had been hoping against hope for some substantive improvement over the years…if not a complete makeover! In truth, though, her observation pleased me a lot.

As I think on it, I had the same reaction on meeting my fellow volunteers after a similar absence. All the good things in them I recalled from four decades ago, and maybe just a few not so good, could readily be seen in them today. It was as if four decades of time had not passed at all. Obviously, while some physical deterioration occurs, we all accrete more experience and polish simply by hanging in there for so long.

Yet, at the core of what people are, who they are, the qualities that center them as unique and special, those factors almost appear as constants in their makeup. I find that quite remarkable and a bit discomforting. I hope that does not mean that I am doomed to remain who I am, that some late-life transformational spurt simply is out of the question. That would be unfortunate indeed!

For whatever reasons, my correspondence changes in tone from this point on to the end of my stay in India. The words and sentiments consistently turn darker, more cynical, and despairing. If anything, they mark someone who is adrift and who lacks direction or hope. And yet, I still could consider and talk of a future…

As for myself, things are as well as might be expected. I have only about six months more to go in India. After that, I am planning to return to the University of Wisconsin's Department of Urban Affairs, that is if the draft does not take me. Actually, returning to school is prompted less by specific career plans than by the necessity to do something. At this point, I have very little emotion in any direction. Perhaps it is the physical distance from everything or perhaps the time of life but nothing is really appealing other than the rather impractical exercise of writing.

The last letters were often very reflective in character. There was less about what we were doing and more on what I was feeling. Perhaps they were also driven by a growing awareness that my days in Peace Corps were coming to a close and that a sobering reality loomed on the horizon. We all had to face the horrific prospect of picking up our real lives again.

It is hard to imagine now, but we were watching the world from what seemed like the end of the earth, with scant information coming from an occasional edition of *Time* or *Newsweek* magazines as well as the desperately appreciated letters from home. There were no phone calls, no internet, no Facebook, and no Twitter. From the information we could get, the war in Vietnam had long spiraled out of control and life in the United States was rent with savage disputes, assassinations, riots, and a kind of cultural implosion. The only positive news was that a sexual revolution had taken place back in the States. Most of us guys, though, feared that it would likely be a short-term phenomenon (women would surely come to their senses) and that it would surely be all over by the time we got back.

My words increasingly reflect the ennui that was taking hold…

…life is atrociously singular. But after close to twenty-five years of enduring it, I suspect that my physical organism has adapted well enough to survive. Occasionally I feel a closeness and warmth with the people or am lightened by the heady physical beauty of a sunset or the harsh, yet seductive, desert. But in general I feel rather removed from the place and the people, both Indian and American. I guess it is the loneliness which I doubt will end when I return to the States nor a loneliness which I feel particularly upset by. It is like being able to, if not stand outside everything, then at least observe all from the periphery.

What I see I would like to comment on, not that such observations would contain penetrating insights or any sort of edifying validity but because .... it would fit my essentially passive, reflective nature. But all this must amuse you. Here is a physical adult who, after twenty-five years of so-called growth, still has not arrived anywhere. Ah, but the capriciousness and incomprehensibility of life yet retains a useless, yet seductive, charm.

All of the uncertainties, the two years of loneliness and often frustrating effort, had taken a lot out of me. Moreover, we were back in the hot season, our constructive work largely over. My words dripped with fatigue, doubt, and a just a bit of despair...

Perhaps I shouldn't start this tonight. For one thing, I've been drinking. For a second, my stomach is slightly screwed up which, in view of the big dinner I foolishly ate tonight, probably means I'll be hustling out to the latrine soon. In view of the fact that there is no light out there, it would be quite a trick to hit the hole even if I were sober. But being slightly plotched and laden with the urgency of diarrhea, one's marksmanship tends to become less than perfect in the later runs. It is also goddamn hot and I am excruciatingly bored. How about that for a sympathy-evoking beginning... was I always a narcissist?

Right now, I feel pretty washed out. I kind of feel like a hunk of fruit that's been squeezed dry. The juice is gone. The only thing left is a bitter emotional residue (rind) that is stale and repugnant. Nothing much is left of the idealism, the kinds of commitment that occasionally made me a bearable (or perhaps unbearable) person.

At times, I can still sense the processes that seem to make the whole thing go but like many others I reject the acceptable labels (probably political) and

systems that define our little world. Unfortunately, my
rejection is complete to the extent that the possibility
of replacing the rotting thing with new generative
institutions or of achieving any kind of adequate escape
from the impact of reality is amusingly absurd.

You and I and every single other person, we are
all alone and, by the curse of God, we must face the
total intensity of existence in that state. And not even
the local booze I pour into my body can dull it into
anything approaching acceptability. There is a kind of
ultimate frustration that hovers about me, that makes
me reject so much yet does not provide me with the
illusion of escape or the delusion of utopian possibility.
There is just this incessant Pascalian sadness at the
immensity of the world and of the infinity of absurdity.

Wow, seriously now, can you believe that Lee could reject such a total, raving lunatic? I mean, really, what the hell could she have been thinking…?

I finished the draft of my novel sometime during this period. I even managed to get a portion of it typed up, somehow managing to charm one of the Peace Corps secretaries in New Delhi into typing at least some of it up for me as a favor (in the States, the spouse of a friend typed the remainder). So ok, I did have a certain amount of charm. It comes with that being Irish thing, along with that damn dark cloud, and along with an unfortunate inclination toward an excessive intake of alcoholic spirits (now, fortunately, an historical footnote).

The manuscript might not have been all that bad if memory serves me correctly. At least I remember one fellow volunteer issuing audible signs of approval as he read passages in an adjacent room. Either that or he was suffering from a painful attack of indigestion.

I think I still have a few chapters of that draft stuffed in a draw somewhere. As I think back on it, she (the secretary) was a native Indian and the manuscript contained some pretty steamy sections. Let's face it, male Peace Corps volunteers (in India at least) have a lot of time for fantasizing and so few opportunities to...oh, never mind. But I do wonder what she thought as she typed up those sections.

That urge to write kept coming back as it had ever since I was a young boy....

> *It would be nice to touch this futility to make it real for others. I'd like to do it as a kind of revenge, as a way of exposing the preposterous joke that has been played upon us. Yet, in a kind of ultimate irony, I am not foolish enough to take even my own confrontation (more like my interpretation) with the world seriously. It is a product of my inherited pessimism (the Irish curse) and cynicism (my pseudo-intellectual pretensions). But if out of this maelstrom of contradictions a literary style could possibly emerge which could touch others with an emotional impact, an interpretation of existence which makes no pretense of coincidence with the actual world but could possibly make a few people stop and breathe a bit deeper, then maybe I might be satisfied. But that is the classic pipedream and all I really have is that kind of gnawing hunger, that loneliness, which leaves you driftless, and that very intense suspicion that frustration is programmed into the whole damn tragedy and no one, no one at all, ever gets to the pot of gold.*

Mostly, the final letters reflected a very tired person...

> *...graduate school, careers, things like that don't seem terribly important. My cynicism, my amorality, my lack of practical ambition has left me with a huge void that only suggests more drift. Find something else to take up the next year and something else the year after that. And after you've successfully completed the prerequisite number of solar revolutions you can withdraw in some complete sense. There doesn't seem*

to be any real place to go and, on top of that, it really probably isn't worth getting there.

It might not turn out as bad as it sounds. I still may very well drift into grad school (Wisconsin because you can get an MA in a year and they will give me enough money). Maybe I should have tried Harvard but it would have required a great deal of resolution to hack my way through. Most likely, though, the Army will lay claim to my body which raises all the classic questions once again. It is even more difficult to confront that decision now since I feel I possess a less convincing system of ethics.

The overwhelming ambiguity of it all at times makes me somewhat anxious. Things seemed a bit easier back in the days when the big sweat was a paper for Bernie Kaplan (a former college professor) or some other such nonsense. Perhaps if it were not so faddish I would retreat to some religious ashram high in the Himalayas where I couldn't possibly be bothered by revolutions, air pollution, spiritual alienation, war, sick societies, traffic jams, starvation, middle-class neuroticism, or four years on the road back to Republican normalcy. But then again, I probably wouldn't like that either (sigh).

Perhaps a trip through Europe will get me out of these funky blues. It is just here where such futility prevails and the days are eternal sessions of sweat. The vacuum has taken something out of me. ...I am tired, very tired.

As my time in India came to an end, I decided that writing to Lee really did not make any sense. She had embarked on a new life. It was selfish and immature to continue or so I thought at the time. I really did enjoy using her as a sounding board, and she was gracious to let me continue to do so. Perhaps she even got something out of it. But I felt, in the end, that she was doing it out of some sense of guilt or pity. After all, the notion that someone might actually like me was patently absurd on the face of it.

Now, let me be totally honest here, I am not beyond using guilt or pity with women, which, I am certain, is much more likely to succeed than my so-called charm. In this instance, however, my better instincts took over. I just hate those instincts.

I believe the following passage represented the final paragraph in the last letter I wrote to her.

PS...Got your books. Loved Updike but I'm not
sure just what kind of image you had of me when you
picked these out. Oh, by the way, I've finished the
first draft of mine. I am rewriting now. Will be leaving
Salumbar around the second or third week in June.
Leave India around the 22nd.

And so it ended... my stay in India at least as reflected in my letters to Lee.

DECISIONS

Some decisions seem to come easily. My professional career started with a job interview that I learned about the very night before it was to take place. The formal panel interview was for a State Civil Service position that I knew absolutely nothing about when I arrived for the interrogation of sorts...I did not know the job title or what skills were required or what I might be expected to do if they were actually to hire me (hardly likely!). But I said 'what the hell' and went with the flow.

After several years, I left that secure civil service job (yup, they exercised atrocious judgment and hired me) to take a position at the University of Wisconsin, one which offered no career security whatsoever. I made that life-altering decision after thinking hard on it for four, maybe five, seconds. Over 35 years later, I am still there (Emeritus status) and never did enjoy any real job security in all that time.

I vaguely recall seeing Lee for the first time as she crossed a room and saying to myself, 'that's the one,' before she even made it to the other side. I had one date with Mary, my wife and wonderful partner of 40 plus years, and sort of moved in. For some unfathomable reason she has never gotten around to throwing me out. Mary and I have often bought houses to actually live in on a whim, only checking out one option before saying 'oh, what the hell'. We bought our current second home in Florida after a one-afternoon blitz search.

The big decisions have always come easily to me (us). Deciding whether to buy a new putter, however, can be a long and agonizing process even though I know full well it will not help my game in the least…technology simply cannot trump total ineptitude on the golf course, or in life, for that matter. And buying a new set of boxer shorts, don't even get me started on how long that might take.

I have often wondered how Mary managed to get through my defenses against commitment and marriage, which were, if anything, even more entrenched upon my return from India. As best I can figure, her secret was that she appeared indifferent to me and, more importantly, to the institution of marriage…a fact that set her apart from most gals of that era.

Now, let me be clear. There are uncountable hordes of women who have, over the course of my life, evidenced total indifference toward me. That is the norm. So, simply treating me with indifference never automatically elicited a marriage proposal. Hell, if that were the case, I would have been proposing to someone every half hour or so.

No, Mary feigned indifference so well that it looked authentic to me and not like the inauthentic feigned indifference evidenced by many women who would not be caught dead appearing to care but, in fact, really do care. Now, if any of that makes any sense to you, perhaps we can move on to a discussion of the technical intricacies of welfare reform or health care financing.

But I digress.

As suggested earlier, on reconstructing our long-ago past, Lee and I concluded that my decision to leave for India proved the final death knell of our youthful relationship. In ways not always obvious at the time, we had been moving toward marriage in fits and starts. She acknowledges that bringing me home to meet her boisterous Greek relatives was an incredible 'commitment' on her part, one she did not take lightly. And I must admit, getting to know her relatives was a definite trip for me, no question. For one thing, there seemed to be thousands of them. For another, they were all into that hugging stuff (except for her Irish dad who, of course, struck me as the only sane one in the whole bunch). Really, all this hugging and affection was a total shock to a guy like me. Hell, I grew up in a household where any kind of touching was considered verboten, if not somehow against the law.

Yet, despite evidence of strong, even compelling feelings for me, she managed to filter out all my written expressions of affection from the 'other side of the world.' Her letters back to me were, for the most part, the kind of perfunctory notes you might expect from a distant cousin who most days has trouble recalling your name. Some four decades after all these events, she cannot recall feeling any guilt when she dumped me and, believe me, she is a hyper-sensitive person who might just match me in the guilt-feeling department. That level of detachment is remarkable for someone like her who is ordinarily so caring of others.

It would appear that she had convinced herself that I had moved on in life. She could not believe I cared for her. Therefore, it never occurred to her that I might be hurt if she decided to marry someone else. To her, I was beyond hurt, perhaps incapable of feeling personal pain? She apparently believed I would simply get on with my life and would seldom (if ever) think of her again.

After digging through the surviving letters as she prepared to send them on to me, she kept expressing total bafflement, and embarrassment, at how she could have missed all the feelings embedded in those long-ago letters. She simply could not reconstruct what might have been going in her head at the time, or how she could have so cavalierly dismissed me back then.

Her obsequious and hourly apologies, though, were just a bit much I thought.

The decision to join Peace Corps, indeed, was the critical moment. Leaving for India cemented her belief that I was not committed and probably could not commit. She vividly recalled a small observation that I included in one of the lost letters. Apparently, I went on at length about how easy it was to divorce in India. It was something about the husband clapping his hands three times if the wife burnt his dinner and then out she was. Who knows, I likely made it all up but, apparently, I argued at the time that this was the greatest societal advancement since the introduction of sliced bread.

There is a lesson in all that. As a man, it is very easy to believe that women never, ever listen to you. But, damn it, sometimes they do, even if they hear the wrong things. I once suggested to my spouse that she might have a 'hearing problem.' After extensive testing by a specialist, she was informed that, indeed, she had a condition well known to audiologists called "Selective Spousal Hearing." Her hearing was perfect, except when her husband was speaking.

And there may be another small lesson here…we all hear what we want to hear and ignore the rest. In any case, it mattered not what I said, my actions in the mid-1960s were way more powerful. I simply was gone…that is what she 'heard.'

Now, knowing all that, would I still have gone off to India?

Of course… that chapter of my life in some sense having already been written somewhere, by someone, and likely was unalterable.

MAKING SENSE OF THINGS

What might be drawn from the passages selected for this chapter? One obvious interpretation jumps out. An idealistic young man joins the Peace Corps with the best of intentions and brimming with ennobling idealism. After two years of unrelenting heat, frustration, cultural friction, disease, loneliness, technical futility, and romantic disappointment, the young man

174

leaves India depressed and disillusioned and drifting without any direction. While it sure looks that way, I suspect that interpretation might just be a tad off, if not dead wrong.

There is a wonderful scene in the movie *A League of Their Own*, the story of a woman's professional baseball league that was started during World War II when many thought the real major leagues would be shut down. The team manager (played by Tom Hanks) confronts his team's best player (played by Geena Davis) who had decided to leave the team just before the start of the new league's first championship series (also, her wounded fiancé had just returned from the fighting in Europe).

Jimmy (the Hanks character) tries to change her mind. "Baseball is what gets inside you. It's what lights you up, you can't deny that."

"It just got too hard," Dottie (the Davis character) responds.

Jimmy glowers for a moment before spitting out a memorable line that goes something like the following:

Baseball "…is supposed to be hard. If it wasn't hard, everyone would do it. It is the hard that makes it great."

On reflection, it strikes me that the really hard things are what make each of us great, or at least just a little better. The Peace Corps experience in India was hard, very hard. It tested us, perhaps in a different sense than the training experience did, though that surely had its own challenges. But India tested us in a special way, pushing us to the point where our core character solidified and perhaps even grew. Either we grew or, given the challenges we faced, it was likely that one's core would bend and crack.

Why was this 'testing of self' so important to me and, I strongly suspect, to each one of us in India 44? In my case, the reasons are transparent.

In my youth, I may have looked reasonably confident and composed. Thinking back, I can see a tall, not bad looking (something I could not see back then), young man who escaped a very modest working-class background by working his way through a somewhat competitive private high school before next working his way through a private college. In all likelihood, to the outside world, I probably appeared to have my shit together.

On the inside, however, my self-esteem remained some-where just south of the toilet, so to speak. Most days, as inti-mated earlier, I was convinced that I would fail. I just knew that others believed I was not smart enough, or tough enough, or good-looking enough, or talented enough, or sociable enough, or (you fill in the blank) to succeed at whatever I was trying to do. It was only a matter of time before I would be discovered as the fraud I surely was in my own mind. At odd moments, waves of panic would overtake me, attacks I was sure others could readily notice.

Where did this sometimes paralyzing insecurity come from? Well, some tendencies and dispositions are probably hardwired, in part at least, coming along with our genetic makeup. And perhaps, I had just a little trouble escaping that Irish black cloud I've mentioned from time to time. A somber quip made right after Kennedy's death in 1963 by Dave Powers, his long-time personal aide, has never left me. It went something like this, "We Irish always know that the good we enjoy will be taken from us but, in this case, we thought we might have just a little more time."

That cloud is always there and, of course, growing up in a marginal, working-class neighborhood did not help. In that place, a successful kid was one who managed to stay out of jail. Of course, maybe, just maybe, my home life contributed a little bit to what I was back then. My mother, in particular, was con-sumed by what others thought. Unfortunately, as the only child, I was exhibit number one as to whether she was a good parent and a good person. To others, as my older cousin related to me much later in life, my mother praised me to the heavens…her little Tommy was so perfect and surely could do no wrong. To me, however, she issued a continuous torrent of criticism and belittlement…I could do no right. Whether accurate or not, that is the way I saw it, felt it. Eventually, the hard words morphed into a firm script that embedded itself somewhere deep within.

Climbing out of that pit of negativity does not happen over-night. It took many years and tons of positive reinforcement … a virtual stream of upbeat feedback that initially puzzled and confused me but eventually cracked through the wall of denial that had been erected to defend my impoverished self-image. That road to a healthier sense of self started at Clark and, believe it or not, began to accelerate in Peace Corps and India. At the same time, I finally began to verbalize the dark sentiments I had long felt on the inside.

I also sensed something else. I had survived my tenure in Peace Corps in perhaps that program's most demanding site. I had survived, in fact probably performed fairly well, in a program that even formal Peace Corps evaluations recognized was designed to fail (see Chapter 1). In spite of everything the program, the culture, and our own sometimes laughable ineptness could throw at us, I did ok. Now, all this may not have been apparent at the time but eventually I came to recognize and accept it.

The dark passages that flowed out toward the end of my two years were not the ravings of a young man unraveling in the face of pressure and failure. Rather, they were a cathartic expression of deeply sensed anxieties that enabled me to start in a different direction. The words did not lead me further down but rather toward a new direction in life.

As I described in our first book, my new direction eventually would lead to a marvelous career in the academy, one that included a heavy dose of exciting public policy stuff. I was like the proverbial 'kid in the candy' store, working with the best and brightest in universities, in government, in think-tanks, in top evaluation firms, and in the philanthropic world. It was beyond what I could ever have dreamed of as a teenager hanging around street corners when I could not imagine who would ever possibly hire me or why. On those street corners, it was inconceivable that I had anything to offer anyone.

In the end, the most remarkable thing is that I felt I really belonged in my new world as an adult. I would look around some meeting in which I was involved, whether in academia or the so-called real worlds of policy formulation and government, surveying a room filled with the best and the brightest and I would realize…damn, I actually belong in this room! Surely, the 'rite-of-passage' that was India deserves some credit for this small miracle.

Now, whether anyone else in that room agreed that I belonged there…that is quite another story entirely!

CHAPTER 8

What Was I Thinking?
or
Who Did I Think I Was?

David Dell

HOW COULD MILWAUKEE BE INTENSE? We found out in the summer of '66 when some 80 or so smart, idealistic, healthy, and hormonally-charged college juniors suddenly were dunked in a rather amazing socio-educational experiment.

We were volunteers in an experiment within the larger Peace Corps experiment. The experiment's mission: To see if the Peace Corps could use a little more time and some leadership development and psychographic tools to first profile, then either select or deselect people who were initially considered to be emotionally ready and trainable. On paper, at least, those of us who endured all that faced us would head off to India and be effective volunteers in a demanding, alien culture.

I was one of the subjects and I thought I was getting a bargain—an amazing education, an all-expense-paid trip to India and a chance to put my own idealism into action. I got my bargain and much more and much less.

In essence neither I, nor the Peace Corps, knew what we were doing. Yet, we certainly thought we were being smart about it.

Almost 45 years later, some of our group met in Washington, and I was challenged to write (as many of them already

179

India 44 reunion, McLean, VA, 2011

had) some kind of memoir of my India adventure to share with my peers as well as with others. In that all too brief reunion I was struck again by our diversity and by the rich array of backgrounds and ways of thinking we brought to Milwaukee so many years ago. I regretted anew how poorly I used the opportunity to get to know some fantastic people while I plowed blithely into the rich new fields of ideas we were absorbing.

Now I find myself more moved to write about myself within our group experiment than about my personal passage to what Whitman called "more than India." That was when I was most visible and present to each of you and fit at least a little better into what you also experienced. What makes it hard to do this is that I don't really know what matters, and my memory is composed more of patterns, flavors, and essences than it is facts. It is more about what I was thinking than what I experienced.

So I ask you all: Is it more relevant that I remember we built a chicken coop in the back of our training residence or that we played Frisbee in the front? Is how I felt when I first dreamed in Hindi more important than the classes on the lawn where we practiced speaking our Hindi and Marathi? Is it the t-groups and sensitivity training sessions at night and yanking off chicken heads by day or the barrage of psychographic tests and peer-to-peer rankings used for possible deselection that we should recall more vividly? Just how significant is it that we were supposed to get to know and celebrate the individuals in our group at the same time there was pressure across individuals to compete for the approval of our trainers?

We knew we were in an experiment. And we didn't need hindsight to know the experiment didn't make sense.

It was nuts to think they could help us enjoy every opportunity for addiction to being part of an exciting and committed group, then turn around and be deposited one or two at a time in a completely unsupportive environment, and still embrace the process. It was ridiculous to think we could learn about poverty in India from a quick tour to Milwaukee's inner city (where many of us saw the same kinds of poverty we grew up in) or to live in communal tents on an Indian reservation where we were well fed and celebrated as an honored cadre of guests and, from that experience, suddenly know how to cope with living alone in India.

It was bizarre that we would read books about cross-cultural experience and get lectures from the finest theorists when we were bombarded with challenging cross-cultural issues amongst ourselves. There were enough differences just among the Californians to keep an anthropologist busy for years; almost all of us were vastly different from anyone I had met before.

But what could the Peace Corps have done that was better? The staff members were almost as young and innocent, and surely just as idealistic, as we were.

Yet with all the wrongness, what we were immersed in was so beautiful. The intensity of some one-on-one moments, the endless debates, the intimate times, the all-night emotional highs, the mental stretching from hour after hour of training in richly crafted curricula, and the exchanges with really stimulating minds and mentors on the staff were irreplaceable opportunities not likely to be repeated later in our lives.

So what did it matter if it was all a joke? It matters because it changed us and because it failed to change us. It matters because it was real and yet surreal.

At least, that's how it was for me.

I was a junior at Columbia University and felt trapped and cheated. I had been working as much as 60 hours or more a week to pay tuition, earn spending money, and, most importantly, eat. The first two years I had my pick of intro classes and was in a curriculum designed to let me learn as much as I could about anything and everything. I loved it.

Then the curriculum shifted from small classes and discussions to big lectures. Now, you had to drill down on something substantive like English, Political Science, or choose one of the physical sciences, etc. It wasn't me, and I hated it.

Suddenly, I saw a loophole! Majoring in Oriental studies (I had liked the core courses I took) let me pick a country, study some language, and basically take any course in the whole university at any level I wanted that might be relevant to that country. As I considered this, Peace Corps recruiters came though the campus with an offer—take part in an intensive summer experience, get a teachable skill, study a language, learn about an intriguing country, and even earn more college credits. That tipped the balance… I applied and changed majors the same day.

Why would I do that? Here I was a kid from a smart but very poor family, completely oblivious to the career paths opening up to him via an Ivy League education, who changes his future so he can learn the way he wants to learn. In today's world I would likely have been diagnosed early as being in the autism spectrum addicted to "knowing it all" and mentally/physically unable to see other people's socialization and reactions. My mind was everything to me, and the joy I felt in how I learned and what I learned transcended any other rewards. I did not know any other way to be. I had even made conscious vows to myself that this was how I wanted to be.

So I went to Milwaukee. First time on a plane, I flew to Chicago, was met by Marcia, a former girlfriend. I stayed with her

David Dell, training, Milwaukee, 1966

and her mom before they drove me up to the training site in her mom's Cadillac convertible. We arrived at the steps of Holton Hall to see many trainees outside waiting to see who might arrive next. And what they doubtless saw was a Cadillac convertible, top down, tall blond student with a Columbia-labeled bag, and a beautiful blond girl giving him a passionate goodbye kiss. I wish all my first impressions could be like that... or should I wish that?

I may never know who assumed I was arrogant from that first moment. Or, did they conclude that later on, whenever I was moved to say what I thought was right without any social awareness or notice of who I was cutting off. It speaks to the wonderful nature of the group that I was accepted at all and included in so much given the diverse array of outspokenness, strong opinions, and self-proclaimed leadership that existed among our marvelous group of trainees.

As I sit here today, I wonder what I simply don't remember or just didn't notice in the first place. I remember odd things like our competing to see who could squat best on their haunches. I remember drown-proofing exercises and chicken debeaking lessons and building a chicken shed. I do not remember sitting in classrooms, but I remember flickers of our teachers in poultry, our psych coaches, and our language team and feeling observed by them and oddly invisible to fellow volunteers. I remember arguing a lot about important global things, especially with Bill Whitesell and Jonathan Schiesel but don't remember why we argued or what about.

I remember the train to the Indian reservations, sleeping on the luggage racks, and all of us being so tired. I recall the confusing babble about what it meant to be in different groups and whether we were being pitted against one another in mini-exercises to see how we would react to stress.

For me, the reservation, was a chance to decompress, climb up to the hills, and get swooped on by a bald eagle. It was a chance to learn I was a bad example for cursing in front of the kids, to throw up from swimming in their polluted cow pond, to marvel at their motorcycle skills, to inspect their garbage and see how little they had, to fail to appreciate their country music (which oddly I can still remember), to fight a prairie grass fire that threatened to consume our tents, to be taken aside into her tent by our psychiatrist and told I had no clue who I was while I was hoping that she might actually be hitting on me. At least on that trip it felt like there was time to remember and reflect and grow as a person. There was finally time to develop a sense of being with friends...

And then back to wrap up, pack, and head off to school with some "see you next summer" goodbyes and some we didn't know yet were final goodbyes. There was even then a sense we had missed some times to talk, to become friends, or go off alone and more than flirt, or come close to intimacy.

Our experiment continued over the winter with meetings and communications, then another summer in Wisconsin, and then more group training in India with our numbers fewer at each step. Finally we were dropped off on our own by our experimenters, actually thinking we were prepared.

Donne said no man is an island, but the Peace Corps made us an instant archipelago.

Here's how I summarize the experience on linkedin.com:

Volunteer

US Peace Corps
1967—1968 (1 year)
Became fluent in Hindi, was trained as a chicken farmer, was sent to vegetarian village where people did not eat eggs or speak Hindi, coped and consulted with farmers and ag agents on new best practices in green revolution.

I find it matters less who went to what village or if we went at all. I find myself now drawn to know the people we were and became and not caring much about who had the worst cook or the funniest story or the closest call with some disease. We all have our stories and stories within the larger story.

I returned to so many shocks, as did we all. I didn't get drafted and did get a Ph.D. in Indian languages. I went back to India several times, and then did a lot of interesting work that had nothing to do with India. Forty-five years later, I find the real wonder is that we mostly all grew and became more interesting and accomplished despite some highly dysfunctional experiences in India.

I think if we all could pick a time in our Peace Corps experience and go back and experience it again more richly and more wisely, it would be to Milwaukee and not India. No need to be young again, but to pick up on who we are and how we think and feel with each other and perhaps enrich each other as friends.

CHAPTER 9

Snapshots from 44A

Sylvia Bray
Kathy Kelleher Sohn
Lynne Graham
Carolyn Jones-Cullen

Editors' Note:
This chapter is comprised of several short vignettes
developed by four members of India 44A. Each story
represents a favorite memory or impression or insight
that the author chose to share.

Arriving Unarmed in the Land of B.A., Fail
Sylvia Bray

It was considered quite a feat in India in the mid 1960's to have gotten to the university level to qualify for your exams for the Bachelor of Arts. So if you failed that final requirement, you might still be noted as "Mukergee Nipal, B.A., Fail" on the plaque on your door or on your business card to let people know the level of education you had achieved.

If I could have just had a designation, "B. A., Fail, Public Health," it would have been more helpful than was my B.A., Pass in Political Science. You see, my Peace Corps assignment was in the field of rural public health and nutrition. Confused looks would follow when I answered questions of people in the village about my university studies. What was I doing there? A hard question to answer!

While it may have been true that living in America in the 1960's gave me a good grasp of germ theory and an understanding of basic nutrition, I was woefully unprepared to really be of help in providing health care to the village of Risod, a desert town located in the geographical center of India in the state of Maharashtra. I very much envied the two RNs in our Peace Corp group. They not only had street credibility, but had done rotations in hospitals and benefited from hands-on experience.

Kathy Kelleher and I arrived in Risod in the fall of 1967. It was considered a very progressive village, though somewhat off the beaten path. We were assigned to work with Dr. Hore, our Public Health Officer. He was from a very interesting family of doctors, beginning with his grandfather, who was an Ayurvedic doctor, and aunts and uncles who had been educated in British medical schools. One uncle was a pharmacist.

On one of the first days after we arrived in Risod, Dr. Hore called us down to the clinic to show us a patient he was treating. He told us that this young woman was dying because the untrained village midwife had attempted to deliver her uterus during childbirth. By the time she was brought to him for treatment, it was too late. He was sending her on to the hospital in Washim, expecting that she would not survive the journey.

I remember thinking, "How can this woman be dying; she looks awake and alert?" I had had very little experience with the dying, and my image of death was one of long decline from illness or perhaps the drama of violent death. This young woman didn't fit any concept I had of someone dying. She was not moaning or groaning, yet the doctor whom I respected was telling us she was dying. It just seemed too ordinary to be real. We heard later that she had indeed died on the trip to Washim.

During our Peace Corps training, we had heard examples of untrained village midwives killing patients by cutting the umbilical cord with dirty field tools, causing sepsis or cord tetanus, and here was an example of lack of medical expertise proving deadly to a young woman.

Not long after this, we were attending the local Bollywood cinema with a trained health worker when we got called to the clinic. Two women were in labor and needed help. This was my first experience of a live birth, and I had never even held a newborn. So when a newborn was thrust into my arms, I felt awkward and concerned that I would be a danger to that new little life. Plus, I was expected to wash it in the chill of the night outside of the birth room. What a shock to this new little life—to go from the mother's warm womb into a chilly world to be bathed. We all survived, though, and embraced the positive, magical experience to counter the shocking one of seeing the life of another young woman end.

Our education continued as we shadowed the trained health worker. Sometimes we were able to help with a vaccination campaign or visit a school. One day, we were puzzled and alarmed when we followed the health worker around a medical ward, really just a room with six or eight beds of female patients, and saw her give each patient an injection with the same syringe, which she only dipped in water between patients.

Did she not understand or believe in contagion? Each of the patients had a different condition, some potentially contagious through the sharing of a contaminated needle. What was her education/training? And what could we do with the knowledge of what we had just witnessed?

That frustrating event paled in comparison with the day a mother presented Kathy and me with her starving baby wanting us to tell her what to do. Her milk had dried up and she didn't know what to do. Where was my B.A., Fail in Health Care? Never have I felt so helpless, useless, and such a fraud. What was the Peace Corps staff thinking when they decided to send young college graduates out to villages pretending they were healthcare workers?

India continued to educate me and give me an array of fascinating, sometimes maddening experiences throughout my time there. Still, I am grateful for the experience of living in a culture so different than my own, and for the opportunity to sometimes find common ground.

Sylvia and Kathy with village families

But with the experience came the taint of failure associated with trying to fulfill an undefined mission with inadequate training and qualifications. How I longed for that B.A., Fail....

Christmas in India
Kathy Kelleher Sohn

Reading over the letters my mother kept for me from my time in India, I was delighted to come across my description of my first Christmas in India, beginning in my village and later in Goa which, as a former Portuguese colony, was a good choice for a Christmas getaway given the area's Catholic influence.

Christmas is always a difficult holiday when you're away from home, but it was particularly so for me since it was the first Christmas in my life that I was away from my seven siblings, my parents, and my extended family. With no cell phones or cordless phones available, I had six months earlier booked a trunk call to my family, calling them from the Troutman's, a Peace Corps staff person in Bombay. It was 4:30 in the morning in the States, and Mother had everyone around the phone to wish me Merry Christmas. What a wonderful gift!

I had received my Christmas package, which Mother had mailed three months earlier because of shipping costs, and among the gifts was a tape on which Mother had recorded all of the family singing as she played the piano. Always one for the dramatic and nostalgic, she threw in music from the Bing Crosby and Gene Autry Christmas albums for effect. Hearing all of my family sing was a real treat; I played that tape time and again until I needed to record some music from BBC and taped over it. My mother never forgave me for that; it was the production of her lifetime and a tribute to me.

I also received that Christmas an 8x10 portrait of my boyfriend, Brian Morley, who had broken up with me two months prior to Christmas. He, too, had sent a package three months ahead. It gave me great pleasure to tear the photo to shreds.

Sylvia and I had planned to leave for the holidays on a trip to Bombay and Goa, but the night before we left, we had a Christmas party for our friends in the village. Sylvia had bought some decorative materials and had Santa and reindeer hanging from a decorated coat hanger on one window. The tree sat on a poinsettia printed cloth, and Christmas cards hung on the walls in the form of trees. We wore our American frocks, sang carols, gave

Dressed for Christmas, 1968

small gifts to the children, and then served snacks and drinks. After our program was over, Mr. Joshi, a friend of the doctor, our Health Officer, got up to make a speech about this being our first holiday away from home and how he hoped we were happy. He wished us a Happy New Year on behalf of everyone there.

We had supper later with the Revenue Inspector—chicken, rice, fish, and mutton. We dressed in our best saris, and the villagers stopped in their paths to watch us walk to his house. Someone almost got run over by a bullock cart gaping at us. We left the next day for our Christmas holiday in Goa, but stopped for lunch with the Christian missionaries in Washim, two hours away. Later at the train station in Akola, the district town, we met four other Peace Corps volunteers on their way to Bombay as well.

In Bombay, we met Jerry Weiss and Don Nordin for the trip; Don and I went to the Elephanta Caves and took a flight to Goa since we heard the boat was full. For only 100 rupees, we flew, taking our lives in our hands. In addition to being noisy, we had no air-conditioning, and our landing was eardrum splitting.

In Goa, we stayed at the misnamed Palace Hotel since finding spots in Goa was impossible and there was literally no room at the inn. This place was as bad as a stable; I was sure that rats were everywhere. We went out to eat and, on our way to Midnight Mass, we heard a group singing. Santa Claus came by on a float, adding to the holiday ambiance.

The Mass was at the foot of the stairs of the cathedral, the altar on the first level facing the congregation. The most beautiful part of the Mass was the Gloria when all the bells were ringing including the huge bell at the top of the cathedral. The choir added much to the solemnity of the moment. It was a little like heaven, and it made me nostalgic for my family. Jerry Weiss and I braved the mobs of people to take communion. While Don was, in fact, Catholic, he had fallen asleep on the steps, and Sylvia had gone back to the hotel because she wasn't feeling well.

The rest of the vacation consisted of riding bikes to the lovely Goan beaches, meeting other Peace Corps Volunteers and two Australian women who eventually came to our village. I then traveled to Bangalore, another lovely town, and met some India 30 volunteers who had been in Milwaukee training during our Advanced Placement summer of 1966. It was great to hang around with them. I got some wonderful ideas from interchanges with other volunteers I met along the way and came back to the village a few weeks later with lots of ideas.

I often think of that first Christmas in India as a milestone for my own education in cultures: the juxtapositioning of a treasured festival for us in a country 12,000 miles away from my own. I also learned about Hindu festivals and found their Diwali feast similar to our Christmas. Now I have learned that family celebrations can happen in so many ways, and that flexibility comes from the decades of Christmas celebrations since that first exotic one in India, 45 years ago.

RAMBLINGS IN A DUSTY MEMORY BANK
Carolyn Jones-Cullen

I sometimes feel pain and frustration at the poverty and disparity in the world. In my innocence, I thought we would be able to make a tiny move toward making a better life for all. I thought those in political power wanted that, too. But on a one-to-one perspective, I knew there were connections, particularly with the children and, of course, there was that poor doctor's wife.

As I ramble on, I'm beginning to reach into my dusty memory bank to reclaim some of those distant flashpoints. Perhaps they may be of interest to others, perhaps not. And sometimes I think I have a story but wonder if I'm actually remembering it correctly after all these years.

Perhaps I could say these are my best recollections...

I hadn't thought about Mr. Ogale and our eye camp for some time. Mr. Ogale's family had a whole village named after them...Ogalewadi. He lived in a huge compound and often

Tai and Sungi, Vita 1968

Mokundrao Ogale

spoke of his nephew who was at the University of Chicago and apparently was a great tennis player. Through a series of conversations, my uncle talked his Lions Club in Detroit, as well as the Rotary Club, into helping us get an eye cataract camp going in our village. Mr Ogale also provided the first 50 rupees to launch our polio vaccination program.

I purchased many Frisbees that I brought to India with me. Oh, the joy of seeing kids of all ages whirling those discs with such excitement. I used to wish I had a 100 frisbees to give out. Maybe I can yet start a frisbee drive for rural India!

I also remember being totally disgusted and repulsed by Dr. M., our Muslim physician who had trained at the Sangli-Scottish Presbyterian Medical School. He spoke excellent English and was quite aware of western ways. He pocketed promised government incentive money that was intended for those who had undergone vasectomies or tubal ligations. Another shortcoming was the inhumane way he treated his new bride who came from a well-to-do family. He would beat her and isolate her in the compound. He did seem to enjoy sparring with me during our conversations. However, when he began taking advantage of a nursing student, that was enough, and I diplomatically intervened.

I now remember the patient with a distended abdomen in our UNICEF operating room. I had to crank up the petrol autoclave and hand Dr. M. the instrument to tap the belly. Out spewed a galvanized bucket of TB fluid. It spouted in an arc as I tried catching the fluid in a bucket. Unbelievable! It's truly a wonder I never contracted TB.

And then there was the young pregnant woman who was carried into the exam room and placed on the floor. A flock of wailing, hysterical family members surrounded her while a Shaman cut off the leg of a chicken shaking blood all over her rigid body. He was in a trance-like state, chanting unintelligible words…no doubt issuing healing requests to the spiritual world. Eardrum piercing bellowing could be heard in all the stillness but for this one stage. Then they were gone, replaced by a morbid silence. We moved her obtunded body to the exam table while protecting her protruding belly. I held my breath as I was skillfully coached to assist with the delivery of her baby.

As I forced myself to breathe, I suddenly realized that I now believed in miracles. I knew I could do this…I could work in medicine. I didn't even think of fainting. I was a doer, a responder, a nurturer. I could be another kind of healer. I was called right then and there!

I learned how to tie the umbilical cord with alcohol soaked cotton string under the expert guidance of our much experienced midwife. I learned how to wrap the tiny baby in rolls of UNICEF cotton. With no incubators in the village, we made do.

But many suffered. Dr. M. took note of my growing interest in medicine and showed me a female patient with a rigid, frozen jaw. He explained that she had lockjaw caused by *clostridium tetani*, a bacterial infection called tetanus, which sadly claimed her short life. For all his faults, he was a competent physician who, along with the midwives, taught me many medical lessons.

On another occasion, a crippled man was trying to make his way up the dusty path to our health compound and no one was helping him. I ran out to the driveway, put my arm around his shoulder, and helped drag him to the men's side of the clinic. He was a leper. He was ostracized. No one wanted to treat him.

They isolated me in a stone room where I had to strip off my sari, which was burned. I then had to scrub and redress. This motivated me to study anything I could find on the topic of leprosy and its cultural ramifications. Of course, there was no internet. Wouldn't that have been wonderful!

I went to Sangli to ask advice from Nancy Ramer, the Presbyterian Scottish nurse instructor at the missionary school. I was so touched during my visit to the Leprosy Colony outside the Sangli district. I forget exactly where it is but do recall it was affiliated with a World Christian Outreach program. I was given a tour and met both patients and residents. As I gazed into their saucer sized soulful eyes I almost had to divert my attention elsewhere for fear I would read their pain.

But I could also see their pride. Yes, and as they showed me their work, they grinned beyond any disfigurement. They were not typically assimilated back into their communities at the time. But they did have several small businesses that originally had been advocated by Gandhi. I bought hand-loomed cotton placemats and napkins to bring home as gifts. My heart liquefied into tears, and I knew the meaning of the word 'charity' at that moment.

A similar thing happened when an old *baba sadhu (holy man)* appeared at our front door appealing for alms. I quickly came to the door and saw this almost apparition with a drawn but sweet betel stained full-toothed smile. His turban and dhoti were dusted red with saffron. While I sat with him on our stoop, we seemed to be in a world without boundaries. It was probably only a few moments, I really don't know, but I was lost in the exchange. Somehow, I came to know the meaning of another word…brotherhood. The spell was then interrupted. I gave him bananas and rupees and he disappeared. Yet, the memory is perfectly clear to this day.

And there was the time I met the banker of Vita who was highly educated and spoke perfect English. He engaged me in conversations about Indian politics and banking (I don't know anything about banking and little of Indian politics except that the Home Minister was born in Sangli district, which gave us some perks). He recommended I visit an elder in the village who spoke some English and who could teach me about the Mahabharatan philosophy, and the principles of Yoga. I was amazed! Unfortunately, I didn't see him much as he was visiting, and the language barrier prevented further learning.

There was still another shocker when I was visiting Andra Pradesh. I was talking out loud about wishing I knew the origins and history of certain historical ruins. There, sitting lotus-like on a ruin was a sadhu-appearing man. He looked at me directly, not a side-glance, and then started instructing me about the history of the place in excellent English. I was so taken aback; I barely remember what he said. It all seemed so surreal. Here we were in this strange time warp, almost like a science fiction novel in which I was a lucky participant. It was like seeing the movie *2001* at the only theater in Poona, then walking outside to 1960s India with the sound of bullock hoofs plodding off somewhere in the distance and catching the faint sounds of chanting. Another rush was watching Apollo 11 land on the moon in 1969 while in India. Such strange and enchanting contrasts of technology and place!

India has now achieved huge technological advances and makes many contributions to the world's economy through the computer sciences and in so many other ways. That is India… ever brimming with surprises at the most unexpected times.

And what did I learn from all this…rambling through that dusty memory bank of mine? Well, maybe it is that kindness became a kind of mantra for me in India. I guess I came to realize that it is the best kind of healing.

A Gracious Way to Shop
Sylvia Bray

From the time I landed in New Delhi, I was dazzled by the beautiful textiles of India. Its long history of making beautiful fabrics had resulted in a dizzying variety of materials that were a feast for sight and touch. The choices were wonderful. I was smitten. Much of my monthly allowance went to feeding my new mania. And it didn't hurt that the very experience of purchasing fabric had a lushness of its own.

For instance, to purchase a sari, one needed to go to a shop that specialized in saris and other related fabrics. Upon arrival at a shop, one was invited to be seated on soft cushions on the floor with bolsters on which to lean. Tea was ordered and a variety of fabrics or saris were brought out, one by one, from which we could choose. And what choices! There were lush silks with gold metallic borders, rough cottons that washed up to a soft

Cloth bazaar, Hyderabad, 1969

A ribbon wallah in the bazaar

clingy material that flashed different colors when one moved, finely hand woven cottons, and synthetics.

In addition, the borders were as varied as the colors and fabrics. Borders were important as they defined the edges of the sari but also the trim at the end of the fabric which hung over one's shoulder. This end piece often told of the quality of the sari, with the most elaborate designs being the most expensive. The material came in brilliant, pastel colors; busy patterns, solid colors, hand woven fabric, and machine woven fabrics. And each of these choices necessitated a choice of fabric for a floor length petticoat, the base garment on which the sari was wrapped, as well as material for a *choli*, or short blouse that matched the sari, though often of other material. These then required a separate visit to the tailor, who would measure one for the petticoat and for the *choli* and have them ready for you in a couple of days.

One of my favorite purchases was tied to one of my nicest memories of India. My roommate, Kathy Kelleher, and I were invited by our supervising doctor to go with him to his hometown for the Diwali festival. There his family warmly welcomed us into their home and showed us a wonderful time. That town was famous for its hand-loomed saris and while there, I purchased a royal purple, hand-loomed cotton sari. It had a gold metallic woven border with a tiny detail of orange. For the *choli,* I purchased a piece of royal purple silk with gold trim. I loved that outfit.

I sigh with pleasure today when I think of those lovely fabrics and the experience of purchasing and wearing them.

Skiing in India!
Lynne Graham

After six months in my hot dusty village I was READY for vacation! And coincidentally a newsletter from PC India arrived with the mention of a ski festival in Gulmarg, Kashmir. Wow, snow, coolness, this Michigan gal has a chance to ski again…I decided to go!

After scrounging clothes from local missionaries and volunteers, I made the 24-hour bus and train trip to Bombay and then flew to New Delhi. The next morning in Delhi I was again at the airport for an early flight to Kashmir. Oops, the flight was to make a stopover in Jammu, below the mountains that enclose Kashmir and the weather was socked in! Twelve hours after taking off from Delhi I was back in Delhi!

Day 2 was a repeat of Day 1. Where was my vacation going…was the dream of snow to remain a mirage? Fortunately, I had found several other volunteers and a staff member on the plane all heading to Kashmir to ski.

Day 3, fly to Jammu, flight cancelled… again!!! BUT now we thought we were smart and hopped off the plane and onto a "luxury" local bus (complete with statues and tassels) to continue up the road to Kashmir! That plan was good for a few

View from a State Transport bus

hours until the road ended at a landslide and we could go no further that day. Fortunately the Hindi-speaking volunteers booked us all into a decent tiny hotel.

Day 4 was a long wait, and word was the road would not open; the ski festival was starting the next day! Late in the afternoon, our problem was solved as the Indian army was driving a convoy of trucks to test the road, and we could ride in the back! Just at dusk we were dropped off at the edge of Shrinager, caught a taxi to Gulmarg, and completed our journey by pony. I was so tired I only remember the pony tender running alongside in the snow while I barely clung to the saddle. But we made it after 5 days on the road and were welcomed into our rooms where there were fireplaces for warmth.

The festival next day was a riot as many locals from Shrinager came to participate and bravely strapped on skis to give it a try. They fell everywhere! Fortunately, the day was warm and sunny. There were several races and I did get a lovely tablecloth for coming in third (out of three contestants). If the crowd hadn't overrun the hill as we were racing, who knows, maybe I would have won! It was a small ski hill with a rope tow and skis with old fashioned cable bindings and leather boots but I was, in fact, actually SKIING! It was bliss…

The next day the Peace Corps group hiked up a nearby mountain and skied down for some more recreation. And then it was time to leave.

This time, Mother Nature was kinder…the snow was melting and our journey back to Delhi proved uneventful. It was a very original yet, in some ways, typical Peace Corps vacation … testing… but very much worth the effort!

Coming Home
Sylvia Bray

Everything was moving so fast. The commuter bus must have been careening down the highway at 60 miles an hour. The others on the bus seemed unconcerned. They weren't time travelers like I was, having just returned from some century past. I was used to horse carts, bullock carts, antiquated buses overflowing with people and goods, and trains that spewed coal dust and cinders through the open windows. But it wasn't just the speed of the vehicles that unbalanced me. Everything was in flux. The ground seemed to have shifted while I was away in India, and I returned to an altered universe.

My personal identity had been constantly shifting in India as I was an honored guest one day, a polluting infidel the next, and a strange curiosity the next. I had also recently married and was now a wife, daughter-in-law, sister-in-law, and Returned Peace Corps Volunteer (RPCV), unemployed, and with no established home.

We had left New Delhi in a driving monsoon rain, proud that the big TWA jet cut right through the bad weather to take us home. Pride in all things American began to get murky shortly after we arrived in Washington, DC. Having been medically evacuated from India, I was being put through a round of difficult medical tests in the daytime, followed by watching the Chicago Democratic National Convention on the hotel TV in the evening. I watched in horror as Chicago police beat peaceful demonstrators bloody, while Mayor Richard Daley acted the arrogant potentate inside the convention. Then there were the more radical demonstrators threatening to put LSD in the city's drinking water, adding fuel to the blazing inferno.

It was madness. What to do? Go back to India to start over? There was really nowhere to run to escape the reality of what was happening. Even before we left India, we had gotten word that Martin Luther King and then Bobby Kennedy had been shot and killed. The Vietnam War was increasingly unpopular, and there was the fear that my young husband would be drafted to fight in that war.

I felt like I had left one culture to go live in another and then returned to yet another culture. We chose to start our new life in San Francisco, which threw me into the vortex of the changes going on in1968. The ground continued to shift beneath me. My husband reveled in the change; I was shell shocked by it.

There were things I loved: the intense idealism, great music, "free universities," colorful clothes, and people trying to do things in a new way. And there was the sadness of seeing my generation pulled apart by the war—those going to Vietnam to fight—so many killed—and those refusing to fight and resentful of those they felt supported the war machine by going. There was also fear of where our country might be headed or that it might implode entirely.

I became a mother, later divorced, remarried and am again part of a different culture through marriage.

How did Peace Corps/India play out in my life? The idealism that led me to Peace Corps stayed with me as I moved from San Francisco to Berkeley to Sonoma County. Not only did I choose to work in non-profit agencies for the causes of health, child care, and affordable housing, volunteerism has also been a constant in my life. I learned a flexibility living in a village in India that has served me well throughout my life.

I feel an amazing camaraderie with those who were part of our Peace Corps groups (44A and 44B), having shared our idealism, frustrations, and experiences and knowing we were truly changed by our brief time trying to be helpful to those we thought might need us. I suspect that sense of connection shall remain a constant for the rest of our lives.

CHAPTER 10

The Me That Nobody Knew

Haywood Turrentine

After two years of living in an Indian village, I would finally get to go home to see family and friends. Not surprisingly, I was a bit anxious to get back. Many of our group discussions over the last few months in India centered on three things: (1) where we planned to attend graduate school; (2) where we were going to travel on our trip home; and (3) what kind of love life had we left behind, including how much, if any, would still be there awaiting our return.

I am not entirely sure how much of that thought process I remember today, some 40-plus years later. I do know, though, that I did not want to return to the United States and not take the opportunity to see some of the wonderful places the world had to offer a poor tenant farm boy from Durham County, North Carolina.

After all, this might well be the last opportunity I would have to visit these wonderful places. No one that I knew from our little rural existence had ever traveled abroad, other than while serving in the armed forces. You just did not up and go overseas if you grew up like I, and so many others like me, did in the late '60s. Hey, we were lucky if we got to travel into the big city of Durham once a week or so. Let's face it, travel was a luxury and not the normal thing to do if you lived on a fourth of what you raised and/or produced. Funds were simply not available for such extravagant jaunts. As a result, even though I was anxious to get home and see family, I knew I needed to stop off and see some of the world's sights.

Don Nordin and I started out traveling together. We went to such places as Istanbul, Belgrade, Rome, Athens, Mykonos, Amsterdam, Copenhagen, Nicé, Paris, and finally London. At that juncture, I was really getting homesick and a bit low on cash, so I decided to head on home. I would not see Don again until we got together in Oakland for our 40-year reunion. Did we have fun during our return trip home? You bet your life we did!

Things got started in Istanbul when we encountered a couple of local entrepreneurs. We must have had "stupid" written on our foreheads because it seemed that everyone tried to take advantage of us. Not to worry, we survived and made it through Europe relatively unscathed, though a bit wiser to the ways of the world.

We were able to visit up close and personal some of the most magnificent wonders of the world. We climbed the Acropolis in Athens and visited the Parthenon along with other iconic monuments of ancient Greece. We saw the Louvre, the Eiffel Tower, and so many other important French sites. We drank great French wines and room temperature beers in Europe. We attended a Russian circus in Tehran, and made it out without incident. Nevertheless, home was calling and, after London, I flew to Boston and then to Washington, DC.

Culture shock really set in quick, fast, and in a hurry, if not sooner. I landed at Dulles International and needed some money to pay for my cab ride to my sister's house in NW Washington, DC. I only had traveler's checks, but did not see any banks that were open. Back in 1969, there was not a great deal of activity at Dulles International, and it seemed as if the airport was located somewhere in no man's land. I think that cab ride ended up costing me almost $50…shock! Hell, that was fairly close to a month's pay as a Peace Corps Volunteer.

Eventually, I navigated my ride to my sister's house and reunited with family. The moment I walked in the door, my sister just finished baking the best biscuits I have ever tasted. I can still see her taking that pan of golden brown biscuits out of the

Parthenon, Athens, 1969

oven; not from a can, but the ones made from scratch. Why is that important? I had not had any home cooked bread since I left the States some two years earlier. She proceeded to ask me what I wanted to eat, to which I replied, some peanut butter and cold milk. That was the first meal I ate on returning to the States, and it was awesome!

You must remember that we did not find fresh, cold milk very often in India. In addition, the peanut butter in India was quite different from what we were accustomed to eating in the States. That was one heck of a meal. Later that afternoon, we dined on a juicy steak and a baked potato with all the trimmings. Home at last, and I was already trying to acclimate myself to another pace and lifestyle than the one I had known for the past two years.

I spent a few days in Washington, DC mostly sleeping in a comfortable bed and watching television. I was content and a bit secure in the knowledge that I was safe and at home with family.

I did not go out of the house very much other than to sit on her front porch. I did go to High's, the local convenience store, to get a pint of hand-packed butter pecan ice cream. My brother-in-law had some first class libations in the house, and I would partake of them freely.

My mother called and said it was time for me to come all the way home to Durham, NC. Yes, I still did what my mother told me to do, and I caught a flight to Durham. I do not remember an awful lot about my reunion with my parents and siblings in Durham. That is a bit strange for me because we had such a close relationship. My guess is that my mother, in her infinite wisdom, tried to make my homecoming as normal as she possibly could. In any event, I cannot remember much of anything about my return home. What I do know is that the person that returned from two years in India was very different from the person that left Durham County two years earlier.

I left North Carolina a person who was largely impulsive, a hothead, somewhat self-centered, perhaps even selfish, and yet a team player who could be extremely loyal. In general, I was persistent, somewhat dogmatic, yet demonstrating some tendencies toward leadership, and one who spoke with a slight southern accent.

I returned two years later with a very different accent; one that I did not realize I had, but one that fascinated my family and friends. After all, I had spent the past two years living in a small village where no one spoke very much English. I had to learn Hindi in order to communicate and I had to learn how to enunciate this newly learned language in ways that the locals could comprehend. In addition to the pronunciation and enunciations of the vocabulary of the new language, there were a number of gestures and idiomatic expressions one learned as an adjunct to communicating effectively. Unbeknownst to me, I brought back all of those expressive nuances to family and friends. After much introspection, I labeled myself *"The Me That Nobody Knows."* That is, I had become a stranger who was coming home to Durham County…a guy who truly was "returning to the other side of the world," just in reverse.

Haywood Turentine, Tom Corbett, and Bill Whitesell

I can imagine most returned volunteers experienced a similar culture shock upon their return. The adjectives I used to describe the person that left Durham County two years earlier were replaced by another set of adjectives. In addition to speaking with an unfamiliar accent, I was now much more committed to accomplishing both my career and personal goals. I had set goals in both areas, and now I was doggedly determined to achieve them. Having a newfound sense of worth, I was now someone to be reckoned with.

My new self-esteem was evident in all I did and manifested itself in a new sense of reliability. If I told you I was going to do something, you could go to the bank on my word. I was as dependable as they came...deliberate, analytical, yet thorough. I took responsibility for my actions and set out to be an example others emulated. I led by example and would readily take charge of a situation when something needed to be done. Being less impulsive and more tolerant of others and their views emerged as strong personal traits. I genuinely enjoyed teaching and mentoring others while being out front, providing direction, leading others to desired conclusions.

The person that returned from the other side of the world was a stranger to those who knew him two years earlier. Thank God I had the opportunity to leave home right away to attend graduate school. There I would be in a place where I no longer had to explain who this stranger was, because no one in this new setting, Cincinnati, knew the old Haywood Turrentine. As far as they were concerned, I was who I always was.

It was funny what my mother said to me one day when I came home from graduate school during the summer. I had planned to spend a month or so at home relaxing with my family. After a couple of days of restlessness, Mother approached me and asked if we could talk. I said, "Sure, what's up?" She said, "Son, I love you and I love having you come home to visit, but you are miserable. Why don't you go on back to Cincinnati, where you are comfortable?" She went on to say, "You are very uncomfortable here, and I cannot stand to see you that way. By all means, do come home and visit but not for an extended period of time because you are not happy after a few days." Though I now thought of myself as the 'me' that nobody knows, my mother still knew me, even though I was a thoroughly changed person.

The person that returned from India was a person that no one in North Carolina knew, with the possible exception of my mother. I do remember wanting to reunite with the girlfriend that I had left behind so many months ago. As it turned out, we did indeed reunite, but no longer as girlfriend and boyfriend. She had met and fallen in love with someone while I was gallivanting through Europe. She had no way of letting me know, so I came home to quite a surprise. I was disappointed, but not really upset with her since she had not done anything wrong. Falling in love is a natural thing for a man and woman to do. It was not as if she had concealed that from me. She had no way of letting me know. Today, with cell phones, that would have been different. However, the cell phone did not exist back then. We remain friends to this day, and she and the young man did get married.

I went off to Cincinnati to attend graduate school and to put that painful turn of events behind me. I eventually met and married a wonderful young lady, who is the mother of our only son and still my wife and very best friend after some 40 years. Life with her has never been better than it is right now.

How does all of this tie into Peace Corps Training and serving as a volunteer? The training we received prepared us for a life of dependability, in which we accepted responsibility for things. We might not have realized while we were in training, but I challenge anyone from India 44 to point to any other experience that has had an equal or greater impact on their life. The way I approached my relationship with my wife, my graduate studies, my approach to childrearing and the world of work, my leadership abilities, and my overall success in life were all deeply shaped by what I was taught in my Peace Corps Training. All these things were influenced further by the life I lived as a volunteer in that small village in India.

No, I did not realize how much those events had affected my life until I started to reflect and ask myself the question: Why did I do certain things the way I did? Without exception, I inexorably would be drawn back to what I learned and what I was engaged in while in Peace Corps and in India. In those grueling hours of sessions with the "shrinks" during our training days, one developed a stronger sense of self-esteem and self-reliance. You hone in on your self-worth, establish yourself as an example to others, and try to be of service to those around you.

During our training, we engaged in exercises that focused our attention on being dependable, being responsible, making and keeping commitments, taking charge of situations, analyzing problems and providing solutions, teaching others to do likewise, being thorough, providing leadership, and being tolerant of others. All of those traits have served me well in my personal as well as professional life.

Some of those attributes surely were a part of what I was exposed to during my youth. At the same time, they were things that we zeroed in on during training and service as volunteers in a much more focused manner. To the degree that any of them were perfected, it happened either in training or during our service or both. I am eternally grateful for the training and subsequent service in India and how they influenced and informed my life.

A resume of my life might better illustrate what I am suggesting and why I make these claims. This truly is a "return from the other side of the world" in living color. I am sure we each had a certain amount of drive and ambition when we first met with the recruiters on our respective campuses. I suspect that if we were as honest and as candid as Dennis Conta (see the Postscript), we all might relate and agree that the same bravado and artifice that saved him as our young training director played a significant role in our surviving a tour in India. I know that when I went to my village of Thur, I pretended I knew much more than I did and perhaps tried to use form and style to overcome a lack of content.

Whom did we really deceive? I actually started to believe some of the crap I pretended to know. I am glad I did because without that belief, I might not have taken as many great qualities from the experience as I did; qualities that shaped my later life.

For example, during my undergraduate days at North Carolina Central University, after our first summer of training, one of our Western Civilizations instructors became ill. Dr. Thorpe, the Chairman of the History Department, came to me and asked me to sit in for the sick professor. I was President of the History Club and a History major. However, I had never taught any one anything, except basketball plays in high school. I went into that classroom and taught that course for the remainder of the semester. It was an invaluable experience, but even more, it was an opportunity to repay Dr. Thorpe for his confidence that I could, in fact, do the job. I was there for every class meeting, did my lectures, gave and graded exams. Did I display leadership? Perhaps, but I know it was a test of my willingness to take responsibility for an assignment and to be responsible for the results. I took charge of the assignment and followed through to completion.

While in my Indian village, the Peace Corps Office needed someone from India 44 to serve as an all-volunteer representative for the Tunisia Region. The details of how I got the position are a bit fuzzy for me now, but I was the representative until Mike (Simonds) replaced me a year later. For the life of me, I cannot remember very much about the assignment. However, I do know that the position required that I fly to New Delhi periodically for meetings.

Of course, anything that got me out of the village was welcome, and I made the best of it. I befriended a couple of the Marine guards at the Embassy. They would take me to the PX and buy booze for me to take back to Udaipur. When I returned, I would let the fellows know, and we all would come into town for a party where Johnny Walker Red and Black, along with Canadian Club, would be shared by all. I had fun and rewarded my fellow volunteers for being supportive of me by bringing back the goodies.

When I enrolled in graduate school at the University of Cincinnati, I was ready for the rigors of graduate school because of a number of good habits I formed in India. While there, we would frequent the train stations and buy the latest books on the *New York Times* bestseller list, read them, and then pass them on to others to read. Thus, I developed good reading habits and therefore did not have a problem with extensive reading assignments in school.

After my first year of graduate school, I was offered a position tutoring Project Upward Bound and special services students in history and geography. The next year, I hired on as a counselor working on financial aid and academic advising with students from the University College and the Educational Development Program. The next year, I signed on as the Counseling Coordinator and designed an academic and financial advising program to counter the revolving door experience many students encountered at the university. I hired the counselors and trained them to work with special needs students.

I worked very closely with the Reading Coordinator because the majority of our students had to enroll in remedial reading classes. She and I had to arrange course schedules that permitted the students to enroll in her classes. She told me one day that the thing that separated me from the other Black faculty and staff on campus was that I had a real sense of who I was and where I was going. She said that made it infinitely easier to work with me. While I am not sure I knew all that, I am sure I gave her the impression that I did. That earned her respect and her willingness to work through all the problems we encountered. I, along with my fellow volunteers, learned to problem solve in India trying to grow a new form of hybrid wheat in an environment of limited water for irrigation, among other challenges. We not only had to sell the farmers, but the government officials as well. This was certainly not an easy task, but a necessary one.

I met my wife during my time working at the university while writing my thesis. Talk about an ability to make a decision! When I first laid eyes on her, I just knew that she was going to be mine. I had to use everything in my arsenal to get her interested in me since she had just broken off an engagement. Her roommate finally persuaded her to accompany her to a party that some friends were giving. After much cajoling and arm twisting, Lelani agreed to accompany her to the party. Her roommate told her that there would be a number of graduate students at the party from the University of Cincinnati. Well, for someone who just broke off an engagement, meeting some new guys might not have been a turn on, but thank God almighty, she did go to that party.

She walked in with Sharon, her roommate, who introduced her to a few of us. Lelani loved to dance and proceeded to spend a healthy portion of the evening on the dance floor. I was right there dancing every chance I got, but not finding a heck of a lot of time to talk to her. Finally, I was able to get in a few words with this beautiful, graceful lady. I told her a bit about myself, you know like where I was from, where I had gone to undergraduate school and what I had done since undergraduate school. Naturally, I started talking about Peace Corps and India. That conversation fascinated her, and as fate would have it, someone came over and asked her to dance. Off to the dance floor she went and danced a couple of songs. When she finished, she came back to me presumably to continue our conversation. However, before we could get back to the conversation, someone else came and asked her for a dance and off she went again.

By now, it started to get late, and I knew I needed to get her number before she decided to go home. Figuring out some way to isolate her so that we could talk without interruption became the challenge. When she finished dancing, she came back to resume the conversation. I took her by the hand, led her into the bedroom of this two-bedroom apartment, and locked the door. Then, we were able to talk more about my experience in India and my travels home at the end of my stay in India. She was fascinated with my experiences. I asked her to tell me about herself. She said there was not a great deal to tell because she had not done very much. She had been out of college one year and was teaching high school across the river in northern Kentucky. She told me that until that week she had been engaged to marry a young man she had met at Eastern Kentucky. I asked her what happened. Though she told me, I do not remember much of what she said. I then asked her if she would give me her telephone number and if I could call her.

She agreed to give me her number, but, she said she never expected to hear from me. In fact, she said she was so sure she would not hear from me that she actually gave me her real number. She told me later that she never gave out her real number when meeting someone for the first time. I asked her why she thought I would not call her and she said because of my breadth of experiences. After I secured her digits, I told her that I wanted to dance with her, and we rejoined the party. I could then relax knowing I could follow up later if necessary. We danced and had a marvelous time. At the end of the evening, I asked her if I could walk her to the car, and she said yes.

In walking her to her car, I asked her again if it would be okay if I called her, and if so when? She said it would be okay, but that she would be away part of the Christmas holidays. She told me when she would be back at her apartment and I could call then. I did not want to appear too eager, so I waited

215

an additional day before calling her. She said that she had not expected to hear from me especially since I did not call the day she returned. I was honest with her and told her why I had not called earlier. She laughed, and I asked her if I could come over. She told me I could and gave me directions to her place. The rest is an integral part of our history together as man and woman, husband and wife, father and mother, the world's best friends. I love her more today than ever and would be worse for the wear if anything ever happened to her.

I had to take control of the situation when I saw her and determined that she was the person with whom I wanted to spend the rest of my life. I knew what/who I wanted and just had to put everything aside and go after her. Where did I develop that decisiveness and ability to take charge? I suspect the answer can be found somewhere in my Peace Corps experience. I have returned from the other side of the world, but have brought with me much of what that experience taught me. The challenges did not stop with her love for dancing. About a year after we met, I accepted a job with the Laborers International Union in Washington, DC. Lelani felt challenged by that decision, telling me that she felt that my move would be the beginning of the end of our relationship. I told her nonsense, that I wanted to marry her. I told her to go on back to Western Kentucky University, complete her Masters Degree in Communications, and come to DC at the end of the summer.

She did, and we were together again, this time for good. We had our challenges, but nothing we could not work through because we had made a decision to be together. My father loved Lelani and on his dying bed asked me to do three things for him. I told him that I would. He said (1) keep the family together, (2) marry Lelani and always take care of her and (3) wear his wedding band. I made him those promises and vowed to keep them no matter what. I had an older brother, but my father called me to his dying bed and asked me to keep the family together. Keeping my word is important for me. If I tell you I am going to do something, I stick to that through thick and thin.

When I moved back to Washington, DC to take that job, I was sure I wanted to spend the rest of my life with Lelani, and I set out to make that happen. I worked hard trying to be the best employee I could possibly be. In my job at the training arm of the Laborers' International Union of North America (LIUNA), I traveled extensively and experienced things that were unheard of for a poor farm boy from Durham County. I was able to make presentations in front of thousands of people; I was able to write and develop scripts for numerous training films. I was instrumental in the writing and passage of legislation that affected countless numbers of people residing in low-income housing through the Lead and Asbestos Abatement Programs. Additionally, we were able to provide those residents with a roadmap to union membership and training which led many of them to finding employment and earning a pension and health benefits. I was able to take Lelani and our son, James, with me on numerous trips all over this country.

When my son was two or three years old, he had already traveled to 27 states. He had experienced things that it took me a lifetime to experience. I am forever grateful for the experience I got while working at the Laborers. I was able to exhibit my leadership, my teaching and mentoring, my dependability, my ability to take charge of a project and see it through to completion. Whatever I am today, whatever I have achieved to date, I owe a lot to my Peace Corps training and my work for the Laborers' International Union. Had the Peace Corps not provided me with all this invaluable training or if the Laborers refused to allow me to utilize those skills, I would not be the person I am today. Thank you LIUNA.

LIUNA General President Coia then nominated me to serve as a representative from an NGO on the National Environmental Justice Advisory Council, an advisory council to the Environmental Protection Agency. Then Administrator Browner appointed me to the Council, where I served with pleasure. After my first year on the NEJAC, the council elected me as their Chairman, the first Black to hold that position. I mention that because of the road I traveled to reach that point. Those traits/adjectives I outlined that described the person that returned from the other side of the world are the very attributes that catapulted me to the position of chairing the NEJAC and helped me as I provided advice and counsel to EPA Administrator Carol Browner. If it had not been for General President Coia nominating me, this experience might never have been available to me. Others can and do help open doors for you, but once you walk through those doors you must perform. These experiences were some of the more rewarding I had during my professional career.

Many of those same traits/adjectives have proven invaluable in my personal and family life. I am never too low or never too high regardless of the situation. I learned how to remain calm and in control even during a crisis. Leadership demands that, and life will accept no less. I guess I really did know who I was, where I wanted to go, and what I wanted to accomplish. I knew myself because I became what I was trained to become. Since family and friends did not know how I had been trained or what training I had received, it became increasingly clear that they could not relate to the person I had become. When I went home, I was a stranger in the home I grew up in and to the family I loved. Coming home from two years in Peace Corps was truly "a Return from the Other Side of The World" for "the Me That Nobody Knew."

CHAPTER 11

A Little Chat with My Innards!

Tom McDermott

Oh unfaithful companion, what happened so suddenly between us? We lived together all these years—more or less at peace. Okay, I did a few bad things to you and you did a few to me, but neither of us went out of the way to humiliate the other. We were buddies, I thought. So why today—after all our time together—did you decide to betray me like this?

And it's not as though either of us has a choice about the future. Like it or not, we are stuck with each other for life. True, for the past hour or so, "til death do us part" seemed not such a bad proposition. In fact, in the last couple minutes, I started to think, "the sooner the better."

Thanks to you, here I am squatting over an open drain along the side of an alley in Banaras, while you empty out your rage and last night's dinner. People are passing by, walking slowly, keeping their distance, but also grinning at the sight of my lily-white tail hanging over a ditch in their village. Not that you would care! Soon they will be calling their friends to come and watch the show. How could you? How could you reduce me to this state of abject humiliation?

No, sorry, we have nothing left to drink now. We finished the last of our water a long time ago. Nothing left now except the last few drops of paregoric. Good that I thought to bring it, huh? Okay, the taste is ugly, but boy it does pack a kick. And the doc says it is good for you, too. Yeah, I know—"tincture of opium— use in small doses only—not more than one teaspoon per hour,"

A busy thoroughfare

but there have to be exceptions for emergencies, right? No doubt about it, we are way past "emergency" here.

Yes, I know. We shared more than a few gulps of that concoction in the past hour or so. Okay, okay—they may have had little effect on you, but those gulps sure helped me— at least in terms of inhibitions. How else could I manage to squat here in a daze as folks wander by to watch you do your dirty business?

And of all days, why today? Here we are on our way to meet my lovely cousin and her husband, the big-shot professor from Princeton. Yeah, you know— the guy who is here doing his sabbatical year at the university. Quiet down a minute and listen. Maybe this guy could have helped me get into a good grad school. But now—well, look at us—would a respectable family let anyone who looked like me or smelled like you into their house, let alone into some Ivy League college?

Okay, are you finished now? Can we please get back in the rickshaw now and make the rest of our way over to the university? Okay, here we go. Behave now. Will you PLEASE BEHAVE?

Yes, I know it's hot. I'm sweating, and wondering what in the world inspired me to wear a suit and tie. It's not like the professor is going to take one look at my suit and say, "Welcome to Princeton, son." Anyway, not now for sure!

The rickshaw winds its way through the back streets. My mind looks back to those first days in India—how we once sat in the Peace Corps office in Delhi while the doctor started his lecture with something like, "On behalf of the United States Government, the Peace Corps and the Medical Service, I want to welcome you and your "virgin gastro-intestinal tracts" to India.

"Virgin?" Who was this guy to call you a virgin? Did he have any idea of how "experienced" you already were—of the weird things we have chewed, sucked, and swallowed? The "normal stuff" alone pushed you well beyond "virgin" status. Just think of all those Twinkies, the three day old pizza, the sloppy Joes in the school cafeteria. I can't (or won't) even begin to recall the even weirder stuff we, as kids, stuffed down there. Humph—what did this guy know about us and food? You had a rock-solid history of handling anything I stuffed down there.

The good doctor went on showing us slides of "normal" intestinal walls of Westerners six months before moving to India and six months after the move. Then he showed us similar before and after slides of Indians who had relocated to western countries. His point was that after only six months the intestinal wall undergoes a radical transformation. In the west, you need lots of little pockets in the intestinal wall where bacteria can lodge to help digest your food. In India, the pockets disappear—there is no shortage of bacteria to do the job, often giving food an express ride to the bottom, sometimes with barely a pause on the journey.

Of course, a couple weeks into training in India demonstrated that indeed food often enjoyed an express ride to the bottom. So long as there was a toilet somewhere near, though, we could handle it. True, learning to balance over one of those squat latrine pans was a challenge—staying upright, not to mention trying to stand up afterwards did wonders for our thighs. And then there was always the issue of aim. But at least, water was plentiful and we always had a roll of toilet paper handy.

Life in the village changed all that. Latrine pans became a distant memory, replaced by a communal place to squat and chat. No doubt, it was a good place to practice Hindi with your neighbors, but let's just say that I didn't show my best side to the village. And I don't know which made them laugh more—my feeble attempts at Hindi, or the loud accents you added to every conversation. So instead, we had to seek out quieter, more private times and places for our bouts of self-expression.

Fortunately, our period in the village only lasted a couple of months before we moved to a small town where I could rent us a house. Yes, this time we had a real latrine. Okay, I admit, this latrine too had its challenges. No, it was not a latrine with a nice white pan and water to flush. It was a "drop and plop" design—a hole in the apartment floor, one story above a basket strategically placed in a dark smelly room below.

Remove cover, hold nose, squat, wait for a satisfying plop to tell us whether you had hit the target. Somewhere down there in the dark was a basket, which a sweeper came to clean out each day. Yes, I felt for that guy given all those times you missed. Social injustice, no doubt, but who was I to change the caste system? And it sure beat squatting out there in the bush, hoping no one would decide to take a shortcut through my private hiding spot.

Think too of what those mornings did for our sense of balance! And what a good way to wake up each morning…just imagining a possible misstep virtually ensured that any hint of sleep was erased before assuming the position.

Back to the good Peace Corps doctor for a minute! Early on you might remember how he persuaded us to join his study of steroids? Of course, back before steroids became the supplement of choice for athletes, neither of us had ever heard of them. Actually, it was easy to persuade us to sign on. What the hell!

We thought by volunteering we could get a paid trip to Udaipur once a month, turn in a urine sample, and give some blood. It was the inducement of a paid night in Udaipur, not so much our potential contribution to science that attracted us and many others.

The problem, of course, immediately became clear in the test results. A night spent in Udaipur, away from our strict vegetarian and alcohol-free life in the village, meant a long session of meat-eating and beer-guzzling—a night that sent the next day's test results in unexpected directions. Moreover, we soon found out that "giving some blood" meant sitting in an Udaipur hospital while some guy in a dirty white jacket tried to find the veins in our arms while using a needle as blunt as an unsharpened pencil. Yes, that ripping sound really was our skin finally giving way. No doubt, there was more blood on the ground than in the test tube.

But for you and me, the worst was the urine sample. "The Doc" soon decided that to avoid the confounding effects of all that beer (who knows, maybe Kingfisher and Golden Eagle added in some steroids with all those other chemicals?) we would take a huge lab jar back to the village and fill it for 24 hours BEFORE coming to Udaipur. That meant loading this well-filled monster jar on the back of our bicycle and CARE-FULLY pushing bike and bottle up the rocky path that led to the nearest town with a bus station some 10 kilometers away. Then we waited in the shade, if there was any shade, until finally we made it onto the back of the bus for a three hour ride to Udaipur.

All around us I could hear people whispering, "I wonder what the CIA guy has in the bottle this time. It looks like…no, it couldn't be. What do we do if it explodes? Let's get off at the next stop? Better to be safe than sorry!"

It really was amazing, just how quickly all those bottles were reported broken! Pity about the study, but I suppose the march of medical research and the progress of modern athletics moved on without our blood and urine. Science always finds a way.

But all those trips to Udaipur had their positive side in the chance to meet other volunteers and to eat, drink, and swap stories

Berry's Restaurant

at Berry's Restaurant. Oh, there were so many "latrine stories" of diarrhea, of the attempts to find a private place to go, of failed attempts to convince landlords and village leaders to allow construction of a modern latrine, of the water impossible to filter and which when boiled only turned more brown, of the tainted food, and of our attempts to convince the cook to wash his hands.

Housing in town

Who was it who came up with that reply to any story, "Yes, you remembered to boil the water, but did you remember to boil the cook?"

But you and I were proud above it all. We had moved to town and a house with a latrine. Okay, it was just a smelly drop down to a basket, but it was a big step beyond squatting outside. Life seemed good, listening to the stories of the problems of others with a detached sense of having sorted out our own problems.

Among my favorite stories was one someone had collected from a volunteer in an earlier Peace Corps group. It concerned two guys in the first generation of India volunteers. After a year in their village, the boredom had just became too much to bear. They wanted out, but neither was willing to be the first to send "that telegram to Delhi."

Inhibitions, however, dim with alcohol. One night after much drinking, one suggested, "Listen, we go up to Delhi, blow off steam for a few days, and then show up at the office and tell those SOBs to give us something worth doing or get us the hell out of here." Both knew, of course, that they were more likely to be sent home than reassigned. Yet, neither of them wanted to admit that this might be the real, though hidden, goal for the trip.

But how do you finagle those few days in Delhi?

Their answer lay with those little kits the Peace Corps Medical Service had so naïvely provided. Back in those days, Peace Corps provided little kits to collect stool samples, if and when you got sick. The idea was that you filled the sample tube with little swabs, wrapped and sealed the tube in a special envelope and mailed it to Delhi. The office then sent the sample on to some U.S. military hospital for testing.

It was nearly morning and their stock of beer had run out. They watched from their porch as a little kid did his early morning business by the road side near their house. Alcohol fueled, they went out in the dim pre-dawn light, scooped up two samples, came back to the house, and, dutifully following instructions, applied the mailing labels Peace Corps had provided.

Then, while they slept, their ever-efficient cook turned up for work and, as usual, set about cleaning up the mess of empty bottles and dirty dishes. On the table he spotted the two neatly labeled envelopes. When he went to market later in the day, the cook dropped both envelopes at the post office, just as "the young sahibs" had told him to do with their mail each day. That evening, over dinner, one of the two volunteers asked the cook about the envelopes. "Oh, yes, sahib, I sent them off, just like always. Not to worry, sahib, market money was enough."

Panic raced through the minds of both volunteers. They hadn't really planned to send those—it was just a drunken lark. Yes, they wanted out, but not this way. They started to consider what going home might really mean—Vietnam, looking for a job, and oh yes that girl to whom they had foolishly given a ring.

First thing the next morning they sent off desperate telegrams to Delhi, "Feeling fine now." "Fully recovered." "No problem." They even phoned and were reassured by someone in the Medical Office that all would be okay. "Don't worry. It happens all the time."

A week later, however, they received telegrams ordering them immediately to Delhi. It seemed that a parasite scale had gone through the roof. No matter that they confessed to their scheme to escape India. No one believed them at this point.

"Oh, what dedicated volunteers! So sick and yet they love their assignments so much that they'll say anything to stay."

So, ready or not, they soon found themselves on a flight off to some military hospital in Germany. No surprise, either, that by our day the Peace Corps had stopped giving out mail-in sample tubes.

Okay, a story perhaps more sad than funny but somehow it appealed to my sense of fantasy during my own long, hot, and boring afternoons in the village. "Escape by medical necessity" seemed thoroughly dishonorable but, hey, honor on those torrid afternoons was not often high on my agenda.

There were also other forms of escape, less permanent, while only slightly less dishonorable. The easiest of these short-term escapes was travel outside the village.

Little did I realize that dishonor, even when short-term, always has a price. This time the price would include squatting in a squalid alley in Banaras.

My invitation to the present disaster arrived in the form of two aerograms from my family. My father wrote about a Catholic missionary with whom he had been corresponding for a few years. The missionary was from south India, but was working among tribal people in a remote part of Madhya Pradesh. My father had been sending money to the missionary and now wanted me to visit the mission and report.

"How did he find this guy?" I wondered. "Dad seldom left Pittsburgh, let alone had a clue about some place called 'Madhya Pradesh'."

My mother wrote in a second aerogram in which she mentioned a cousin of mine who had recently come to India. I had never met this cousin, but it seemed that she had married a college professor some years before. He now was spending a sabbatical year at the university in Banaras. "Must be somewhere close to you," my mother wrote. "Could you visit and say hello from me?"

"Mom, Banaras is nowhere close to Rajasthan," I said aloud to myself. But then after a moment's reflection, I thought, "What a good excuse to get out of the village for a week!"

You didn't protest my plans to escape. You were as bored as I was. More important, you had been behaving very well lately.

I planned the trip carefully. Planning escapes was my thing; after all what else did I have to do in those long, hot afternoons? Like all those earlier escapes I had planned, but never taken, I began by pouring over the Indian Baedeker, that master time-table for sale in Indian rail stations. The Baedeker showed the times of every train and bus in the country— the essential guide for every Indian escape fantasy.

When the day came, we headed off, one train leading to another, the gauges of track becoming narrower as we went. The smoky carriages became fewer as the train became shorter at each major stop until at last the train was just the steam engine, the coal car, two carriages, and a caboose. The forest in that part of Madhya Pradesh was heavy and the trees seemed to close behind the train as we slowly chugged deeper into the jungle.

We reached the final stop, a tiny rail station near where Madhya Pradesh meets the borders of Uttar Pradesh and southern Bihar. The missionary met us and took us back to his mission.

We spent a couple days. It was inspiring—something out of one of those movies about missions in Africa. But it wasn't for me, and I was anxious to move on quickly to Banaras. The missionary arranged for us to spend a night on the way at a Catholic school just outside Banaras.

So it must have been there at the school that I gave you something that caused you to behave so horribly. Okay, sorry… I didn't mean any harm. The food looked good, and both of us were hungry.

The night went fine, but the day did not start well. I had brought along this silly suit and tie. God knows why I would include a suit and tie among the meager things I packed to use in village India. But having brought it, I decided that a visit to "the professor" and his family was finally an occasion to use my formal attire.

I put on my suit, shoes, and tie and checked it all in a full-length mirror (a while since I had seen one of those). How thin I looked! When had I last worn this suit?

Then I heard you begin to groan a bit. Troublesome, but no real problem—off to the nice modern toilets—still of the squat type, but clean and each with an overhead tank with a chain to pull when you wanted to flush. Flushing toilets—now there was something we hadn't seen for a while!

Everything seemed to come out okay. I stood. You seemed quiet and happy. "Okay," I thought, "Now we are good to go."

I turned to flush. Nothing happened. So I pulled again harder. And again, harder still. The result was that I, rather than the latrine pan, got flushed. Yes, a gush of cold water I would have enjoyed as a morning shower, were I not fully clothed in suit and tie, while standing there in a toilet.

I did the best I could to dry off; hung the jacket, shirt and pants out. These were, however, the days before "stay-pressed" fabrics. To say "wrinkled" somehow doesn't capture the state of crumpled rumpled cloth that was left after drying. Now, the wise thing would have been to change back to my dirty jeans and even dirtier shirt, both veterans of that long smoky train ride across Madhya Pradesh. But no, I had brought that suit and damned if I wasn't going to wear it.

So, off we went to see "the professor" and family. The people at the school warned us that it was a long and hot trip across the city by cycle rickshaw and that a cycle rickshaw was the only way to go; no taxis come out to this part of town. They also repeated that there would be nowhere to stop on the way across the city—no water and no toilets. On the other hand, they said, "Once there you will be in heaven." They described the campus of Banaras Hindu University as a place that didn't really belong in India, certainly not in Banaras, a beautiful green campus of European and American style buildings.

About a half hour into the journey, you started complaining. I told you to shut up and be quiet. Okay, I'm sorry now that I spoke to you so roughly. Whatever I said, it didn't deserve your reaction. Every bump of the rickshaw brought a rumble from you. I started looking desperately, anywhere for a place where we might find a toilet. Left and right, I saw nothing but thousands of mud-brick buildings interspersed by tiny alleys. I asked the rickshaw driver where to go. "No way, Sahib…no way except the street here."

I grabbed the paregoric and took our first swig. No reaction. Soon you couldn't hold it any longer. We found a spot that seemed relatively quiet by Banaras' standards. Of course, no sooner had we stopped and squatted than people started to wander over to gawk at the sahib in the suit, doing his business beside a Banaras street. Hey, why not? If I saw some scene as weird as this in my town, I would gawk as well.

Another swig of paregoric…and still no reaction! On we went. Again, we had to stop. Again, a repeat of this nightmarish scene. Again with the paregoric which might not be doing much for you, but it was sure helping me by this point. I was easing past any sense of dignity or sense of shame. It became what it was…absurd, ridiculous, and yes, flat-out hilarious.

Somehow, we got to the university—no thanks to you, of course. The rickshaw finally pulled into the gates of the campus. As promised, there was green grass, neat buildings, virtually another world. The faculty housing area included a line of domiciles that could have graced any American suburb.

I was beyond seeing house numbers by this point, but fortunately the rickshaw driver wasn't. I paid, took my bag, and staggered up to the front door. I rang the doorbell—a door bell! Since when did houses have doorbells? Someone answered. I managed to say, "Hi, I think I'm your cousin." I don't remember much after that point, except a lot of very kind care, a long shower, and a bed. And eventually, yes, even you eventually settled down and started to behave.

It was a nice American family: husband, wife, and two kids. There were university guests at dinner that night. I was super ashamed and therefore super quiet and, thank God, you were as well. Of course, I didn't eat anything, just smiled and passed

Western landscaping

plates. Here I was among these professor types, eating a normal American meal at a normal table. Fortunately, my mind was too addled to recall the horrid details of our trip across town that morning. My hosts, of course, had not forgotten but were too polite to raise the subject, at least at first.

Soon, though, just like those 'gab' fests among volunteers over beer and tandoori at Berry's, the topic changed to India and to diarrhea. They did not speak directly of my story. Instead, they just started telling their own. How "it" had hit them at dinner in the hotel, running to the elevator, then down a long corridor to the room, only to discover that they had left the key downstairs on the table. Or having to flee a class they were teaching, running to a toilet, only to find it blocked and no other in sight.

I realized that we all had our diarrhea stories to tell. Of course, anywhere else but India we would be too embarrassed to tell such stories at dinner. Somehow, India just gets us to "loosen up" in more ways than one.

Look, you have given me one such story to tell, and one is more than enough. So settle down now and behave, will you? No more stories, please…it's dinner time.

CHAPTER 12

On Being "Amreecan" In Village India

Mary Jo (Dummer) Clark

We were the "Amreecans," Carolyn (Jones) and I. This is a phonetic spelling of the corrupted pronunciation of "American" that was rampant in our central Maharashtran village. When you think of it, however, this isn't much different than the twist the British gave to many names in India. Even the name of the country, "Hindustan," as it was known to the British, is a far cry from the way the natives perceived their own country.

Being an American in another land is often a memorable adventure, and our two years in the Peace Corps were no exception. In village India, our status vacillated from honored guest to freak show exhibit to village idiot. All of these roles were colored by the villagers' perceptions of Americans, gleaned primarily from popular movies and occasionally from international news.

We were always on display, and people in the village were curious about every aspect of our lives. The adults were **slightly** more subtle in their curiosity than the children, but not much. We were plagued by juvenile "peeping toms" who thought nothing of peering in our windows at all hours or clambering up to watch us over the wall if we were in our enclosed back courtyard. It got to the point that we kept our window shutters closed, foregoing any slight breeze that might have cooled the

Curious neighbor children

house, in order to maintain a little privacy. We also developed the habit of moving about the courtyard quietly, particularly when headed to the latrine in the back corner, to avoid activating the wall climbers.

The adults tended to restrain their curiosity to questions that would be considered rude in Western culture. The most common question was the standard, "How much money do you make?" Our likely responses, unfortunately, were beyond the villagers' comprehension. If we expressed our Peace Corps salaries ($75 a month at the time) in dollars, they had no frame of reference. If we converted it to rupees, it was an astronomical sum for most people in the village. They couldn't comprehend that by American standards that was well below poverty level, even in the 1960s (an interesting thought in light of the concurrent "War on Poverty" of the Johnson era). In their eyes, again based on the movies, all Americans were rich. So, by definition, we were rich. It's a good thing I never mentioned what I would be making as a new nursing graduate in the States.

Another question frequently posed to those of us who were female (and possible sometimes to the guys as well), was "Why aren't you married?" To us, our age (21-22 at the time) was the time to feel our oats, start a career, and maybe start looking for a suitable life partner. In their eyes, we were far beyond marriage-able age, and our parents would probably have difficulty getting us married off when we got home.

That discussion was usually followed by the twin questions, "How could your parents let you get this old without being married?" and "How could your parents let you go so far away from home?" It did no good whatsoever to explain that our parents generally had no role in our marriages (except possibly paying for the wedding) and that American daughters were not generally cosseted and protected beings, but made independent decisions. To admit that my parents didn't "let" me come to India (and weren't particularly pleased when I did) was to court perceptions of parental disrespect. Fortunately, I stuck with the mantra that American parents let their children, even girls, make their own decisions.

With respect to parental involvement in one's marriage, the villagers had heard about love marriages, but still couldn't grasp the concept of a parental "hands-off" tradition. Yes, it is fine to have a love marriage, but surely your parents made some attempt to find someone for you to love?

The other side of the not-married coin was the universal perception that, if we weren't stuck with one man in the form of a husband, we must be sexually promiscuous. Based on the movies (again!), all American women, especially young women, were fast, weren't they? We weren't usually asked outright if we were virgins, but I'm sure the general assumption was that we were not. We probably went a long way in supporting that assumption by entertaining male volunteers who came to visit. All of those visits were strictly platonic, but that was another concept foreign to the villagers. If men and women are together

Mary Jo Dummer, Roger Edwards, our
house, Vita, India, 1-31-68 (India I-69)

Roger Edwards visits Vita, 1968

overnight, they must be having sex, right? If so, Carolyn and I
missed out on a lot.

At the opposite end of the spectrum was our status as *pukka
sa'bs* (loosely translated as "first class persons") and honored
guests. We became status symbols in the village, and people
vied to have us to their homes for a meal. We conferred particularly high status on a bride and groom if we attended their
wedding. Oddly enough, people were rather circumspect in their
invitations to weddings, but I do remember attending more than
one wedding at which I knew neither the bride nor the groom.

At Hindu weddings, guests are separated by gender, with
the men seated around the wedding couple and women behind
a screen to one side. As honored guests, however, Carolyn and

I were seated with the men. Once again we saw the influence of western (not exclusively American) movies. The couple's families scoured the village to come up with two metal folding chairs on which we perched among the men seated on the floor. Although we appreciated their attempts to make us comfortable, it actually had the opposite effect. But Westerners sit on chairs, right? Therefore, we must have chairs—no matter that we didn't have a single chair in our own house.

Many of even the poorest families in the village invited us to their homes, if not for a meal, at least for tea. I'm sure the basic impetus was hospitality, but it didn't hurt the family's status with their neighbors for us to be seen in their home, either. We were treated as *pukka sa'bs* in the local stores as well. Most upper class customers were offered tea by store owners, and we were no exception. However, in our case the offer was often a Coke instead. After all, Americans drink a lot of Coke. Fortunately for us, bottled Coke was one of the few soft drinks (along with Orange Fanta) considered safe to drink. Unfortunately, if you needed to visit several stores, you experienced an extremely full bladder and a need to return home at a rapid pace. The public latrines in the village were considered off-limits by us since not even the locals used them.

Visits to other people's homes for dinner also provided occasions for our village idiot role. Due to concerns about water contamination, Carolyn and I always brought boiled water from our own house. Try explaining the concept of water contamination and resulting bacterial infection to people who have no concept of basic germ theory! We finally had to settle for the explanation that the water at home was different and our stomachs reacted badly to the difference, so we had to bring our own water. I'm not sure anyone ever understood, but at least they accepted our accompanying *lotis* (water containers) gracefully.

Some other typical American behaviors also cast us in the role of village idiots. In India, women (and maybe men as well, I never actually asked) put coconut oil on their hair to "protect" their heads from the sun. After several visits to Taiwan, Hong Kong, and Korea, and watching the Vietnamese and Laotian immigrants to San Diego, I wonder now why Indian women didn't adopt the concept of sunshades seen so frequently elsewhere in Asia. Women in our village, however, were very concerned that we didn't use coconut oil to protect our heads from the sun's rays, and they constantly encouraged us to change our unhealthful ways. Carolyn's hair was longer than mine, and she was able to braid it in the traditional braid (albeit a short one) used by the village women, so at one point she succumbed to their entreaties. Even to be culturally congruent, I wasn't going down that road. I liked my chestnut (then) hair soft and shiny, not glued to my head. Perhaps my occasional memory lapses these days are a result of sun damage to my brain while in India.

Another bit of evidence for mental incompetence lay in our habit of doing things for ourselves, rather than leaving them to servants. If one of our string of cooks (Asha, Pandu, or Maggie) was busy when we needed more water, Carolyn and I would go to the well in the health center compound and haul up a bucket or two. This, too, was beyond the comprehension of the villagers. "You are *pukka sa'bs*. You have servants to do that for you. Why are you drawing your own water?" When we tried to explain that in the U.S. most women don't have servants and do all their own work, we were met with blank stares and shaken heads. "Maybe," we said, "the **very** rich have servants, but the rest of us do our own housework including cooking, washing up, washing clothes, and even scrubbing floors." I never could decide if they thought we were lying or just plain crazy, most probably the latter because that was one of the behaviors we heard described as "another crazy American habit."

We made one further foray into taking on lower class work when (mostly out of boredom) we started washing the windows in the health center. None of the houses in the compound (or in the entire village) had glass windows, but for some reason, the health center did. When Carolyn and I started washing them, we were met with the usual stares and questions, the foremost of which was "Why do the windows need to be clean?" Our response to that was pretty much on the order of "because we said so." We didn't really want to admit that we were doing it out

Mary Jo cooking, Vita,

of boredom. The subsequent question was "Why are <u>you</u> doing it? This is work for the health center's fourth class *peuns*." Only in hindsight does it occur to me that they might have seen our efforts at the well and with the windows as attempts to overturn existing class boundaries. Who knew we were going to be revolutionaries when we left the States? No wonder many people in India thought all Peace Corps volunteers were subversives, or at least CIA agents!

Again, we tried to explain that manual labor was not considered below anyone's dignity in the U.S. (well not **anyone**, but you get the picture) and didn't decrease one's status or the degree of respect in which one was held. In fact, in many instances, being willing to pitch in to do the dirty work often increased the respect in which one was held. As usual, our explanation was inconceivable to the rest of the health center staff. At the same time, they couldn't very well let the *pukka sa'bs* do the work alone, so they all pitched in (I don't think Dr. M. did, that was

239

Washing at the well, Vita, 1967

too far below his dignity) and the windows were duly washed. As I noted in our prior book of personal reflections, the staff forestalled ever having to wash windows again by whitewashing them. So much for a light and airy environment in the wards!

Some of our experiences of being "Amreecans" in a foreign setting were funny; some were embarrassing; and some were frustrating, but they were all growth producing. What did I learn? My experiences reinforced the fact that our interactions with others are influenced by preconceived perceptions and that considerable effort is required to change those perceptions. I also learned that, in some cases, when the perceptions are harmless, that effort may be unnecessary. What did it matter that the villagers attributed our attempts to fend for ourselves as craziness? They were at least exposed to differences in cultures that when encountered again, might seem somewhat less bizarre.

Above all, however, I learned to be comfortable in my multiple roles in the village. I learned to accept gracefully my status as an honored guest. That has made subsequent interactions in other Asian countries more comfortable. I no longer resist having a former student carry my luggage or purchases when I visit Taiwan. In her eyes, I will always be the respected teacher who is due deference and assistance. I also learned that it was okay to be myself unless my own cultural behaviors would be considered offensive or cause someone else to lose face. I don't have to "go native" to fit in or to be effective in whatever role I am playing vis-à-vis another culture (e.g., as a consultant or educator). In some instances, being different may actually increase my credibility in those roles. Finally, I learned that being considered a village idiot doesn't do lasting damage to my psyche. Prior to my Peace Corps experience I would have been mortified to have my ill-wrapped sari disintegrate around me in the village street. Now I calmly put myself back together and go on about my business.

You know! Sometimes it is not a bad thing to become part of the local folklore.

CHAPTER 13

Far Side of the Dawn

Michael Simonds

Editors' Note:
What follows is a fictional piece inspired by the author's
service in India 44. It was largely written during his
Peace Corps service in the late 1960s and thus serves
as a real-time depiction of his India experiences. The
character of Steve, as well as his experiences, will
be recognizable to any and all volunteers who did
agricultural development in rural India.

It was early. The sun had yet to fully rise over the parched and barren hills of Rajasthan as Steve pushed his bike to the crest of the last hill and stopped for a moment to look out over the plain. This was his favorite spot. At this point, the jagged, abrupt hills that surrounded his village came to a sudden halt before the broad, flat plain that stretched out 50 miles toward the legendary city of Udaipur. Below him he could see the sandy river bed that had not known a steady flow of water for centuries. Three small villages could be identified in the foreground, their mud huts blending with the fallow fields. Throughout the landscape a dozen goat paths and bullock trails were woven, many of which ultimately merged with the paved ribbon of road known as the National Highway which, in turn, led to the town of Kapasan, his goal for the day.

Steve propped his bicycle against a tree and removed his canteen from the rack. The water was already lukewarm but it was all that he had. Turning to replace the canteen he caught the hint of a cool breeze as it flowed across his arms. It was a rare and exceptional pleasure that he knew would disappear as the sun rose higher and the hot desert wind began to blow in from the west. The sky was a stark, unyielding blue absent any evidence of a cloud. It had been like that for three months, and he knew from experience that there would be no relief from the blistering heat until the monsoon clouds appeared from the south.

He was late. He had hoped to be well down the valley before the sun was fully up over the hills. He had completed the hardest part of his journey through the hilly passes and it was all downhill from here to Kapasan. But it was hard to move. In the gully to his left he heard the fresh sparkling voice of a young girl singing a Mewari folk song as she strolled down the slope, basket on her head, searching for piles of cow dung. She wore the colorful Rajasthani dress; a red ankle length skirt, a brief blue halter with a yellow veil wound around her head. The large silver bracelets she wore on her arms and ankles rang out in a syncopated rhythm as she stepped sprightly between the rocks. A small boy completely naked scampered along behind her. He stopped once to throw a rock at a lizard before running to catch up again.

Steve watched them as they made their way around the hill until they disappeared from sight leaving only the fading notes of the girl's song to be lost amid the whispering of the breeze through the brush and the coughing of an old tubercular cow. The cow, with every one of its ribs showing through its diseased and pockmarked hide, wandered toward Steve and regarded him curiously for a moment before coughing again and drooling its' way on down the trail. Behind the cow came a herd of perhaps a hundred goats and sheep being driven into the hills by a young Mewari and his wife in search of ever more elusive fodder. As he approached Steve, the goat herder joined his hands together in the Indian sign of greeting.

"Ram, Ram!" he shouted to Steve.

"Namaste."

View from the top of the hill

"What are you doing?" the goat herder asked in Mewari.

"Looking at India."

"Oh, for that you should go to the highest mountain." He pointed to one of the hills behind Steve.

"Can you see all of India from there?" Steve asked with a smile.

"From that mountain you can see the whole world!"

"Including Chicago?"

"Where?"

"Never mind. That's in a different world anyway." Steve noted the puzzled expression on the Mewari's face and laughed. "I'm going to Kapasan."

Ah, the Mewari nodded. That he understood. He grinned a big toothless grin at Steve then hurried to catch up with his goats which were already beginning to scatter up the hillside.

Steve waved at him then started down towards the valley. A blazing, golden crest appeared on the eastern hills as he peddled through the first village...the sun was in its full glory by the

Highway traffic

time he reached the main highway. There is nothing subtle about the tropical sun, it seizes center stage and dominates both heaven and earth as a true Oriental monarch. Steve began to curse himself for not having started earlier as he felt the sun sear his back through his shirt.

The road, a one-and-a-half lane paved highway linking Udaipur with Jaipur and then New Delhi to the north, grew more crowded as he approached the town. He passed several bullock carts which wove in and out among a small herd of camels crossing the road. In turn, he was passed by several trucks and a bus.

Coming to the outskirts of the town he passed a large barren plot of land, surrounded by a fence and dominated by a large,

245

official looking sign which said in both Hindi and English "Site of the Mavli Saman Cement Plant: A Government of India Undertaking." The sign had been there ever since Steve arrived in India fifteen months before. So had the empty lot! Nothing had changed, nothing was being done, and no one in the town seemed to know anything about it. The phantom plant had been the source of many humorous analogies developed by frustrated volunteers and applied to various aspects of India's official economic-development plans.

Kapasan itself was a confusing contradiction of activity and despair, of growth and decline, development and decay. It was the district capital, a town of about 10,000, and the center of what light industry there was in the region, mainly sugar cane processing and peanut oil pressing. There was also a genesis of a future slum growing up in the cardboard and tin shacks which dotted the fringes of the settlement.

The town was at the height of its midmorning bustle as Steve arrived. A high-pitched whistle blast told him the morning local was leaving the Kapasan station for Udaipur. Women clustered around the wells drawing water for the day's needs while smoke chugged from the stacks of the makeshift peanut oil mills and merchants bargained with farmers gathered in front of their shops. In a few hours these streets would be deserted as the people fled the vengeful summer heat of the afternoon.

"Namaste Americkan! Namaste!"

Steve twisted in his seat and caught a glimpse of Raceda as he glided by. He had almost missed her. She was carrying a clay jug of water on her head and she looked so much like a grownup woman that he'd almost overlooked her. He managed to give her a wave before she disappeared back into the crowd. He knew she would go straight back to her father and that the two of them would be waiting for him when he came out of the district headquarters. It was a tacit arrangement they had fallen into their very first day in Kapasan. Fresh off the train from Delhi, he and Mark had found little to choose from among the dozen pushcart *wallas* that clamored for the privilege of carrying their belongings to the government buildings. All had been

Mischievous minx

equally obnoxious in their desperate pushing and jockeying for the Americans' business. Exhausted from the train trip, Mark had retreated in despair while Steve had struggled to gain some control over the situation with his classroom Hindi.

And then Raceda had appeared.

"You are an Amera-rickan?"

Mark had looked up to see a young girl, certainly no more than twelve move out from behind his trunk. She wore a dirty peasant pajama so filthy and faded that the original color could only be guessed. Her hair was matted and a scar cut into her right cheek. But her eyes flashed a vitality alien to India and her impish grin hinted at a gift for mischief. She had thrown him off balance with her approach—uncharacteristically bold for a female of any age in this country.

"Yes," he had answered weakly.

"My father will move them for you." Her Hindi was flawless, the kind learned in the classroom, without as much as a hint of the local Mewari dialect. "Wait here!"

And that was that. She walked past Steve, shouted with the other pushcart *wallas* for a few moments, and held them at bay until her father appeared and began packing their suitcases on his flatbed cart.

Steve and Mark had exchanged gestures of wonder as they watched this young girl intimidate her father's competitors. There was something mysteriously substantial about this frail little thing in rags. She had a talent for a kind of beguiling intimidation, which they found all the more impressive when it was turned on them.

"Ten rupees!" she demanded when her father had finished unloading their belongings in front of the district headquarters.

"Two," Steve had countered, prepared for some tough bargaining.

"Okay, two rupees," she agreed. And they knew that they had been had. They were not at all surprised when Kadar had told them that two rupees was five times the normal rate for such a job.

Ever since that day Raceda and her father had held exclusive rights over goods transport for the American volunteers operating out of Kapasan. And every time Mark or Steve had come into town, they had known that she and her father would be there waiting, just in case they were needed.

"Is the BDO in?" Steve asked the clerk at the door to the office.

"No, Sahib, he is in Ajmer."

Steve nodded. Although he was officially under the supervision of Jawalia Putik, the Block Development Office, he inwardly detested that fat, fawning, corrupt political animal. Luckily, he was usually away "on tour" somewhere and Steve could work directly with his staff, a younger more professional crew. He crossed the compound and entered one of the smaller offices behind a huge propaganda sign extolling the virtues of hybrid corn. There, in a starkly whitewashed office littered with old yellowing reports and official documents under a lazily turning fan, he found Talik, the Agricultural Extension Officer.

"Ah, Mr. Steve." Talik rose, extending his hand for a western-style handshake. "So nice to be seeing you. Please being comfortable sitting down."

Steve took his hand then seated himself in one of the straight, hard wooden chairs.

"You will be having some tea, yes?"

"Certainly," Steve replied. He disliked drinking hot tea on a day like this. But he knew how much trouble he would cause by attempting to depart from the accepted social routine.

"Boy!" Talik snapped his fingers and a grey old man who looked more than his forty odd years rose from his squat in the corner and scurried out into the bazaar to fetch the tea.

"It will be very hot today." Steve tried to make conversation.

"But of course. It is May, isn't it?" Talik leaned back in his chair and lit a cigarette. He was a short, wiry young man in his late twenties. He was very dark, almost black, and was often subjected to indignities by the lighter, color-conscious Indians on the staff. He generally ignored their petty slights and threw himself into his work as compensation for his social isolation. He was the Agricultural Extension Officer and the most competent member of the block staff; Steve had a great deal of confidence in him.

"It does not get this hot in your country?"

"Not where I come from. Rarely over a hundred degrees, never does it just hang around 110 for weeks."

"I see." The bearer had returned with two small dirty white cups of tea and handed one to Steve. The tea was so hot that he couldn't hold the cup in his hands and set it down on Talik's desk.

"I was reading your report, Mr. Steve. You are having such lovely English. I wish I could be speaking it only half so good as yourself."

"Thank you. Actually the report is what I came to see you about."

"Well, as I said there I will have two hybrid maize demonstrations in my village. One of those will be sponsored by CARE and the other by the University Extension Department. Now since I'm supposed to have at least one demonstration with Government funds I was thinking that I might conduct it in Sinyalpu, Mr. Mark's old site."

"Oh yes, and how is Mr. Mark?" Talik seized the first opportunity to reverse the terrible American tendency to rush into the official discussion of business. "Have you heard from him?"

"No. He is just now arriving in America." Steve caught himself slipping into the Indian phrasing the volunteers often termed "Indish." "I don't expect a letter for some weeks yet. But before he left we discussed it and he wanted some work carried on in his village…"

"Yes. Yes." Talik dismissed this whole line of conversation.

"He had this one very progressive farmer and..."

"Yes, of course."

"So you don't mind then if I do some work outside my circle?"

"Of course not. Whatever!"

"Mr. Steve!" The source of the interruption was Kadar, the Government co-op officer for the district. An unusually tall Indian, he stood just over six feet and towered over the rest of the staff. A native of Delhi he was more sophisticated and well-travelled than the average staff member and felt more at home with the American volunteers in the district than with his fellow Indians. He made no secret of the fact that he considered this assignment in a cultural backwater to be a necessary, if unpleasant, step on the typical civil service career ladder.

"I saw you come in on your bicycle this morning. Have you come for a game of Scrabble?"

"Of course. Why else? But also to talk with you about my water project. We're almost at the point where we can submit the forms to the co-op office..."

"You Americans! Rush...always rushing. First we will play a game of Scrabble. Then my wife will make some little snacks. Then we can talk of projects."

"It sounds very good, but I really can't. I don't have the time and..."

"Baba, where will you go? It is summer. It is hot. You will relax. You can return to village in the evening when it is cool."

"Yes, but..."

"Ahray Jodu! What are you doing?" Kadar scolded Talik. "You have given him tea again. So many times I have told you he is an American. He drinks Coca-Cola!"

"I am sorry. I am forgetting."

"No, no. It's alright. I like tea," Steve lied.

"Come on Baba. We'll have some Coca-Cola at my house while we play the Scrabble."

"But I have business here. There are forms and..."

"Ahray Baba! Talik will bring the forms and we will teach him to play Scrabble."

250

"No, no. I am not liking the game. But I am watching you two play."

"See there, Baba. Come on now."

Steve shrugged and yielded, following Kadar to his quarters. "You sound like you no longer wish to play the Scrabble."

"It's not that," Steve protested. "But I do have a lot to do. And besides, you always win. And you beat me in my own language."

"It means nothing. This Kapasan is a no social place. Before you and Mr. Mark came, I spend all my evenings playing Scrabble with only myself and the dictionary. So many words I am using I do not know the meaning for."

"You would rather be back in Delhi?"

"Of course! My family is in Delhi and my sister's family. There are so many things to do. Here, there is nothing. No family, no cinema, no shops, no doctor. Just last week my daughter had the fever. I had to ride all the way to Sanwar for the doctor. For this I am in government service? So my children may have typhoid with no doctor?"

"She had typhoid?"

"Yes, but she is now better. Still very weak, but better. But I will keep trying for a transfer to Ajmer. Here there is nothing."

It was late in the afternoon before Steve emerged from Kadar's quarters. They had played two games of Scrabble and eaten a big Rajasthani lunch of dahl and eggplant. Talik had appeared around two in the afternoon with Steve's authorization forms and joined Kadar in a fascinating discussion concerning the effect of the phases of the moon on one's bowel movements. Since all the business Steve had come for had been completed in three minutes, they spent the rest of the afternoon playing "Flash," an Indian card game vaguely similar to cut-throat poker.

A year ago, Steve would have bristled and fumed at all the delays. Now he accepted them as part of the system he had to work within to be effective. He had known before setting out that the morning and most of the day would be spent in games, social amenities, and bull sessions. And yet he had accomplished all he had hoped for. The authorizations he carried would provide him with enough useful work to carry him through the next three months.

As expected, Raceda and her father were waiting for him. They had parked the push cart—a flatbed on four bicycle tires— against the compound wall and were squatting underneath it to avoid the afternoon sun. The gray little man hung back as his daughter ran out to greet Steve. He never talked, rarely so much as raised his eyes to meet the American's. Wisely he left it all to his daughter—for he knew well that it was only because of her that he had the lucrative American franchise.

"Namaste Amer-rickan! You have some service for us?" she asked in Hindi.

"I do. Come with me." In an impulsive gesture he swept Raceda up in his arms and placed her on her father's cart and began pushing the cart himself. People turned around in the street and the bazaar to catch a glimpse of the spectacle of an American Sahib doing physical labor. Raceda's father followed a few steps behind mortified that someone was usurping his function as a hauler. Only Steve and Raceda really enjoyed it. She seized the moment and dominated it. Sitting cross-legged on the cart she assumed the arrogant pose of a rich Indian mogul shouting orders to her American slave. "Jeldi! Dine hot purr! Dayko! Dayko!" Faster! To the Right! Watch out there!

"Okay, enough now! Come down little princess." Steve lifted her off the cart when they reached the government warehouse.

"No, sahib. More! Let's ride some more. Just a little more…"

Steve looked down at her. For the first time he realized how really young she was. Until then, he had thought of her mainly as a flirt with a fantastic flair for business…an enchanting imp who would rob him blind while making him enjoy every minute of it. Now he saw her as a little girl reluctant to surrender an all too rare childish game. He was touched and saddened, and for a moment off-balance.

"No, no," he said gently. "Maybe some other day?" Then he turned to her father and continued in a too self-consciously authoritative tone "We will get many bags of fertilizer here to carry to the bus."

"Yes, Sahib," the man mumbled without looking up.

Steve hesitated for a moment then went up to the watchman at the warehouse door. "I have a requisition for some fertilizer and some pesticides."

"Mr. Husain handles this. You will have to see him."

"Where is Mr. Husain?

"Udaipur."

"When will he be back?"

"Soon."

"When? Today?"

"No, not today. Soon."

"I must have these supplies today. Is there anyone else who can get them for me?"

"Yes, Mr. Gopal can."

"And where is Mr. Gopal?"

"He is in Udaipur with Mr. Husain."

"Who else?"

"No one else, Sahib."

"You, do you have the keys?"

"Yes, Sahib. But I cannot open the door."

"Why?"

"It is not my duty, Sahib. It is Mr. Husain's."

"But he is in Udaipur."

"Yes, Sahib."

"If the BDO needed fertilizer what would you do?"

"I would give it to him. But he is in Ajmer."

"I know, and Mr. Talik?"

"If he writes on a piece of paper that it is his responsibility for you, then I will open the door."

Steve sighed. He'd been through it all before. He went back to Talik and got a special authorization to open the warehouse, then watched as Raceda's father loaded the bags on his cart. It was all so stupid and inefficient. He knew that he had secured his supplies only because he was a white foreigner. This system was supposed to work for the local farmers but for them there would be no special treatment. If Mr. Husain happened to be in Udaipur, they would have to wait until he returned. And if they waited more than three days past the authorized date, they would have to apply all over again, going through three different officials before their request was fully approved.

Steve shook his head. He could almost see Mark laughing at him. Mark had always been the pessimist. Even if everything works out now, Mark would likely say, it will all fall apart the first season you're gone. Well, maybe he was right. But he was in America eating hamburgers and leering at girls in miniskirts. Steve was still in Rajasthan and knew that he had to believe he still had a chance to make a dent somewhere, if only to survive. That was basic. Questions were luxuries. Luxuries were for people in America. People like Mark.

The transport of 80 kilos of fertilizer posed a few problems. Steve would have to take it by bus to Sangli, the closest the bus would pass by his site. Tomorrow he would hire a bullock cart to take it up the trail to his village. It was still hot, he was tired and his mind raced feverishly as he thought about the problems of the transporting, storing, bargaining, and bickering that faced him.

The bus stand was an open lot between three buildings. Two sides of the lot served as open air latrines for the non-self-conscious travel weary. Hawkers sold molasses covered figs and other sweets crawling with lazy flies while beggars displayed their deformities to the more prosperous looking passengers. One glance told Steve there would be no seats. He would have to stand for the two hour journey to Sangli—a cruel fate for an American too tall to stand upright on a small Indian bus.

Raceda's father helped the conductor load the bags of fertilizer on top of the bus before Steve paid him the now standard two rupees. He felt he should say something more but it was late and hot and he was tired so he simply waved to them. "Good-by princess" and boarded the bus.

Every seat was taken. Several women were already squatting in most of the extra space in the aisle. There was just enough room between the woman breastfeeding her child and the goat tied to the last seat for Steve to put his feet as he hunched over beneath the low ceiling. He had just begun to contemplate the horror facing him when he heard some of the Indians in the back

Village transportation

call to him. He looked up to see several men waving from the back seat of the bus.

"Come here. Come here," they said in Mewari "We have plenty of room."

He looked at them incredulously. The back of the bus was a solid wall of people. He could see no trace of the lightly padded wooden bench on which they were seated.

"There is room," they repeated, and then they twisted and squirmed until a tiny space appeared between two of the men. It didn't seem as if a child could fit into such a small space but they kept on encouraging him until he shrugged and decided to give it a try, if only as a diplomatic accommodation.

He grabbed the pole and swung himself over the goat, aiming carefully for the tiny unoccupied spot and then let himself down slowly. It was no use. He found himself suspended several inches above the empty stretch of board resting on the thighs of two Desi farmers. They squirmed and jostled some more, and he sank another inch or so, but it was obviously hopeless.

They held an emergency conference jabbering suggestions in Mewari far too fast for Steve to follow. Finally it was resolved that one of the larger men in the back would trade places with a boy a few seats up. When this was accomplished through a series of highly complex maneuvers, Steve finally found himself resting on solid board. Everyone cheered although Steve could only wonder how much advantage there was in this position with their pelvises wedged so tightly together.

He had exerted himself in the process of gaining his seat, and now Steve found his clothes dripping with sweat. There was no ventilation on the stationary bus, and the people jammed so closely together made the heat unbearable. The woman squatting on the floor in front of him, unable to move because of the crush, simply held her child out in front of her so he could urinate on the empty space on the floor, and Steve just barely moved his foot in time to avoid the boy's poor aim. He yearned for nothing so much as some sign that the bus was about to move.

It was another ten minutes before the driver appeared and climbed into his seat. He was a big fleshy man in a greasy undershirt. He turned to give the passengers a contemptuous glance then kicked the old machine to life. Two blasts on the horn announced their departure, and a dozen more people piled on to the already over-crowded bus, filling every available space, and then hanging from the open doorway. To Steve, it seemed as if he was engulfed in a solid mass of humanity intent on blocking any hint of ventilation that might filter through the bus once they started moving.

The old engine coughed and sputtered as the bus rumbled slowly down the streets of Kapasan, picking up yet another bunch of passengers who hooked their arms through the windows or grabbed hold of the people already hanging from the doorway. The horn blew once again, and the bus began to pick up speed.

Just as Steve heaved a sigh of relief, the bus ground to a halt at the outskirts of town. The burly driver dropped down from his seat, spit out a mouthful of beetle juice into the dust, then strolled across the road to where several women were busily engaged in stringing flowers into garlands. He paid one of them a rupee and collected two long colorful garlands of wild flowers. Climbing back on board the bus, he carefully arranged the flowers around the pictures of the God Ram and the Goddess Lakshmi that adorned the front of the bus. Then, making a little bow with his hands folded, he uttered a brief prayer to Ram for a safe journey and threw the old bucket into gear. The bus jumped forward with a lurch and then began to pick up speed as it rumbled out of town onto the open road.

Steve sighed. In just another three hours he would be home.

CHAPTER 14

Fatehnagar: Eight Years Later

William Whitesell

In 1977, eight years after I left India as a Peace Corps Volunteer (PCV), I returned for a visit with my wife, Dale. It was her first experience of India. So, when we arrived in New Delhi, I was proud to show off what remained of the Hindi I had once spoken every day in my Rajasthani village. We stayed at the Oberoi, a place I had once visited as a PCV. In the 1960s, I had found the Oberoi's coffee shop way too expensive for my $55/month pay from the Peace Corps. By 1977, though, my financial circumstances had changed; I was now an investment banker living outside of Paris.

I was surprised how quickly my Hindi came back. Indians are so grateful for someone who tries to speak their national language (northwest Indians at least, given that other native tongues predominate in other areas of India). I could get along in the street well enough in Hindi. But maybe it's not surprising that shopkeepers boost your ego when you try speaking the local tongue. (Shopkeepers in France, of course, don't bother to indulge your ego; you buy from them because of *their* ego.)

One well-dressed young Indian man we found walking beside us on Connaught Place was particularly friendly. After an exchange of greetings, he congratulated me on my Hindi—using his own impeccable English. He explained that he was a graduate student home visiting his family for the holidays. We asked some questions about tourism opportunities and even stopped to take tea together. My wife was particularly interested in seeing a performance of native dances. The young man said he could get us tickets for a performance that he was himself going to attend with his family the next evening. We were thrilled. He told us he would come to our hotel to pick us up at 7:00 pm. As he left, we gave him money for the tickets.

Of course, we never saw him again. The experience reminded me of my first trip to New Delhi as a PCV ten years earlier. I had heard that the dollar-rupee exchange rate was much better on the street than in banks. Naturally, I looked for somebody who could make an exchange for me as I walked around Connaught Place. One young man agreed to do the trade. We went into a tiny cafe. He said he had to make the trade in the back room. He took my money and went into the back room. I waited for him to return. And waited and waited and waited. Evidently, there was a hidden back door to the cafe. You can guess the rest of the story…I never saw him again either.

"Don't write about that!" Dale is now saying while looking over my shoulder. "Tell them how wonderful our trip was!"

"Okay, okay," I promise. "But shoo!"

Well, to fulfill my promise: Everybody knows what the Taj Mahal looks like from a distance. In the moonlight, in person, with your lover, it is an experience of heaven. And up close, in the light of a full sun, the Taj is even more breathtaking with its myriad symmetries of inlaid semi-precious stones. I recall running from one side of the mausoleum to another, thrilled to see that each of its four facades held the same intricate patterns. New patterns of symmetry kept emerging the longer I looked.

It was Dale who brought me back from my aesthetic trance back then in 1977: "Sure, it was an achievement for Shah Jahan to build it," she said. "But don't forget the achievement of his wife, Mumtaz, who inspired him and died giving birth to their fourteenth child in nineteen years."

Ah, romantic India! For a PCV stuck in a dusty, purdah-shrouded, caste-fragmented village, it seemed an oxymoron. But here it was. And there was more. The palace of Fatehpur Sikhi, built by Shah Jahan's father and grandfather, Jahangir and Akbar, proved to be another extraordinary vision. In the heat of

Taj Mahal (side view)

India, I was most impressed by the baths, fed by cool under-ground waters. Not to mention the haram where Jahangir's 800 "wives" resided: For Moghul emperors, clearly, quality did not supersede the need for quantity.

Dale and I then moved on to Khajuraho. It is the Kamasutra in 3-D with temple after temple covered from top to bottom with sculptures of sexual bliss states. Every position depicted… multiple partners, perfectly formed bodies, and melon-breasted goddesses at every turn. Just imagine living there in those times. Your teenage kids would be begging you, "Dad, can we please go to church today?" As a visitor, I do recommend you bring your lover with you.

We then moved on to Varanasi (formerly called Benares or Kashi), the holy city on the banks of the Ganges. Even on the trip into town from the airport, many family pilgrimages could be seen. Bathing in the Ganges or, for some, drinking its water, is thought by many Hindus to be a blessing. Being cremated on the banks of the Ganges at Varanasi is especially auspicious for your prospects in a future life. All along the river bank, there were wooden platforms and steps down to the river (called ghats). Yogis, their faces smeared with sacred ashes, could be seen chanting, moving through ritual postures, or just standing or sitting in unnatural poses. Many people were wading into the water. Funeral pyres could be seen every few hundred feet along the bank.

When we arrived at the airport in Varanasi, I was still smarting from being cheated in Delhi. I was also remembering how, as a PCV, my cook used to harangue me about how much I was overcharged every time I bought something from a local shopkeeper. Of course, my cook may have had his own reasons for wanting me to put him in charge of all my purchases.

As we exited from the airport terminal at Varanasi, I saw numerous buses loading up tourists for the trip to the city center. My Hindi had come back fully by now, and I wanted a more deshi (local) experience. So I bargained with a cycle rickshaw *wallah* to drive us to our hotel from the airport. I kept knocking down his price until he finally agreed to accept a pittance. It must have been the equivalent of couple U.S. dollars at most to take Dale and me, including our luggage. The trip into the city was much longer than I had expected (it's actually about 10 miles). By the time we got to the hotel, I was thoroughly embarrassed at having bargained so hard.

And yet, I was not quite finished being hard-nosed. So far, I had spared Dale from any GI-track troubles by making her drink only bottled water. At the hotel's reception desk, however, they said they had no bottled water. They claimed instead that they boiled all the drinking water for guests. I was skeptical. Up in our room, a hotel staffer brought us a complementary jug of water and insisted it had been boiled. I didn't believe it. I made them take it away. About a half hour later, they came back with a *mutka* (large clay vessel) filled with water that was still steaming. I had to give in. It was almost like drinking tea, but without the tea. And Dale maintained her enviable record: She may be the only Westerner to have visited India in those days with the sole gastrointestinal complaint of a case of constipation.

Our next stop was Udaipur. I must admit; it was great to be flying into this historic city as opposed to enduring once again

Clay water pots in the bazaar, 1969

the 24-hour train ride of our PCV days. We stayed a couple nights in the gorgeous Lakshmi Vilas hotel, with its spacious marble bathrooms and beautiful view of the lake. We rode bicycles through the city. And on New Year's Eve, we took a boat out to the Lake Palace Hotel, which emerges almost magically from the midst of Lake Pichola, for a sumptuous Indian dinner.

We then rented a car for the one hour trip north to my old PCV village of Fatehnagar. It used to take me well over two hours to make the trip by bus. How strange to arrive in that small town in an automobile. It wasn't the first time I had seen one in Fatehnagar. Buses did stop there, and the town had a train station. But the arrival of a private automobile was a rare and special event in my Peace Corps days. By 1977, the town had clearly grown. A few more shops and residences were evident, but the streets were as dusty as ever. The shopkeepers still recognized me. Someone went to tell my cook from the old days, Mohammed, that I had returned.

The Lake Palace

When I first met Mohammed, in 1967, he had been working as a traveling salesman. He visited the tiny villages surrounding Fatehnagar on a rented bicycle, selling whatever small household utensils, medicines, and toys he could carry. When he got a job as my cook, he set up a little wooden cupboard on a side street in the town and made sales from there. His wife prepared most of the food, and he just carried it over to my apartment in the town. Mohammed lived with his wife and six kids in one rented room in the Muslim section of town.

In 1977, Mohammed was overjoyed to see me again, and thrilled that I had brought my wife. He insisted we both come to his home and take tea with his family. Mohammed had really come up in the world. He now lived in a three-bedroom apartment and proudly pointed out that he even owned a radio. After brief introductions, he huddled for a moment with his wife and daughters before announcing to me that Dale's cotton sari

263

(which we had purchased in Delhi) was not really suitable for our visit to the village. The women took Dale into one of the bedrooms and fitted her with a more expensive sari of polyester blend. Now the *mem sahib* was ready for display in a walk through the village.

When the village mayor (*sarpanch*) learned we were there, he also invited us over for tea. In my two years there as a PCV, I had never met his wife. But she appeared while Dale and I were having tea and even sat with us for a moment (though didn't take any tea with us herself). It turned out she was a college graduate. This revelation made me wonder about how much I missed when I was living there as a PCV.

Dale and I also took our rented car to the village of Sunwar, two miles away, where I had spent my first year as a PCV. We pulled into the dusty little courtyard of the fort-like residence of the Rajput who once owned the whole village. While Fatehnagar had bus and train stations, Sunwar was more remote. And while Fatehnagar had grown and prospered in the eight years since my Peace Corps service, Sunwar was the same as before. Indeed, it had remained unchanged—except for political control—for many centuries. Well, in truth, there was one change since I left. My pilot poultry project, housed within the Rajput's courtyard itself, had not been continued. So sad...

We encountered another unfortunate development when we returned to Fatehnagar. We asked Mohammed about his brother, Kasim, who had been the cook for Fatehnagar's other PCV at the time, my good friend Mike Simonds. Evidently, Mohammed and Kasim, though both Sunni Muslims, belonged to slightly different minor sub-sects that were active locally. Because of a feud between the leaders of these sects, their followers were not allowed to talk with each other. Therefore, although the brothers lived just around the corner from each other, they had not exchanged a word for over nine months. May their reward in heaven be great!

Mohammed had some business in Udaipur, so we gave him a ride back with us. As we bid him goodbye, I handed him an envelope that I had stuffed with rupees. He declined, saying proudly that he didn't need it now. I pressed it on him, saying, "Well, pass it on to someone who does."

Dale and I finished our trip to India with a short visit to Bombay (now Mumbai). It was a typical tourist visit—a snake charmer on the beach and a drive by Malabar Hills, where the Parsis leave their dead exposed for vultures to consume—along with a side trip to the Ajanta and Ellora caves.

Aside from a lasting attachment to India and an interest in economic development, one final note about how PC service affected me: I had grown to know my fellow Fatehnagar PCV, Mike, through umpteen repetitions of our life stories as we wiled away two years in the village. After our return to the states, Mike found himself a bride within a few years. I was honored when he invited me to be his best man. He also told me he was looking forward to introducing me to his fiancé's sister. He had actually dated the sister briefly before the better matchup with his fiancé materialized. Ironically, the sister and I had each been complaining to Mike about the people we had been dating—it seems we both felt that our relationships were not giving us enough space and freedom to be ourselves.

Well, I met the sister at Mike's wedding. And she became my wife Dale. Married since 1975, we've built a beautiful life together. So, thanks brother-in-law Mike. And thanks, Peace Corps.

Postscript:

I had a chance to return to Delhi and Mumbai in 2011 and found it a different world. There may now be more cycle rickshaws in Washington DC than in Delhi and Mumbai. The traffic in those cities, especially Mumbai, is overwhelming. As before, no one respects lanes, and your driver must be aggressive to get anywhere. But drivers do give way where you have maneuvered yourself into a slight edge ahead of them. There are no cows and goats on the roads anymore, and fewer open markets with row upon row of giant burlap bags full of spices and other goods. Now, you see everywhere the extraordinary sight of a man on a motor scooter, weaving his way through the traffic, his wife on

Today's city traffic

Bombay street dwellers, 1968

the seat right behind him, her sari flowing out behind her in the breeze as she hangs on with one hand while gesticulating forcefully with the other, making sure her husband gets the point of her harangue.

Among the many signs of development I noticed while strolling around Connaught Place in 2011, two really stand out: First, I saw no beggars. Not one! They had evidently been vastly up scaled; street vendors now weave their way among vehicles stopped at every intersection, selling such things as magazines and windup toys of dancing movie stars. Second, the stray dogs had changed. I remembered those dogs—they slept anywhere on the streets during the day. At night though, as I knew from the experience in my village, they took over; they **owned** the streets. They jealously guarded their turf from each other and from people, too. They pounced viciously on any rodent, insect, or piece of refuse that came their way to try to eke out a meal. In 2011, however, although I did see many stray dogs taking their midday snooze in the streets around Connaught Place; they were not at all like those I remembered from 1967. They were fat, as fat as pigs! They were the fattest dogs I have ever seen.

CHAPTER 15

Reflections

India 44

A man may die, nations may rise and fall, but an idea lives on.

John F. Kennedy

According to an old African proverb, *"No place is too far for a bird."* For some of every generation, distant places and seemingly insurmountable obstacles beckon with some strange and irresistible allure. Like those wandering birds that range over nations, if not continents, some intrepid individuals easily embrace challenge and change where others settle on the familiar and the ordinary.

Few moments in time capture the sense of personal exploration as completely as the early 1960s. Just as we emerged into adulthood, the world seemed to teeter on the cusp of a dramatic transformation. The old world of common sense and conformity mutated into some new and exciting alternative whose potential and form could hardly be apprehended. Life suddenly seemed more like an adventure as old certainties disintegrated. All around us, convention and set ideas were confronted as new rights were being asserted against racial and gender and ethnic stereotypes. National interests around the globe were rising as colonial oppression first wavered and then fell away. We boldly established ambitious national priorities to put a 'man' on the moon and to wipe out poverty in America.

Everywhere, seemingly archaic forms of authority and rigidity were first questioned and then confronted as all of our "truths" appeared open to debate and reinterpretation. Of course, much of this was discomforting, if not bewildering. After all, we were formed in the 1950s when conformity was a prized virtue and the prevailing institutions evinced largely unquestioned power and authority. We thought we knew 'right' from 'wrong,' did we not? And in case there was any confusion, the good guys would always be wearing the white hats. And even when we were presented with conflicts to our often optimistic world view, we were still quite certain that, in the end, we as young Americans represented something special and had something unique and valuable to bring to the wider world.

During his academic career, Tom Corbett taught undergraduate and graduate students at the University of Wisconsin. He was always struck by a contrast between how he had experienced the world while in college and what he saw in his students several decades later.

To his young eyes back in the 1960s, the world offered fresh opportunities and great adventures, even as the broader society around him was buffeted by war and civil strife. Somehow, we just knew that our generation could make that world a better place. In contrast, the college-aged students he encountered later in life seemed worn and anxious. Burdened with debt and an almost paralyzing concern about their economic futures, they seemed far less likely to challenge prevailing norms than to wonder if there would be a place for them at the economic table. They appeared much less likely to want to change the world than simply find their niche in that world.

No matter what was happening around them, their full attention seemed focused on making sure they got a piece of the pie when society's goodies were being distributed. And these were students of Social Work and Public Policy, not those studying to be the next generation's captains of industry and finance. Did the world change that much? Had too many in recent generations lost that sense of adventure and seeking that he, and so many of both his college peers and fellow volunteers in India 44, had felt so strongly? It is impossible to say.

Of course, broad statements encompassing a whole generation are certain to be misguided, at least in part. A number of us have come across individuals in recent years just as committed and idealistic as we were so many years ago. Some of us can tell stories of young people we encouraged to look at the Peace Corps as way to make a contribution, budding idealists who subsequently went on to do wonderful service oversees. And yet, the overall feel about how recent generations see and react to the world seems quite different from our own experience so long ago.

Certainly, the numbers seeking to serve in developing countries have substantially declined. Young people do volunteer to do good for their communities but too often the sacrifice seems oriented toward filling in their resume for a top college. We do see occasional protests against inequality and injustice but those bursts of indignation now seem ephemeral and almost quaint. We still witness youth drifting toward the helping professions but they strike us as more concerned with pay scales than with the contributions they might make to others. Or maybe it is we who have become too cynical? Again, hard to say!

And so, intriguing questions remain ... was our generation somehow special and different? Even if that were true, how do we understand how each of us responded to what appeared to be new opportunities and challenges as we found our way in the world? Were we more socially conscious, more willing to sacrifice for the common good, more sensitive to social inequities or to the failure of public and private institutions? Or do we simply think we were? In the end, no one can answer those questions, certainly not us. After all, we are surely not immune to a self-serving bias.

Understanding Our Decision

What is clear is that few of life's opportunities provide such a venue for personal growth as did the Peace Corps in its early days. The Kennedy concept arrived at a time when those of modest means had few, if any, chances to expand their world view through a primal interaction with new cultures. Thousands of young Americans, many whose parents and friends had never strayed beyond the comfort of their known world, responded to this new opportunity. But many more did not. What can explain all those individual choices? Why did some take the road not often traveled while others stayed on the well-trodden path?

Perhaps a story can help us understand our choices as college students some half-century ago. One member of India 44 recalls two friends, twin sisters born in an Irish, working class Chicago neighborhood. Long ago, they told him a story about their childhoods that stuck with him. As very young girls, they both vividly recall looking out on their surrounding world through the front window of the upper-level tenement in which they were raised. They would spend many hours looking out on the street below. It was a magical place for them…one that teemed with all sorts of sights and sounds and magical delights.

It was not until many years later, as adults, that they discovered they had been viewing radically different worlds. One sister always looked straight down on the street below. For her, that street represented a familiar Irish world that she found comforting and comfortable. The other sister would look as far down the street as she could see. As she did, she could not help but wonder what amazing and undiscovered delights were there just beyond her view, just around that next corner, just beyond where her ordinary experience ended. She kept wondering…Just what might exist beyond the edge of her known world?

The sister who found such comfort in the street below never strayed far from her known world as she matured into adulthood. She married, had children, and spent the rest of her life in the Chicago area. Her life was as she wanted it, successful in a comfortable and conventional way.

The sister who was inexorably drawn to distant worlds, even as a very young girl when those exotic places could be found just around the next corner, matured very differently. Like those

Shivaji Fort, 1968

migratory birds in the African proverb, she eventually flew off to Georgetown University to pursue a doctorate in Russian Studies. She then engaged in a professional career in the demanding worlds of national politics and public policy. And while she also married (at least for awhile) and had children, her adult life was a whirlwind of causes to be pursued and political battles to be fought. For several years, she served as a principal advisor to Senator Edward Kennedy.

In some ways, this story is not very remarkable since siblings often choose dramatically different life paths. But on another level, the simple story of the Irish twins strikes us as quite illuminating. It might just be that the need to 'fly from the proverbial nest' is hardwired in some way. Some of us evidence a 'need' to strike out and discover new worlds for ourselves, both figuratively and literally. We need the excitement that

Shore Temple, Mahabalipuram, 1968

comes from novelty, from testing ourselves, from embracing change…even when those challenges are tarnished by a touch of the absurd and perhaps a little futility. And we need to believe in things beyond ourselves and outside our own provincial worlds, in visions of a better world that we can help erect.

Mary Jo (Dummer) Clark, though shy and introverted as a young girl, was caught up by an adventurous spirit that appeared to touch her family at various times in the past. After pondering the question of why she chose the Peace Corps, she concluded that "…the quest for adventure was genetic in some family members." She tells the story of an aunt who often commented on the "…wanderlust that surfaced in different ways in different generations of the family," starting with those that pushed westward to farm the Midwest prairies to those who kept moving west to seek new adventures and fortunes on the West Coast before World War II. For her generation, the lure of the unknown was overseas.

We have pondered the question of just how many of us were driven to explore new vistas by something inside us, something in our very makeup. How many of us would have found some way to express a sense of adventure and a commitment to a broader vision of the good society even if Peace Corps did not exist? There is no way to know how we would have responded in such a counter-factual world. We remain grateful to this day that we had Peace Corps as an option and an opportunity.

The good...and the not so good!

Some of us will recall George Bernard Shaw's iconic quote popularized by Robert Kennedy in the 1960s that went something as follows: *"You see things; you say, 'Why?' but I dream things that never were and I say 'Why not?'."* In some ways, how each of us reacted to this saying while in college tells us a lot about who we were at that time. Some of us would be inspired by the underlying sentiment, pushed to change a world we saw as very imperfect. And others in our generation would find the saying to be insufferable, and surely highly forgettable, drivel and would move on with life without any doubt or regret.

As we look back, it is easy to conclude that each generation has some common experiences that inform their formative years...war or peace, economic boom or bust, national crises or triumphs. In some small part at least, such formative input serves to shape a kind of collective view of the world. Heterogeneity surely does not disappear but we, as a cohort who come of age at the same time, are imprinted with some common emotional memories.

Those of us raised in the 1950s, for example, would never forget the safety drills where we hid under our school desks to prepare for when the Russkies would drop the 'Big One,' as was assumed in our young minds to be virtually inevitable at the time. That sense of impending threat, if not doom, would stay with us for a long time. Still, how the hell a flimsy wooden desk was supposed to protect us from nuclear holocaust always remained somewhat of a mystery to those of us who pondered such conundrums.

Of course, we recognize that assigning some kind of generational response to the world would be overly simplistic. Every age-cohort evidences extraordinary variation in how they view life and in the choices made. As we confronted the decisions thrust upon us by the 1960s, some of us shipped out to Vietnam while others took to the streets to protest that war; some of us sought social justice and economic equality and others happily ran off to Wall Street to make their fortunes; some of us responded to Kennedy's iconic call to "...ask not what your country can do for you..." while others never gave his eloquent exhortation a second thought. Undeniably, though, that call for personal sacrifice and contribution from a martyred President somehow captured the hearts of so many of us who managed to find our way into the Peace Corps family.

And so, in 1965, each member of India 44 responded to the world we encountered at that moment with a singular decision....the choice to apply to this thing called the Peace Corps. We chose to apply for wildly different reasons. Some of us wanted adventure. Some of us sought to make a contribution to the world. Some were moved by the Kennedy mystique and his untimely death. And some wanted to expiate what they saw as their country's 'sins' in Southeast Asia. Whatever the motivation, each of us decided to spread our own figurative wings. We went down a path, one surely more popular at that time than it is now, which remained a choice that only a few pursued despite all the glamour surrounding this new program, which promised so much adventure and, at the same time, so much risk.

And maybe, just maybe, we were meant to start on this adventure by some internal drive, something locked within each of us at birth. Perhaps there was something in our makeup, our DNA, which made our choice all but inevitable. We can never know for sure. What we do know is that the choice, having been made, would change our lives and our futures beyond measure. Now that we have had the opportunity to reflect on our experiences and discuss the meaning of that decision and our service, most of us believe that we were quite fortunate to be in that time and place at that moment in our lives. On the other hand, a retrospective look back might just reveal that our options and choices were, at best, a mixed blessing.

There is little question that our training was intense and transformative. Sam Rankin (India 44A) points out that, unlike today's Peace Corps Volunteers, we were immersed in an exhaustive, absorbing period of preparation that spanned, with gaps to allow us to complete our senior year in college, some fifteen months...from June, 1966 to September, 1967. Of the 200,000 plus PCVs to have served overseas, only some 1,500 were exposed to what was termed this 'Advanced Training Regimen', a form of intense preparation and testing both before and after heading overseas. It was an experiment in personal development and growth that was unique and which had a profound effect on those who experienced it. David Dell, after arriving in Milwaukee from New York and Columbia University, still recalls his PC training as an exhilarating and transformative experience some forty-plus years later. As good as it was, however, there was precious little hope of turning us into competent agricultural specialists or public health workers.

From what we understand, today's volunteers are trained far less diligently but selected with somewhat greater care. It would appear that the fewer volunteer sites that now exist enjoy the advantage of being developed with specific skill sets in mind and are staffed with volunteers who evidence some reasonable approximation of those skills. In the 1960s, it was more of a numbers game as we discussed in Chapter 1. We were going to inundate India (and other countries) with enough volunteers to make a difference. Consequently, the careful matching of placement to volunteer skill set was unlikely to occur in practice even if such a commitment existed on paper.

In any event, the Peace Corps of our day had far more young people knocking on their door than they could possibly use. Even getting invited to training was a difficult hurdle to overcome. After that, many more were weeded out during the training process, though not always in ways that made sense to those who made it through this gauntlet. At the end of the day, each of us who made it to India felt a certain pride in our accomplishment. We felt special, as if we were one of the chosen to represent our country in harsh and often remote environments. What was not done, in our opinion, was to match what each individual had to offer with what a specific site needed. That sense of 'feeling special' that came with successfully completing our training did not last long when faced with our obvious technical deficiencies when we finally hit the ground in our villages. And that was an almost fatal flaw for our great Indian adventure.

Thus, we were dealt a hand that put us in the hole from the very start. As rigorous as the training was, as selective as the process for choosing the final set of volunteers might have been, one inescapable reality remained. We were assigned to perform tasks in technical areas where we had no prior experience and with only superficial skills to bring to our work. We were plunked down in sites where, in too many cases, people had little notion of why we were there or how we might be of use. We were expected to do community development work without all the necessary tools to make that endeavor a success...we had no monetary or other substantive resources to bring to the table and no surefire knowledge base upon which to give sound advice. Good will, motivation, and a broad smile can only take you so far.

To make matters worse, we were assigned to one of Peace Corps most demanding countries. As we discussed throughout our two volumes, the cultural frictions Westerners experienced in India were many and often intractable. Relative to other sites, India had a very high PC dropout rate, much higher than the one-third rate Peace Corps has generally experienced over the years. It also demonstrated a higher than average incidence of mental and physical problems as well as high dissatisfaction rates among volunteers. This was not a place for the faint of heart. Of course, India was also a place of magic, beauty, charm,

Golkonda Fort, 1968

and endless fascination. It was the kind of place that easily fostered a love-hate relationship, a tug that lingers for many of us to this day.

Compounding the challenges was the reality that, unlike today, conditions were very primitive. We were in remote sites at a time when there were no cell phones, no internet, no visits home, and virtually no resources at our disposal. We were, for the most part, isolated and alone. Appropriate ways to release frustrations and yearnings were few at best, actually less than that. While there were many joys and high moments of satisfaction and accomplishment, moments in which the beauty of the land and charm of the people touched us deeply, there were also many lonely hours, cruel frustrations, and bitter disappointments! Most of all we could never escape the reality that we too often did not know what we were doing and that the locals knew this all too well. In the end we could not escape the reality that we could screw up oh, so easily.

Two years can be a long time.

And yet, as you read our reflections you see not despair and defeat but rather resilience and triumph. Yes, there were failures and embarrassments galore. But most of us, most of the time, found a way to survive, if not thrive. Most of us, most of the time, found a way to turn adversity and challenge into personal learning and growth. Most of us, most of the time, emerged from two years in the cauldron that was our Peace Corps experience stronger and more self-assured than when we arrived in Milwaukee just three short years earlier. Somehow, Peace Corps and India made us better human beings.

Coming to terms with our pasts

As we put together India 44's two volumes of reflections, we stumbled upon a few fascinating insights about ourselves. One epiphany was the harsh realization that revisiting the past just might not be an easy or carefree journey. On the whole, the members of India 44 evolved into a quite accomplished group. Among our limited numbers could be counted an international banker and Federal Reserve official, university teachers and researchers, business owners and entrepreneurs, medical professionals and attorneys, a UNICEF Station Chief (in some of the world's worst hot spots) and a Foreign Service Officer (who served in Iran up to the Khomeini takeover of the Embassy), a national labor union official, a non-profit CEO, a musician and early employee of Apple Computer Inc., and so many others who left a remarkable imprint on the world. The proportion of our volunteer group earning doctorates or equivalent terminal academic degrees is astonishingly high and well beyond what one would expect to find in the general population of college graduates.

What runs though the stories shared over two volumes of reflections is a deeply felt recognition that, no matter the original motivation, our decision to apply for the Peace Corps resulted in profound experiences that shaped our subsequent lives in so many ways. No matter how difficult our in-country experience might have been, we brought back with us invaluable life lessons. While no one can say for sure, the collective personal and professional record of the India 44 volunteers might well have been less impressive had they chosen differently in 1965.

The PC influence assumed many shapes and forms. For David Dell, as noted above, it was the remarkable mix of fellow trainees he found on landing in Milwaukee as he transitioned from New York and Columbia University that made the difference for him. He remains thankful for his training experiences and what those experiences eventually meant to him later in life. For Carolyn (Watanabe) Adler, it was the finding of a soul mate despite a series of almost comical miscommunications and misperceptions, though why this lovely and intelligent woman chose a mutt from India 40 while eschewing all the wonderful guys of India 44 remains one of life's great mysteries. For Haywood Turrentine, Peace Corps was an opportunity to move beyond the limited life of a sharecropper's son to evolve into an adult virtually unrecognizable to many of his own family. For Tom McDermott, India was a springboard to a life working with refugees who were driven to the brink of desperation by some of the world's worst human catastrophes. For George Wilson, Peace Corps was a precursor to many years of service as a Foreign Service officer.

Bill Muhler has thought hard about how Peace Corps influenced his subsequent professional life. He recently noted that "... operating within the limits of our intelligence, emotional capacity, education, and life-style aspirations, I think that a close examination of our careers would reveal that we brought something special, if not extraordinary, to our 'conventional' jobs based on our Peace Corps experience." Armed with a Masters and a Ph.D., Bill took his three years in India (and later his experiences in Africa and other parts of the globe) into his profession as owner of a landscaping business that is artistic, ethical, and ecologically sensitive. He found ways to make his PC experiences relevant to his life. In general, we all probably found ways to use Peace Corps no matter our later chosen paths in life.

Mahatma Ghandi is credited with saying that *"Whatever you do will be insignificant, but it is very important that you do it."* Few India 44 volunteer thought that their service in India, whether long or short, resulted in substantive contributions that would endure over time. With some exceptions, the general consensus is that we accomplished little, if anything at all, despite all our good intentions and best efforts. This sense of not doing well enough has come to represent a shared understanding for many of us. For a few, the feeling is perhaps a bit stronger, slipping over into a sense of failure that stayed with them. And while a number of us, perhaps most, can recall making contributions for which they still feel pride and a sense of accomplishment, there remains a nagging sense of falling short, of not doing quite enough and certainly not doing it well.

And yet, when some of us had the opportunity to compare our memories with diaries and letters from that period, a rather intriguing anomaly emerges. It would appear that we accomplished more than we recall. If anything, we seemed to have discounted both our efforts and our service and surely did not amplify our accomplishments nor exaggerate our contributions, tendencies which might ordinarily be assumed to be the case. Possibly, we simply could not quite adjust to what was probable given the exuberance of our youth and the difficulty of our situations. Our disappointments may well have been heightened by the expectations we imposed on ourselves based on the image of Peace Corps service we had almost unconsciously absorbed.

Getting our personal narratives right is not only about accuracy. Really, who cares whether we got all the details correct about what we did some four-and-a-half decades ago on the other side of the world. But, in terms of our interior space, how we think about ourselves, remembering our own histories with some felicity is quite another matter. The very effort to go back to our youths and relive our tenure in India was not always an easy endeavor; the emotions and feelings aroused by our attempts were not always pleasant. For some, in fact, it proved a difficult task indeed.

One volunteer, after several attempts at putting her reflections to paper, finally gave up on the effort, concluding that her experience in India had left her too "bitter." In the end, she simply did not want to relive what was for her a sense of failure. Another volunteer who finally accepted the futility of trying to put memories and emotions to paper wrote the following: "...content arises from emotion and inspiration and, for whatever reason, I cannot summon those qualities from my PC experience. It is very painful for me to have failed this..." This volunteer was looked upon by the rest of us as very successful both in his Peace Corps service and in his subsequent professional life. In the end, though, it is one's personal accounting that is most important.

Still others could verbalize harsh memories in more private, one-on-one settings but found committing those recollections to paper an impossibly daunting endeavor. One volunteer confided that at least one of her parents was so antagonistic toward her Peace Corps commitment that she was forced to sneak out the window during the early morning hours where she was picked up by her boyfriend at the time. He then took her to the airport so she could start her journey to India. Another volunteer still carries emotional scars from her stay with an impoverished family in Milwaukee as part of her training. She witnessed instances of domestic violence that she was powerless to do anything about, leaving her with conflicts that are still with her all these decades later. Such recollections might be verbalized but remained too powerful to fully share or describe in writing.

Perhaps those who found it difficult to commit memories to paper also captured a bit of truth about our collective experience. What we took away from our Peace Corps tenure, whether good or bad, uplifting or corrosive, positive or negative, all added to what we were to become in our future lives. Each of us experienced a whole set of epiphanies during our service. What might be critical, though, is that our negatives taught us as much about life as did the positives. Challenge, humiliation, and futility were as good a teacher as was any success and positive feedback received from those with whom we lived and worked. Sometimes our moments of pain or frustration can be as much a positive as our triumphs or accomplishments.

In the end, however, the process of capturing past memories proved liberating for most of us. One contributor noted that "I am really enjoying the process of writing and I think I will have something that is useful for others to understand the transformative power of the Peace Corps experience." Yet another author found the exercise of articulating his reflections to be "...a marvelous method for clarifying what actually happened during my tenure in India." Mike Simonds published what he thought were accurate reflections of his days in village India in volume one. But doubts nagged at him, prompting him to search for long misplaced journals and diaries. Their discovery opened up an entirely new reality to him, a volunteer experience that proved far more constructive and successful than he recalled or had shared with others over the years. Gareth Loy experienced a similar epiphany and sets his personal record straight in Chapter 6. His diary provided him with a deeper, richer emotional content for his stored memories.

After volume one had been completed, Tom Corbett came into possession of letters he had sent to his then college girl-friend. They proved to be illuminating in several respects. For instance, some long-held memories of what happened back then proved to be wrong, or at least incomplete. In other respects, he experienced an epiphany similar to that of Mike Simonds. There were references to projects and his involvement in village life that, in total, shed a much more positive light on his service than he had previously recalled.

Through these recaptured letters, Corbett had a chance to experience some of his inner thoughts from that period in a very intimate and direct way. His written record portrayed a young man undergoing stress and confusion. Upon further reflection, he concluded that his letters were, in fact, indicative of something a bit more redemptive. They intimated a possible transformative moment in his personal development...a point in his life where a confused young man began to evolve into a more confident adult.

Getting the Questions Right

Musician-activist Bono once said that *"We thought we had the answers, it was the questions we had wrong."* As young, naïve volunteers, we conceptualized our Peace Corps tenure as an opportunity to help make a better world. We had absorbed, almost inflexibly, the unchallenged premise that bright, college-educated Americans could improve the situation in what was then thought of as an emerging, third-world economy. It was simply assumed that we possessed skills and attributes that could master virtually any challenge and overcome any obstacle.

Perhaps, though, we should have been asking a quite different question back then. What could India teach us? How could two years living in harsh, even uncompromising, conditions while trying to achieve highly improbable ends with limited technical skills, help us become better human beings? We are not entirely sure but maybe, just maybe, we were the intended beneficiaries of the Peace Corps experience. Maybe, just maybe, that was the unstated meaning of our Peace Corps lives all the time. Maybe, just maybe, we have been too concerned with meeting some unrealistic personal or programmatic standards and not nearly appreciative enough of the blessings we absorbed on the sub-continent.

Confucius is reputed to have said that *"Real knowledge is to know the extent of one's ignorance."* We were, to be honest, very young and naïve, even if equally well meaning. India, village life, and the struggle to contribute in a complex technical area (whether public health or agricultural development) all served to mark our ignorance and define our inadequacies. As revealed in vignette after vignette in these two volumes, many of us described just how quickly and completely we became conscious of our personal shortcomings, at least as we remembered them. And many of us came to realize that we yet could contribute despite our shortcomings.

At one time or another, we reacted to the pain and uncertainty that we felt in different ways. Some of us withdrew into our private spaces, often shutting out the people around us. In some instances, tensions surfaced with the people with whom we shared a site as we struggled to negotiate the demands placed upon us. And sometimes, we lashed out at locals who invaded our privacy in public places or our own homes, or who behaved in ways that we interpreted as communicating thinly veiled contempt or ridicule. Sometimes we escaped in a bit too much alcohol or trips that need not be taken, just to get away for a time. In truth, there is much we have stored in the recesses of our minds that touches on a sense of failure in what we tried to do well so long ago in such a distant land.

What we saw as failure existed in at least two dimensions. We felt impotent as agricultural specialists or public health specialists, with the possible exception of the very few nurses among us and perhaps one or two from the 44B group who were more skilled in the practical arts. The importance of this perceived deficit should not be diminished. It struck at the core rationale for our being there and for making all those personal sacrifices. Beyond that, we absorbed strong feelings of guilt about the way we dealt with our perceived shortcomings. That sense of what can only be termed 'shame' that, on occasion, led some of us to question not only what we accomplished in those years, but maybe even the choice we made that brought us to India in the first place.

Hidden amidst the debris of self-doubt, though, might well lie the real reason for our stay in India and the real contribution we made while there. For all our deficiencies and frailties, we showed the people of India a different kind of America and Americans. From movies and the media, they saw an America of violence and exploitation, a people that too often used power and violence to get what they wanted. They saw arrogance and imperiousness with an occasional touch of excessive narcissism. The notion of the 'ugly American' was not fabricated out of thin air.

In contrast, here were Americans who lived among them, simply and without pretense. Here were Americans who shared their lives and difficulties at the rawest levels. Here were Americans who tried to help, without apparent gain or advantage. Here were Americans who seemed all too human…with little of the arrogance and insensitivity that created that widely-held image of the 'ugly American' in the first instance. If we left only one enduring gift, it might well have been a more balanced and favorable image of who we were in that far side of the world. The few of us who had opportunities to return to our villages have been taken with the fondness with which we are remembered.

Vision and Reality

In retrospect, our legacy may be even more than some residual positive image of our country. Our tendency to downplay our accomplishments, to easily accept this sense of not doing well enough, simply may not be warranted. In fact, that perception likely is misleading. Clearly, we did not visibly transform the villages and towns in which we were placed...an absurd notion in the first place. From the scant real evidence at our disposal, as opposed to recollections of dubious authenticity, we did more than we typically recalled. We interacted more with the locals, often in quite positive ways, than we imagined. We launched more projects than we stored in our memories. And we left more indelible marks on our villages than can be easily resurrected so many decades later.

In short, there existed a large gap between vision and reality. Our vision of who we were and what we might accomplish was expansive, certainly informed by our youth and a certain kind of American hubris. We were raised to simply assume that our society enjoyed some type of inherent superiority. Despite our lack of experience and of any tangible skills in what we were assigned to do, we assumed we would prevail and even contribute. After all, we were Americans.

The reality of village India proved both abrasive and sobering. Intelligence and high motivation were not enough to ensure success. We could not simply go out and transform a culture that had been eons in the making. Hell, we could hardly communicate across human divides that would have tested those older and wiser than we were. And we did, perhaps too often, act and react as the still developing young adults we, in fact, were.

In the final analysis, our experiences in India may have had little to do with what we were expected to contribute. In September of 2011, many of us gathered in Washington DC for the 50th anniversary of Peace Corps. During the festivities, a number of us attended a reception and dinner hosted by the Indian Embassy that wanted to recognize the volunteers who served there some two generations ago.

Comments by one of the Embassy officials struck a chord with some of us. Paraphrasing a bit, the official voiced something like the following, "India, in having volunteers in our country, wanted to expose American young people to the culture that was India…that we had no real expectations other than that." So, in addition to our representing the kindly, well-intentioned American, our hosts were teaching us something invaluable that they hoped would have, and it did, a lasting impression on us.

By that metric, our PC experience was a rousing success… these two volumes are evidence of that.

"Failure is the foundation of success and the means by which it is achieved," according to Lao Tzu. And so it was with us, our perceived failures were also the basis for our successes. Look with care over many of the stories we have shared throughout these two volumes. What theme is repeated time and again? It is the theme of transformation and growth. Mary Jo Clark joined as an insecure and shy young college graduate and emerged from her tenure as a strong, confident woman. Bill Whitesell sought out India in a somewhat confused search for spiritual meaning and emerged with a much clearer sense of what he might become and where he was headed in life. Mike Simonds, through his scrupulous journal-keeping, eventually came to appreciate his own strengths and realized just how much he accomplished as a volunteer. Tom McDermott came within a whisker of giving up before, through imagination and adaptation, he developed an entirely new role through which he could make a contribution in India and, later in life, in a host of world hotspots including Bosnia during the Balkan's civil war in the early 1990s. And these are but a few of such examples.

We see young men and women tested and pushed, sometimes stumbling a bit, but eventually rising to the occasion. Though many of us landed on the subcontinent with doubt and concerns, virtually all of us left India with greater direction and sense of self. We became stronger by being tested.

And India did test us. In one way or another, each of us passed the test. For so many of us, our Peace Corps years were a time out of time. It was a period where we were transported to a place so out of the ordinary from our usual lives that simply getting by was a major accomplishment. We could no longer live by the usual scripts that got us through our lives with so little effort and with such scant attention to what we were doing. We could no longer merely exist. Perhaps, in some sense we responded to the long ago insight of Socrates ... *"An unexamined life is not worth living."*

And so, each one of us, in our own way, took our time out of time to better understand ourselves as well as to figure out the "possible of our own lives." And that, after all, is a gift that few are blessed to receive. In a way, each of us grasped one of Buddha's more famous exhortations... *"Your purpose in life is to find purpose and give whole heart and soul to it."* As we look back from the perspective of four plus decades, each of us made great strides toward figuring out who we were during our India stay.

Visions are typically uplifting but can be quite elusive, perhaps even illusionary. What we expected from India probably was unrealistic from the start. Yet, what we did experience, what we obtained from that marvelous, yet frustrating, land proved precious and redeeming. Even after four-plus decades since our return from the sub-continent, we realized through our shared stories and retrieved memories that our Peace Corps lives were very much a part of us even if that insight had eluded us for all this time.

Reality was so much more authentic than the fantasy of India or the illusory vision of riding into some village as a savior on a white horse or, in our cases, a Superman bicycle. And yet, the reality we did encounter might well have served as a basis for articulating a new vision for our personal futures.

One member of India 44 vividly recalls a recurring image from his early childhood. Snow would fall, whipped into a semi-horizontal slant by bitter winds. Looking up at the grey sky, the snow pellets appeared as planets and stars that streamed by as if one were on some imaginary intergalactic journey. If he closed his eyes, it was easy to visualize an exciting journey to places and worlds where no one had gone before.

In a sense, Peace Corps was our own personal journey into the unknown. Allegorically, at least, each of us traveled to places and worlds well beyond what resided in our conventional understanding of the world. That journey surely was not easy. We struggled at times and, on occasion, found ourselves wanting. But there were also moments of laughter, joy, accomplishment, love, understanding, wonder, and learning.

At the end of our journey, we did not arrive at some specific destination. No, nothing as prosaic as that! We arrived at a better understanding of ourselves and our potential. We found ourselves not at an end but at the starting point of an even greater adventure…one that continues to this day.

Peace Corps Redux?

We end our two-volume journey into our pasts with a few thoughts on the Peace Corps concept. We pause to do this just as this iconic institution, much as we did not so very long ago, approaches a kind of middle-age, at least in some bureaucratic sense.

Recently, a short volume titled *Peace Corps: The Icon and the Reality*[i] was published. The author, Anthony Watkins, joined a number of other critics over the past decade in suggesting that the Peace Corps had lost its way. He notes the following:

> *Over the past decade, however, criticism has been emerging that reveals an agency which prioritizes its own image over quality programming, volunteer support, and the needs of the communities under its care.*

Watkins is the latest contributor to a small, yet perhaps growing, chorus of critics who argue that the uniqueness of the Peace Corps initiative is being lost as idealism and vision are replaced by turf protection and risk-aversion…the sure signs of institutional rigidity. The first clear note of concern was struck a decade ago in 2002 when the United State General Accountability Office (GAO) issued a report that raised

serious concerns about volunteer safety. This critique was succeeded in the following year with a series of scathing articles
in the *Dayton News*. This exposé argued that Peace Corps officials actually blamed or ostracized volunteer victims of physical and sexual violence in an effort to suppress potentially
embarrassing news and preserve the organization's untouch-
able image. In 2005, Phillip Weis published a damning article
about the murder of a volunteer by another volunteer and the
shocking way Peace Corps officials handled the aftermath of
this tragedy.

By 2007, a small reform movement had emerged that was
nominally led by two former volunteers...Chuck Ludlum and
Paula Hirschoff. The drift of their concerns were that Peace
Corps had evolved into a top-down, command and control
bureaucracy beset with vertical rigidities and over-regulation
imposed on field operations by an isolated and removed leadership. Innovation and performance had been replaced by an
obsessive concern with avoiding any negative publicity at all
cost, even if it meant endangering volunteer well-being. The
dominant mission, the critics argued had mutated into the protection of an idealized, iconic image...a blatant milking of the
Peace Corps myth above every other consideration. One critic
mused that the Peace Corps had become a "Peter Pan organization" which had lost its way, no longer really knowing what it
was supposed to be or how to fulfill its mission.

Responding to these concerns, U.S. Senator Chris Dodd, a
former volunteer himself, introduced the Peace Corps Volunteer
Empowerment Act in 2007. This initiative embraced numerous
reforms but the core principle was simple. Reshape the Peace
Corps agency from a typical government agency into what many
believed it had first been envisioned to be. Dismantle the hierar-
chical architecture currently in place and transform the existing
Weberian bureaucracy into a flatter, adaptive, and more responsive structure. Redo the program into a bottoms-up institution,
Dodd argued, where the volunteers could more fully participate
in those decisions that impact how they function on the ground.
Impose fewer restrictions and rules and work to create a culture

that rewards risk taking and creativity while shifting the focus to goals rather than rules.

Official Peace Corps vigorously opposed the Act and it faded from view. But the discontent did not. In 2011, Larry Brown, a former volunteer in India and country director in Africa, wrote an unsettling treatise attacking the current Peace Corps leadership. He, and several other African country directors, had been summarily fired when, according to him, they raised too many questions about the way the program was being managed. He painted a picture of those at the top too often reflecting political loyalties or personal ambitions rather than Peace Corps ideals. These functionaries, he argued, were too far removed from the field and the realities on the ground, more concerned with favorable, if meaningless, statistics, and paralyzed by negative feedback even when those data might well serve as the basis for program improvement. Peace Corps, when asked to do a self-evaluation, prepared a report that argued all was fine, dismissing the rumble of concerns and criticisms that yet continues.

In one sense, the debate about whether Peace Corps management has lost its way sounds so familiar. What agency, public or private, does not defend what it sees as its integrity and core technologies ... what it does as a basic function? Think back for a moment to the image of several executives from tobacco companies declaring under oath before Congress that they did not believe that the ingredients they put into cigarettes were addictive. Is there any greater testament to institutional or personal disingenuousness? We can easily find examples from petroleum companies who fight evidence of global warming and gun companies who actively dispute the meaning of the data showing gun-related homicide rates in the U.S. that are multiple times higher, shockingly higher, than in all of our national peers. Either the surfeit of guns on our streets has something to do with these numbers or we are a remarkably barbarous society.

But this is the Peace Corps! It is supposed to be different. It was not created to be a mini State Department or Foreign Service or U.S. AID organization or any kind of private enterprise whose compelling rationale is to make a buck or appease investors no matter what. Peace Corps was supposed to be an idea, and an ideal, not a program or an agency. It is supposed to be a place where dreams thrive and visions of a better world can be nurtured. In those terms, is Peace Corps now failing?

Pursuing dreams

In the final analysis, we did not develop these two volumes to defend or criticize Peace Corps. Our reflections are about us, about our individual and common experiences and what they meant to us and might mean to our families and acquaintances. Those experiences, however, do give us permission, if not a responsibility, to comment on the meaning and future of Peace Corps.

What made Peace Corps special back then and, we hope, in the future is a firm belief in a set of underlying ends that have persisted through time. Peace Corps, it seems to us, has always embodied three principles…a belief in grass-roots development and self-help, an embrace of the ideal of cross-cultural exchange and understanding, and an irrevocable attachment to peace-building and the fostering of good will among peoples.

Those ends remain fundamental and irrevocable; all else is noise. And even in an age where cynicism, narcissism, and materialism seem so dominant, we cannot accept the argument that our youth, that all of us, cannot be motivated by an elevated call to a greater purpose in life. What we may need is the kind of leadership that can once again ennoble self-sacrifice and the personal commitment to a broader sense of the good. We need a recommitment by our society to the grander vision of a society that treats all with dignity and respect. We need to reassert that a fundamental sense of community is an ideal worth fighting for, that individual avarice and unfettered acquisition are not the highest virtues in our land. After all, many countries around the world yet seek some expression of these traditional Peace Corps principles. They yet seek what the Peace Corps has always sought to provide. Even today, some twenty nations have asked for Peace Corps volunteers to no avail since budget restrictions preclude expanding the program.

The sentiments that Sargent Shriver first articulated in Thailand are no less true today than when he first uttered them in 1964. Peace Corps, he said, actualizes...

> *the idea that free and committed men and women can cross, even transcend, boundaries of culture and language, of alien traditions and great disparities of wealth, of old hostilities and new nationalisms, to meet with other men and women on the common ground of service to human welfare and human dignity.*

Such a simple concept...such a compelling idea! We hope that Peace Corps, as an organization, can reform and reinvent itself every generation or so. It was, and remains, a unique concept and should strive to find a way to remain relevant as time passes and circumstances evolve. But maybe, in the end, what the bureaucracy looks like is not the most important consideration. After all, dreams reside in people, not organizational charts. As long as there are individuals who embrace noble aspirations, who are willing to sacrifice to make them a reality, who are not dissuaded by frustration and failure, the idea and ideal of Peace Corps shall not perish...that particular dream shall thrive.

And all of us who were blessed to be a part of India 44 will continue to take some small measure of pride in our contribution to this vision of creating dreams...to this hope of making the world just a little better for all of us.

After all, as Eleanor Roosevelt once eloquently noted:

> *The future belongs to those who believe in the beauty of their dreams.*

Remembering India 44
Dennis Conta

Editors' Note:
Dennis Conta served as our stateside training director in 1966-67. He put together a memorable experience for us, which a number of authors comment on in their chapters. As he pointed out, he was only a few years older than we were at the time. Through instinct and risk-taking, he managed to put together a training experience that stretched us in so many ways. He tapped into the exuberance and optimism of the 1960s, helping prepare us to be change agents half way around the world. After training several Peace Corps groups, he earned a Masters Degree from the Kennedy School of Public Policy at Harvard before being elected to the Wisconsin State Assembly, where he rose to the position of Majority Leader. He later served as Secretary of the Wisconsin Department of Revenue and subsequently worked on housing and education issues over a long career dedicated to public service.

When we do the best we can, we never know what
miracle is wrought in our life, or the life of another.
Helen Keller

I have read some of the remarkable ruminations that the members of India 44 have gathered together and beautifully eased into reflections on their Peace Corps experience in general and their training program in particular. Given that I served as the Director of Training for this group (at least for the state-side preparation), I have been asked to share some of my own thoughts about the program. This exercise draws me back into time and across distances, momentarily taking repossession of fragments of the past before a maturing mind can no longer bring them back to life.

Most of what happened in 1966/67 is lost and irretrievable or has been altered to meet subjective needs that were never met. What I do remember with the most clarity is the mood and the moment: the decade of the sixties—years of deep discontentment and high idealism—the one dissolving into the other, a merger of thought and engagement that largely drove the nature and purpose of India 44.

As I read the personal journals in these two volumes, the unique influence of that special decade is poignantly addressed in many of the reflections. Instead, what I can offer are impressions of the program, thoughts about the volunteers, and a sense of my own performance as a member of the staff. In so doing, I am pleased to be a part of this thoughtful remembrance of things past.

I wonder how many of the India 44 volunteers realize just how young I was at the time. I was only 25 years old in 1965 when I started training my first PC group, no more than three or four years older than most of the trainees. Moreover, there was little in my background that qualified me to serve as a Peace Corp Training Director. Nor did I have any management or administrative skills to speak of. To be sure, I had been an officer in the U.S. Army for two years and afterwards spent an additional two years working in mental health clinics and inner city poverty programs while earning a Master's Degree in Social

Welfare. Other than those experiences, nothing really qualified me to assume responsibility for the administration of India 44's stateside preparation for India.

As I think back, what saved me was a good deal of bravado and artifice. I pretended I knew much more than I did; I tried using form and style to overcome any lack of content I suffered. In this way I could deceive others or, at least, deceive myself. What kept me going, I suppose, was my drive and ambition and the deep inspiration I drew from political, religious, and civil rights leaders of the sixties, iconic influences that meant the world to me—the Kennedys, Martin Luther King, Jr., and Reinhold Niebuhr. But above all, it was my staff that offset my own lack of experience—it was through their efforts that the program achieved a number of worthwhile training objectives.

The staff of India 44 was blessed with a remarkable group of men and women—a combination of the first Peace Corps volunteers to serve in India, a dozen superb Indian language instructors, respected religious leaders, community organizers, and academics. This talented group led seminars in values, politics, and culture. The technicians imparted their skill and knowledge in ways designed to stimulate technical curiosity and establish a foundation for future learning. I felt then, and feel even more strongly now, that the staff had the qualities and virtues that were a showcase for the high idealism that characterized much of the decade.

As I read some of the reflections that have been gathered for these marvelous volumes, I do recall with pleasure the planning and reasonable execution of the mission of India 44. I remember the days and months that were spent in designing the program... recruiting staff, preparing materials, selecting training sites, and implementing the program. And I recall the demanding hours that drove a rigorous daily schedule. It seems to me that all of these efforts were responsible for modest but meaningful program outcomes. However, what I also remember with a degree of ambivalence and sadness are the program's failures and disappointments.

The early years of Peace Corp training and placement suffered from severe structural problems. Quite simply, we knew too little about so many things, above all how to identify and recruit potential volunteers, evaluate their capacity to serve under conditions of complexity and stress, and then prepare them to meet the technical, cultural, and emotional demands of new environments. In short, resources and knowledge were insufficient to satisfy high expectations.

Given these obstacles and training limitations, the evaluation process used in India 44 to select and deselect trainees to serve as volunteers was clearly an imperfect process. A group of well-intentioned psychologists, India 44 staff, and Peace Corp program officers from Washington were appointed to make judgments about the capacity and capabilities of young men and women to satisfy the extraordinary demands of service in a foreign country.

As I think back on these evaluation sessions, I am reminded how easy and difficult it was to make those life-changing decisions. It was a comfort to make quick judgments about the best and brightest trainees who seemed to have all the qualifications needed to serve with effectiveness and even distinction in India. It was troublesome, even stressful, to try and judge the capacity of trainees who received mixed evaluations or other trainees who seemed to have a very limited capacity to meet the requirements of Peace Corp service. In the case of these trainees, we did our best to make thoughtful and fair-minded decisions.

Some of our deselection judgments were heartbreaking, not only because we knew we were causing pain and disappointment, but because most of us knew or felt in some vague and disturbing way that we were begging the question. A part of us knew we lacked the multi-faceted criteria—the time, knowledge and resources—needed to make complicated judgments about the potential of trainees to serve as Peace Corps volunteers.

So it was that we selected some trainees to become volunteers who left the program early or experienced considerable personal or programmatic hardships. And, no doubt, we failed to recognize the potential of some trainees who would have made a fine contribution as volunteers. We did our best to make good decisions with the knowledge and resources available to us. In many cases, it was not enough. Perhaps it was enough, however, to provide future Peace Corps programs with the benefit of our trial-and-error experience.

I close my impressions by highlighting the valuable insights offered in the preface of this second volume of personal reflections. In these fine and touching remarks, the authors describe the important process of goal displacement that took place for many within India 44, a process in which the means of the program became a noble end in itself:

> *Its significance does not lie in large or visible projects with easily measured markers of success. No, the significance of Peace Corps is found elsewhere... in much smaller things like the personal relationships we developed with those we met in our host sites and in the bonds forged with follow volunteers. It is about modest contributions we might have made in villages and city slums largely invisible to the wider world, tiny gifts to others unnoticed at the time. And perhaps most importantly, Peace Corps is about understanding life in some broader sense including how we came to view ourselves and how willingly each of us embraced subtle lessons that we then treasured for the remainder of our lives.*

CONTRIBUTOR PROFILES

The photos on the left are from 1966; those on the right, 2012.

Name: Peter Adler

Residence: *1966:* Chicago, IL (India-40)
                      2012: Honolulu, HI

Education: *1966:* English, History, Roosevelt Univ.
                      2012: PhD, Sociology, The Union Institute

Career Plans: *1966:* Soldier of fortune; lead guitar in
                      rock band; hedge-fund owner
                      2012: Mediation and consensus building on
                      environment, energy and public health policies

Interests: *1966:* Backpacking, swimming, poetry, fishing
                      2012: Public affairs; writing; swimming

Travel: *1966:* U.S., Canada, Europe
                      2012: Everywhere

Family: Spouse: Carolyn
                      Daughters: Corey, Dana, Kelly

Name: Sylvia (Bray) Larque

Residence: *1966:* Palm Desert, CA
            2012: Santa Rosa, CA

Education: *1966:* CA State Poly, Los Angeles State
            College, Chapman College

Career Plans: *1966:* Government sevice
            2012: Office and project management for
            nonprofit in housing and child care

Interests: *1966:* Folk music, pottery, tennis, softball
            2012: Travel, organic gardening, reading,
            writing

Travel: *1966:* Western U.S. and Mexico
            2012: Thaland, Vietnam, Myanmar, South
            Africa, Mexico, France

Family: Spouse: Bernardo Larque
            Daughter: Sonja
            Grandchildren: Amber, Alexander & Andrew

Name: Dennis Conta

Residence:	*1966:* Milwaukee, WI
	2012: Milwaukee, WI
Education:	*1966:* MSW, Univ. of WI-Milwaukee
	2012: MS, Public Policy, Harvard Univ.
Career Plans:	*1966:* Public service
	2012: President, Conta and Associates
	Former WI legislator, Head of WI Dept. of Revenue
Interests:	*1966:* Public policy
	2012: Education, housing, lowering racial disparities
Travel:	*1966:* U.S., Wisconsin
	2012: Europe, England, U.S.
Family:	*1966:* Spouse: Marcia
	Spouse: Deborah
	Two children, five grandchildren

Name: Thomas J. Corbett

Residence:	*1966:* Worcester, MA
	2012: Madison, WI and Hudson, FL
Education:	*1966:* BA, Psychology, Clark Univ.
	2012: PhD, Social Welfare, Univ. of Wisconsin
Career Plans:	*1966:* Counseling or social work
	2012: Academic, Univ. of WI-Madison
Interests:	*1966:* Golf, baseball, politics
	2012: Social policy, poverty, writing, golf
Travel:	*1966:* Washington DC, Chicago, Canada
	2012: Every U.S. state and 22 countries
Family:	Spouse: Mary Rider
	Dog: Ernie

Name: David J. Dell

Residence:	*1966:* Orangeburg, NY
	2012: Poughkeepsie, NY
Education:	*1966:* BA, Oriental Studies, Columbia Univ.
	2012: PhD, Indian languages and cultures, Columbia Univ.
Career Plans:	*1966:* Something to do with India
	2012: Managing Director, Schrwartz, Heslin Group; Business advisor, management guru
Interests:	*1966:* Golf, reading, bridge
	2012: Translation, global and local sustainability, water
Travel:	*1966:* Northeastern U.S. and Canada
Family:	Spouse: Penny
	3 children, one grandson

Name: Mary Jo (Dummer) Clark

Residence:	*1966:* Whittier, CA
	2012: Santee, CA
Education:	*1966:* BSN, Univ. of San Francisco
	2012: Ph.D. Nursing, Univ. of Texas, Austin
Career Plans:	*1966:* Nursing
	2012: Professor of Nursing, Univ. of San Diego
Interests:	*1966:* Tutoring, traveling
	2012: Traveling, reading, writing, crocheting
Travel:	*1966:* Western and Midwestern U.S.
	2012: US, Japan, Taiwan, Korea, Hong Kong, Canada, Mexico, Europe, Israel
Family:	Spouse: Phil Clark
	Son: Phil Clark II and wife Heather

Name: Lynne Graham

Residence: *1966:* Okemos, MI
               2012: San Diego, CA

Education: *1966:* Albion College
               2012: BA, English/Psych

Career Plans: *1966:* Social work, foreign service
               2012: Hotel & private catering

Interests: *1966:* Mountain climbing, hiking, tennis,
               2012: Kayaking, travel, RPSV music, painting

Travel: *1966:* Canada
               2012: Hawaii, Europe, Mexico

Family: Three cats

Name: Carolyn A. (Jones) Cullen

Residence: *1966:* La Mesa, CA
                     2012: San Diego, CA

Education: *1966:* San Diego State Univ., Social Sciences
                     2012: Registered Nurse

Career Plans: *1966:* Teaching
                     2012: Retired from UCSD Medical Center,
                     working *per diem*

Interests: *1966:* Baton, politics, sports

Travel: *1966:* Michigan, Ohio, Mexico

Family: Spouse: John Cullen
                     Son: John Cullen

Name: Katherine Anne (Kelleher) Sohn

Residence:	*1966:* Greensboro, NC
	2012: Greensboro, NC
Education:	*1966:* St. Josephs College, MD
	2012: MEd, Counseling; MA, English; PhD, Rhetoric and Linguistics
Career Plans:	*1966:* Teaching at college level
	2012: Community organizer, college professor
Interests:	*1966:* Swimming, sewing, guitar, sports
	2012: Exercise, gardening, family
Travel:	*1966:* New York
	2012: U.S., South Africa, Europe
Family:	Divorced, 2 adult children, Laura and Brian

Name: David B. "Gareth" Loy

Residence: *1966:* Diamond Bar, CA
                    2012: Corte Madera, CA

Education: *1966:* Psychology, UCLA
                    2012: Doctor of Musical Arts, Stanford 1980

Career Plans: *1966:* Ethno-musicology
                    2012: Hi-tech guru in music, digital audio, expert witness

Interests: *1966:* Folk and classical guitar
                    2012: Staying healthy, living the good life, playing music

Travel: *2012:* Yes please!

Family: Spouse: Lisa Hauck-Loy
                    Children: Morgan, Greta

Name: Thomas C. McDermott

Residence:	*1966:* West Mifflin, PA
	2012: Santa Fe, NM
Education:	*1966:* Philosophy, Fordham Univ.
	2012: MPA, Harvard Univ.
Career Plans:	*1966:* Social work
	2012: NGOs, United Nations (UNICEF)
Interests:	*1966:* Tutoring, youth recreation, volunteering
	2012: Development, post-conflict, int. politics
Travel:	*2012:* Asia, Africa, Middle East, Europe
Family:	Spouse: Viviane
	Son: Daniel

Name: William M. Muhler

Residence:	*1966:* Oakland, CA
	2012: Oakland, CA
Education:	*1966:* UC Berkeley
	2012: M. Div, PhD, Religious Studies
Career Plans:	*1966:* Community development.
	2012: Landscape design and construction
Interests:	*1966:* Cycling, hiking, climbing, skiing, soccer
	2012: Writing, hiking, road trips
Travel: 1	*1966:* 3 European countries, Sierra Leone
	2012: 42 states, 53 countries
Family:	Spouse: Dede Noll
	2 children

Name: Michael J. Simonds

Residence:	*1966:* Oakland, CA
	2012: Milford, CT
Education:	*1966:* San Francisco State College,
	2012: MLS, Drexel Univ. Monterey Institute
	of Foreign Studies
Career Plans:	*1966:* Not stated
	2012: Nonprofit, CEO
Interests:	*1966:* Chess, creative writing
Travel:	*1966:* Germany, Italy, England, Wales, Canada,
	extensive travel in U.S.
Family:	Daughter: Robin (1975)
	Daughters: Susan (1988)

Name: Haywood Turrentine

Residence: 1966: Durham, NC
2012: Chelsea, AL (Greater Birmingham)

Education: 1966: BA, History, NC Central Univ.
2012: MA, Urban Transportation; Doctor of
Divinity, Cambridge Theological Seminary

Career Plans: 1966: College professor & coach
2012: Education & training administration

Interests: 1966: Basketball, baseball
2012: Education policy & leadership;
published author

Travel: 1966: Washington DC, Virginia Beach
2012: U.S. & 20 countries

Family: Spouse: Lelani
Son: James Lynwood

Name: Carolyn (Watanabe) Adler

Residence:	*1966:* Honolulu, HI
	2012: Honolulu, HI
Education:	*1966:* Butler Univ., INMEd, MSc
Career Plans:	*1966:* Teaching elementary school
	2012: 30 yrs. teaching/counseling/Diagnostic team member Hawaii School for Deaf & Blind
Interests:	*1966:* Hula, piano, volleyball
	2012: Taiko drumming
Travel:	*1966:* From California to DC, Texas, Mexico
Family:	Spouse: Peter Adler
	Daughters: Corey, Dana, Kelly

Name: William C. Whitesell

Residence:	*1966:* Manchester, CT
	2012: McLean, VA
Education:	*1966:* Yale Univ.
	2012: PhD, Economics, New York Univ.
Career Plans:	*1966:* Psychology or business
	2012: Financial Economist
Interests:	*1966:* Sports, reading, bridge
	2012: Climate research, spirituality, biking
Travel:	*1966:* Philippines
	2012: Many countries
Family:	Spouse: Dale
	Children: Lily, Craig

ABOUT THE DEVELOPERS OF THIS VOLUME

Mary Jo (Dummer) Clark earned a Bachelor's Degree in Nursing from the University of San Francisco, a Master of Science in Nursing from Texas Woman's University, and a PhD in Nursing from the University of Texas at Austin. After her return from India, she worked as a public health nurse for the Los Angeles County Health Department before turning to the teaching of nursing. She has held faculty and administrative positions at East Tennessee State University, the Medical College of Georgia, and the University of San Diego. She currently teaches in the PhD and Doctor of Nursing Practice programs at the Hahn School of Nursing and Health Science, University of San Diego. In addition, she serves as an accreditation evaluator and team leader for the Commission on Collegiate Nursing Education (CCNE), the accrediting body for baccalaureate and graduate nursing education programs. She is married to former nurse Phil Clark and has one son and a daughter-in-law, but no grandchildren (yet). In her spare time, she writes professionally and crochets. Her internationally-acclaimed population health nursing textbook is entering its 6th edition.

Thomas Corbett holds a Doctorate in Social Welfare from the University of Wisconsin-Madison (UW). For many years, he served as a Senior Scientist and Associate Director of the Institute for Research on Poverty, a national think-tank focusing on poverty and human services issues located at the UW. He also taught several policy courses to undergraduate and graduate students in the School of Social Work. He spent a great deal of time working with public officials at the local, state, and national level focusing, among other things, on welfare reform and the design of human services systems. He served on a National Academy of Sciences panel on evaluating national welfare reform, spent a year on leave from the University working in Washington DC on President Clinton's welfare reform bill, and most recently co-authored (with Karen Bogenschneider) a book titled *Evidence-Based Policymaking: Insights from Policy-Minded Researchers and Research-Minded Policymakers*. Now retired, he splits his time between Madison, Wisconsin and Hudson, Florida with his wife, Mary Rider, and the best dog in the world, Ernie.

Michael Simonds received a Bachelor's Degree in Interdisciplinary Social Sciences from San Francisco State University and a Masters in Library Science from Drexel University. After working for the Van Pelt Library of the University Pennsylvania and the Norfolk Public Library in Connecticut, he became the Chief Executive Officer of Bibliomation, Inc., a non-profit consortium of some 60 public libraries located throughout Connecticut. He served as President of the Connecticut Library Association (1983-84) and has been a speaker at the American Library Association National Conference and the national Computers in Libraries Conference. Mike has two beautiful grown daughters and lives in Milford, Connecticut where he continues his work in library automation.

Kathy (Kelleher) Sohn earned her Bachelor's Degree in English from St. Joseph's College, a Masters in Counseling from University of North Carolina at Greensboro, a Masters in Rhetoric and Composition from Northern Arizona University, and a PhD in Rhetoric and Linguistics from Indiana University of Pennsylvania. After returning from India, Sohn worked for the Office of Economic Opportunity as a rural organizer, a program director for the American Lung Association, and a counselor in the Maryland community college system. After moving to Appalachia in 1975, she initiated and directed the Pikeville College Center for Continuing Education, beginning in 1984 teaching college composition part-time. After she completed her doctorate at the age of 53, she was hired full-time to teach composition as well as to design and coordinate the newly formed Writing Center. Sohn's dissertation, "Whistlin' and Crowin' Women of Appalachia: Literacy Development Since College," won the

2001 College Composition and Communication Conference James Berlin Outstanding Dissertation Award. She has published essays in *College Composition and Communication* and was a contributor to the collected volume, *Multiple Literacies for the Twenty-First Century.* The book, *Whistlin' and Crowin' Women of Appalachia: Literacy Practices since College,* based on her dissertation was published in March 2006 by Southern Illinois University Press. Dr. Sohn took her sabbatical for the 2006-2007 academic year in New York City where she completed follow-up research on the children of the women participants in her original study. Presently she is working to report those results in an article, *Mountain Echoes: Second Generation Postsecondary Choices.*

Haywood Turrentine holds a Bachelor's Degree in American History from North Carolina Central University in Durham, North Carolina, a Masters in Urban Geography from the University of Cincinnati, and a Doctor of Divinity Degree from the Cambridge Theological Seminary. He is retired from the Laborers Training Trust Fund of the Laborers International Union of North America where he worked on the design and implementation of health, safety, and skills training programs. While with the Laborers, he was appointed by the General President to serve on the National Environmental Justice Advisory Council (NEJAC), a National Advisory Committee to the United States Environmental Protection Agency (EPA). During his tenure on the Council, he served on the subcommittee that developed a Model Plan for Public Participation in the permitting and siting of waste facilities under the Clean Air and Water Acts. The Council elected him as the Chairman of the NEJAC. He served in that capacity for four years, providing advice to then EPA administrator Carol Browner. He is retired and spends much of his time writing and volunteering at his church. He recently authored his first book entitled *The Invisible Chain that Enslaves Us: The Clergy's Misuse of the King James Version of the Bible.* He lives in the greater Birmingham, Alabama area with his lovely wife of 32 years, Lelani. They have one son, James Lynwood.

CHAPTER NOTES

Notes for Preface:

[i] Steven Johnson, *Where Good Ideas Come From*, New York: Riverhead Books, 2010, p.60.

Notes for Chapter 1:

[i] See *Jack Kennedy: Elusive Hero*, by Chris Mathews, 2011, New York: Simon and Schuster, p. 120.

[ii] Mathews, p. 304.

[iii] Ibid, p. 311.

[iv] See *Remembering America: A Voice from the Sixties* by Richard Goodwin, (Little, Brown and Co.: Boston), 1988, p. 219.

[v] *The Port Huron Statement at 50*, in the New York Times, Sunday Review, March 4, 2012, p. 5.

[vi] Mathews, p. 330.

[vii] See *Peasants Come Last: A Memoir on the 50th Anniversary of Peace Corps*, J. Larry Brown (E-Book), 2011.

[viii] Goodwin, p. 9.

[ix] See *The Other Side of the World: Vision and Reality* by Mary Jo Clark, Thomas Corbett, Michael Simonds, and Haywood Turrentine (Strategic Book Groups), 2011.

[x] The available roster list seems incomplete.

[xi] Stanley Meisler, When the world calls, the Kennedy chapter...

[xii] Special Report: Business in India, the Economist, October 11, 2011, p. 4.

[xiii] See *India: People, Place, Culture, History*, (DK Publishing: New York), 2008.

[xiv] See *A Life Inspired: Tales of Peace Corps Service*, (U.S. Peace Corps: Washington DC), 2008.

[xv] Meisler, p. 54.

[xvi] As quoted in Meisler, p.44.

[xvii] In fact, President Richard Nixon hoped to terminate the program though only succeeded in scaling it back.

Notes for Chapter 5:

[i] *The Other Side of the World: Vision and Reality,* Strategic Book Groups, 2011.

[ii] (http://www.scholarpedia.org/article/False_memory)

[iii] Ibid.

Notes for Chapter 7:

[i] Chris Mathews, Jack Kennedy: Elusive Hero. 2011, New York: Simon and Schuster, p. 405.

Notes for Chapter 15:

[i] *Peace Corps: The Icon and the Reality* is available at Amazon.Com.

CPSIA information can be obtained at www.ICGtesting.com
Printed in the USA
LVOW080349010413

326825LV00001B/2/P